Electronic Mail

Uyless Black Series on Computer Communications

BLACK • *The V Series Recommendations: Protocols for Data Communications Over the Telephone Network*

BLACK • *The X Series Recommendations: Protocols for Data Communications Networks*

BLACK • *Network Management Standards: The OSI, SNMP, and CMOL Protocols*

BLACK • *TCP/IP and Related Protocols*

HUGHES • *Data Communications*

KIMBERLY • *Electronic Data Interchange*

WHITE • *Internetworking and Addressing*

Electronic Mail

An Introduction to the X.400 Message Handling Standards

Sara Radicati, Ph.D.

McGraw-Hill, Inc.
New York St. Louis San Francisco Auckland Bogotá
Caracas Lisbon London Madrid Mexico Milan
Montreal New Delhi Paris San Juan São Paulo
Singapore Sydney Tokyo Toronto

Library of Congress Cataloging-in-Publication Data

Radicati, Sara.
Electronic mail : an introduction to the X.400 message handling standards / Sara Radicati.
p. cm.—(Uyless Black series on computer communications)
Includes bibliographical references and index.
ISBN 0-07-051104-7
1. Computer networks. 2. Electronic mail systems. 3. Computer network protocols. I. Title. II. Series
TK5105.5.R33 1992
621.39'81—dc20 91-31492
CIP

1 2 3 4 5 6 7 8 9 0 DOC/DOC 9 7 6 5 4 3 2 1

ISBN 0-07-051104-7

The sponsoring editor for this book was Neil Levine, the editing supervisor was Jim Halston, and the production supervisor was Pamela A. Pelton. It was set in Century Schoolbook by McGraw-Hill's Professional Book Group composition unit.

Printed and bound by R. R. Donnelley and Sons.

To Elena

Contents

Preface

Electronic mail has gradually entered the mainstream of corporate life, and many people today take its use for granted to satisfy their day-to-day communication needs. Most users are familiar with electronic mail primarily as a means of exchanging short, interpersonal text messages. Increasingly, however, electronic messaging systems, as they are called in their broader sense, are being designed to handle much more than just text. This may include electronic documents, voice, graphics, and financial transactions such as electronic data interchange (EDI). As such, electronic messaging systems are rapidly taking over as the medium of choice for the exchange of any kind of electronic information. Most importantly, they are beginning to provide a fundamental connectivity channel that supports the flow of information among many kinds of disparate and often geographically dispersed information processing systems.

Electronic mail, however, is only as valuable as its ability to interconnect large groups of users. As people become accustomed to using electronic mail to support their day-to-day communication needs, their desire to communicate on a global basis increases. In order to be truly useful, electronic mail systems must be designed to allow users to be interconnected on a worldwide basis. While this may initially sound overly ambitious, a number of international standards have been developed in recent years to support exactly this goal. Just as was the case in telephony, interoperability is rapidly becoming the key requirement that must be addressed in order to ensure the widespread use and acceptance of electronic mail. This requirement refers both to the need to address mail across diverse electronic messaging environments, as well as to the need for a common set of regulations that can support the deployment of electronic mail services across national boundaries. The X.400 standards for message handling services are playing a key role in ensuring the development of interoperable message handling services that meet both requirements. In order to appreciate how electronic mail systems are being deployed and interconnected today, one must understand about X.400, and the role that X.400-based services will play in the future in providing interoperability among electronic mail systems on a worldwide basis.

While electronic mail systems have been around for a couple of decades now, few books have been written to date devoted solely to this topic. Most of the knowledge and information about the design and overall architecture of electronic mail systems still remains the preserve of a relatively small group of specialists. Much of the information collected in this book about the X.400 standards is typically available only through a direct reading of the international standards documents themselves, not an easy task for people outside the field.

This book is intended primarily for computer professionals who are already familiar with networking and are looking for a rapid technical introduction to the topic of electronic mail and the X.400 standards for message handling services. Computer professionals who will need to actually design and implement aspects of the X.400 protocols will find that reading this book will make it easier for them to move on to study the formal standards specifications on their own. On another level, the book is also intended for nontechnical readers who wish to gain greater familiarity with the overall concepts behind electronic messaging systems, including topics such as how the technology is evolving and its impact on the industry. The book gives a complete perspective on electronic mail and the X.400 MHS standards, and provides readers with enough information to allow them to research additional topics in greater depth on their own.

This book is also suitable for classroom study at the undergraduate or graduate level, or as background reading for courses on distributed systems design or networking technologies. It may also be used as a main text for graduate seminars specializing in distributed systems architecture or network protocol architectures.

The book clearly separates the 1984 X.400 functionality from the 1988 X.400 functionality. This is done in an effort to clarify an area that has become increasingly confusing to many people attempting to approach the standards for the first time, since both versions of X.400 are in use in the industry today and commercial systems often mix aspects of both.

Chapter 1 provides an overview of the evolution of electronic mail and the international standards for X.400 message handling systems (MHS). It describes the standards process and provides a perspective on the economic forces that are shaping the development of electronic mail today. Chapter 2 offers a brief overview of networking principles in general and discusses how electronic mail systems fit into an overall networking architecture. Readers who are already familiar with networking terms and concepts may choose to skip this chapter. Chapter 3 provides a technical overview of how electronic mail has been implemented in a number of operational computer networks and describes in detail the simple mail transport protocol (SMTP) in use in the Internet today.

Chapter 4 introduces the reader to the architectural and protocol layering principles proper to both 1984 and 1988 X.400 MHS. In particular, it provides a concise overview of the differences between the 1984 and 1988 architecture, which is not usually available to people who are not specialists in the field. It gives a technical introduction to the major supporting standards underlying the X.400 MHS protocols. Much of the information presented in this chapter is of an introductory nature and serves to prepare the reader to better understand some of the protocol specifics presented in the later chapters.

Chapters 5 and 6 provide a detailed technical introduction to the 1984 MHS model and protocols, respectively. The 1984 protocols are still relevant as they are still very much in use commercially today. Chapters 7 and 8 are devoted to the 1988 message handling model and protocols and how these differ from the 1984 versions. Chapter 8 provides an in-depth technical description of the message store protocol, also called P7, which is one of the major new protocols to emerge from the 1988 MHS recommendations.

Chapter 9 covers the topic of security in MHS environments. It provides a detailed technical overview of the security standards and mechanisms that have been put in place for use in 1988 message handling systems.

Finally, Chapter 10 discusses at a detailed technical level the issues of interoperability between 1984 and 1988 MHS systems, gatewaying between X.400 MHS and SMTP, and electronic data interchange (EDI) services being defined for use with X.400 MHS. It also introduces the reader to the newer work taking place in the field of electronic mail and a number of techniques being developed to allow different systems to interoperate with each other.

A special thanks goes to the many people who contributed thoughts and ideas to this book, as well as many fascinating conversations about how electronic mail has evolved and where it is headed in the future. In particular, I would like to thank Eric Skovegaard for his thoughtful reviews, and SRI for making some of its library facilities available for research. A special thanks also goes to my husband for proofreading many versions of the text and providing useful suggestions for improving its readability.

Sara Radicati

Electronic Mail

Chapter

1

Introduction and Overview

Electronic mail is the single most visible application of distributed computing in use today. While a great deal of progress was made in the last two decades in the development of technologies to enable the exchange of information between computer systems, most of the benefits provided by these systems have been generally appreciable only to computer specialists. Electronic mail is the first application of computer networking accessible to all users regardless of their level of technical expertise. Electronic mail relies on the simple premise that if two computer systems can exchange information with each other, they can also provide an information transporting mechanism that can be used to exchange human readable, interpersonal messages between the end users of those computer systems.

1.1 What Is Electronic Mail?

Electronic mail systems are typically characterized by two major components: a set of facilities to create and display electronic messages in human readable form, and a set of facilities to reliably transport information from one user to another. A major requirement of any electronic mail system, even in its simplest form, is that the complexity of transporting information remains completely transparent to the end user. Ideally, this means that the users who are creating and sending electronic messages should not need to know anything about the underlying network environment: what protocols are being used, what the network topology looks like, or what communication medium is being employed to transfer the information.

In order to provide this kind of transparent message transporting mechanism, a number of sophisticated electronic mail protocols have been developed over the past decade, culminating with the specification by the Consultative Committee for International Telephony and

Telegraphy (CCITT) of the X.400 Standards for Message Handling Systems. X.400 MHS, as it is commonly called, defines the rules that public service providers (VANs) and computer vendors must adhere to in order to be able to exchange electronic mail messages on a worldwide basis.

Today electronic mail has grown out of the computing laboratories where it was first conceived and has entered the mainstream of corporate life. Many businesses and large corporations rely extensively on electronic messaging to provide a principal mechanism for managing the information flow within their organizations. Electronic mail has thus found a place in the office, much in the same way as has the telephone or the facsimile machine. However, electronic mail offers some important advantages over these more traditional forms of interpersonal communication:

1. *Electronic mail is asynchronous:* That is, electronic mail allows information to be transferred between two parties in a store-and-forward manner without requiring the recipient of the message to be on-line when the message arrives. This is extremely useful in business environments, because it allows information to be exchanged without requiring a simultaneous session between two parties.
2. *Electronic mail supports one-to-one as well as one-to-many information exchanges:* In most of today's electronic mail systems it is as straightforward to address a single mail message to a wide number of recipients, potentially located in disparate geographical locations, as it is to address the message to a single recipient.
3. *Electronic mail can be integrated with other office applications*: Electronic messaging systems run on computer systems that also support a great variety of other applications from spreadsheets to sophisticated document management and retrieval systems. Integrating these applications with the messaging function enhances a user's overall ability to access, manipulate, and transfer information.

However, the use of electronic mail facilities in the office or business environment also introduces some major challenges in the way in which it impacts the social aspects of the office environment. For example, the fact that electronic mail can be easily sent to large groups of users can lead to disruptive behavior on the part of some users, through either ignorance or malicious intent. Also, and perhaps more importantly, the use of electronic mail raises a number of complex issues dealing with information privacy and security. Electronic mail systems, for example, generally lack a signature mechanism to parallel the way in which paper documents are signed. Where mechanisms for signing electronic messages do exist, the legal basis to support these mechanisms has not been fully established yet. More generally, there is still a great deal of concern today about allowing sensitive business or private information to flow unprotected throughout potentially very large networks of computers.

In recent years a great deal of emphasis has been placed on addressing these complex issues both at the legal level as well as by improving the underlying technology. In terms of the technology, solutions range from adding sophisticated encryption techniques to electronic messaging, to embedding whole sets of privacy features within the messaging protocols themselves in order to allow them to more easily accommodate individual privacy requirements. As our understanding of security requirements and technologies grows, we will be in an increasingly better position to design electronic mail systems that can become an essential and reliable part of our day-to-day business life.

1.2 The Evolution of Electronic Mail

The use of computers in public messaging services began in the 1960s when several suppliers of telex and telegraph services started automating their switching functions. In 1965, a study done by Western Union identified as many as 57 organizations with private, computer-based switching systems. These were characterized as follows:

1. Computer-based teletypewriter systems
2. Large military systems
3. Systems for individual corporations
4. Some industry-based systems

Most of these systems were using computers merely as sophisticated "data switches," which relayed messages, but did not provide any message composition capabilities, as well as little or no support for searching through old messages.

In the 1960s several communication suppliers, including Western Union, became interested in selling data processing along with communication services. This resulted in several data processing companies entering the data communications market. However, the merger between data processing technologies and communication technologies never really occurred until the late 1980s. Even then, the driving force behind merging the two technologies came primarily from the user community rather than from either the vendors of communications or data processing equipment.

The steadiest development of networking technologies, and as a result electronic mail, has come from the computer science research community. The evolution of remote, interactive computing in the mid-60s meant computer users were often physically far apart from the computer operators when problems arose. To obviate this inconvenience, computer system builders began developing what might be called "linking tools," which were designed to allow two users to interlock their terminals in order to see what the other was typing. This simple tool was used to exchange short status messages or request that some network administration function be carried out. Similarly, "mailbox tools" were developed to allow users to send short messages to other users on-line on the same system, as well as to the working space of users not currently on-line. The first interactive time-sharing system at MIT's Project MAC offered both linking and mailbox facilities. And so did most time-sharing systems beyond that.

The earliest electronic mail systems were nothing more than standalone bit buckets of information where a user would deposit a text message for later retrieval by one or more intended recipients. This arrangement is very similar in concept to the way in which today's PBX-based voice messaging systems operate, and it can be anticipated that these will also evolve into store and forward systems once voice compression and latency issues are resolved. The name of the recipient was generally expressed as a text string at the start of the message, and the electronic mail message would not actually travel anywhere except from the work space of the sender to that of the recipient. As computers began to be linked with each other, this simple model evolved into a more complex one where host computers actually exchange electronic mail messages with each other. Mail messages are therefore physically transmitted from a host serving the sender to a host serving the recipient (or recipients) of the message.

In the late 1960s, construction of the Advanced Research Projects Agency Network (ARPANET) was initiated as part of a project sponsored by the Information Processing Techniques Office of DARPA of the U.S. Department of Defense (DOD). The growth of the ARPANET spurred a great deal of advanced research into the development networking protocols and technologies leading up to the definition of the TCP/IP protocol suite. Experimentation with the ARPANET began in 1969 and involved many universities and computer research institutions throughout the country. By 1975, the ARPANET was a fully operational computer network, and control was transferred from DARPA to the U.S. Defense Communications Agency.

Experimentation with the ARPANET protocols focused on the development of store-and-forward communication techniques and wide-area networking protocols. A natural outgrowth of this research and experimentation with communication protocols was the development of electronic messaging facilities to improve the level of communication and cooperation between researchers located in different parts of the country.

The development of electronic mail in the ARPANET has fostered research and a level of collaboration rarely experienced before in the academic community. By adding electronic mail, the ARPANET has led over time to the establishment of what might be called a "community of thought," which now reaches well beyond the original academic institutions that created it, to involve industry and other researchers outside the United States. "The largest single surprise of the ARPANET program has been the incredible popularity and success of network mail" from "a history of the ARPANET" (DARPA 1981).

Because interoperability is a key factor to the success of electronic mail, work on electronic messaging was taken up by the international standards bodies in the early 1980s. In 1984, CCITT adopted a standard for store-and-forward messaging services called X.400 Message Handling Services (MHS). X.400 is the first and most widely used application of the architecture for Open Systems Interconnection. The design and architecture of X.400 was based extensively on electronic messaging work done previously by the International Federation for Information Processing (IFIP, Working Group 6.5).

The International Standards Organization (ISO) also began the development of electronic messaging standards in the early 1980s, called MOTIS (Message Oriented Text Interchange Standard). MOTIS was originally intended to converge with the 1984 CCITT work but was not completed in time to do so. This led to an initial divergence in the architectures proposed by the two standards bodies. These differences have now been largely overcome in the 1988 version of the ISO and CCITT standards, where the two organizations have been able to work more closely together. However, some differences still remain between the two standards, and their implications will be discussed fully in later chapters.

Since the CCITT version of the standard was completed earlier than the ISO version, most people in the industry generally refer to the MHS standards as X.400, rather than MOTIS. Throughout the remainder of this book we will use the term X.400 to refer to both the ISO and CCITT versions of the standard, while the term MOTIS will be used to refer specifically to the ISO version only.

1.3 The Standards Process

When talking about standards it is important to distinguish between two kinds of standards: *de facto* standards and *de jure* standards. Technologies represent de facto standards when they are in use by wide communities of users and are based on specifications that are in the public domain. TCP/IP is an excellent example of a de facto standard since it is widely used as a computer networking technology today and is based on specifications that are openly available to the public. UNIX is also a de facto standard in the minicomputer and workstation market segments, since it has been adopted as the leading operating system by many major computer vendors.

De jure standards, on the other hand, are standards that are defined and approved by one or more legally recognized standards setting bodies. OSI and X.400 MHS represent de jure standards, because they have been developed and approved by formal standards setting bodies such as ISO and CCITT. De jure standards have a legal value beyond simply the fact that they are being used by a wide range of people. In particular, de jure standards can be officially referenced by government procurement guidelines.

Every country has a national standards setting body that defines all the standards for use within that country. This ranges from standards for bicycle helmets, to electrical equipment, to data processing, and computer networking. In the United States, the national standards setting body is the American National Standards Institute (ANSI), in the United Kingdom it is the British Standards Institute (BSI), the Deutsches Institute fur Normalisatung (DIN) in Germany, and so on. These national standards bodies converge at the international level into ISO, which is a voluntary organization. ISO members today comprise most of the industrialized nations of the world. Work within ISO's technical committees is carried out largely by technical representatives from leading computer vendors, as well as researchers from the academic community.

ISO has played a leading role over the past two decades in the development of standards for data processing and computer networking. In particular, it was ISO that in the late 1970s adopted the architecture for the Open Systems Interconnection (OSI) as the framework for the development of nonproprietary computer networking protocols and applications. OSI has two very important goals: on one hand, it strives to define and standardize all aspects of computer networking so that systems built by different vendors can fully interoperate with each other. On the other, it strives to accomplish all this by defining an architecture and a set of protocols that can be implemented on any kind of computing system regardless of the underlying hardware or operating system environment. The second goal in particular tends to make the OSI international standards more difficult to comprehend at first reading even to computer professionals since most concepts have to be expressed in abstract terms without referring to specific technologies in common commercial use.

CCITT is what is called a treaty organization in that it has been set up by agreement among national governments. CCITT operates under the auspices of the United Nations as part of the International Telecommunication Union (ITU). As a treaty organization, CCITT defines the standards and procedures that must be followed by all national postal, telegraph, and telephone (PTT) administrations, as they are called, when interconnecting with each other for the purposes of providing telephone and telecommunication services on a worldwide basis. Members of CCITT comprise all the national PTT administrations, plus private service providers such as ATT and MCI, as well as other international organizations, including ISO.

CCITT has largely adopted the OSI architecture as its own framework for the development of telecommunications standards. However, CCITT has also chosen to diverge occasionally from OSI when it has needed to more directly address the specific internetworking needs of PTTs.

ISO and CCITT are beginning to cooperate more closely on all aspects of OSI standardization with the ultimate goal of achieving closer interoperability between the networking services offered by the PTTs, and those provided by computer vendors. In particular, standards such as X.400 MHS and X.500 Directories have been developed in very close cooperation between the two standards bodies. The process for defining and approving standards varies greatly, however, between the two organizations, and this has made it difficult at times for standards approval to be synchronized across both organizations.

CCITT, for example, has traditionally operated in study cycles of 4 years. This rule was relaxed at CCITT's last plenary meeting held in Melbourne in 1988, with the intent to publish new standards only when they are mature. Nevertheless when we talk about CCITT recommendations, we speak about the 1984 study period and the 1988 study period. At the end of each 4-year study period, CCITT used to publish a whole new series of standard "recommendations," as they are called in CCITT terminology. These recommendations represent the rules by which service providers in all the member nations must abide when providing telecommunication services.

On the other hand, ISO does not have a concept of study periods of fixed length. Rather, work on specifications progresses until there is sufficient content to put the standard out to a formal ballot. At that point a balloting process begins which takes the document through various stages from Draft Proposal (DP) to Draft International Standard (DIS), and finally to the International Standard (IS) level. At each step in the balloting process, comments that are received from all the member nations must be resolved before the document can advance to the next stage in the approval process.

ISO and CCITT have strived as much as possible to catch up with each other and sort out any of the incompatibilities that have resulted from the different timing and operating styles of the two organizations. Some technical differences still remain, however, in X.400 MHS between the ISO and the CCITT versions. This is due both to historical reasons stemming from how the standards were developed, as well as to actual differences in philosophy between the two organizations reflecting different views of the commercial benefits that derive from the standards they are developing.

The approval by ISO and CCITT of an international standard represents only the first step in the commercial deployment of the technology. Because an international standard strives to remain independent of any actual implementation details, other standards groups are often involved in defining additional rules and agreements describing finer details of how the international standards should be actually implemented and tested. These groups are called *functional standards groups,* and the task of more closely detailing what options must be followed when the standards are implemented is called *profiling*. Profiling activities deal with specifying more closely any aspect of interoperability that may have been left open to choice in the international standard.

The National Institute for Standards and Technology (NIST) in the United States is an example of a functional standards group. NIST hosts a series of workshops for implementors, whose purpose is to define all the pragmatic rules that implementors must adhere to when developing OSI systems. NIST publishes a new set of documents each year, called the NIST Implementors' Agreements. These agreements are used by computer vendors as a detailed guide on how to implement the OSI standards within product offerings.

Several counterparts to NIST exist in Europe and the Pacific Rim. In Europe, the organizations that have been involved in the development of functional profiles for X.400 MHS include primarily the Standards Promotion and Application Group (SPAG) and the European Workshop for Open Systems (EWOS). EWOS is currently the most active group and has a legal status within the European Economic Community. In Japan, the principal functional standards group is the Interoperability Technology Association for Information Processing (INTAP). A new group that includes many Pacific Rim nations, called

Asia and Oceania Workshop for Open Systems (AOWOS), has also been formed in order to parallel the European cross-national efforts.

The NIST Implementors' Agreements, as well as the functional profiles published by many of the above regional standards organizations also form the technical basis for the specification of Government Open Systems Interconnection Profiles (GOSIP). GOSIP specifications are procurement guidelines published by national governments to guide the procurement of computer equipment by their government agencies. GOSIP specifications have been published by the U.S. government, the U.K. government, and many other European governments. GOSIP is having a major impact on fostering the adoption of X.400-based electronic mail systems within the government sector. In turn, this will undoubtedly also have considerable influence over the adoption of OSI and X.400 by the commercial sector.

The Corporation for Open Systems (COS) is a consortium of the major computer vendors that was set up in the late 1980s to institute a formal process for testing and verification of the implementations which adhere to the OSI standards. COS intends to validate the level of conformance to the standards of individual vendor implementations and issue a mark of compliance. X.400 MHS has been one of the first conformance test suites to be developed by COS. To date, however, COS has fallen somewhat short of its goal of policing MHS implementations, since many vendors have released products on the market before COS could complete its work on MHS testing. Since most of these implementations do interoperate quite well, as demonstrated in a number of major industry events and trade shows, vendors are less eager to go through the effort of having their systems pass COS certification.

1.4 Economic Forces behind Electronic Mail

Several important factors are contributing to the development of electronic mail services, and in particular X.400 MHS. On the one hand, public service providers, or PTTs, are fostering the development of electronic messaging services as a way to introduce new value-added services to the general public. The PTTs see electronic mail as a likely new source of income, given the relative saturation of the telephony market and related services. Electronic messaging is, thus, the new frontier. It opens up almost limitless possibilities for value-added services ranging from the exchange of a few lines of text to the exchange of complex documents and other forms of information such as Electronic Document Interchange (EDI), voice, or even images.

The computer industry sees electronic mail as the first application of networking and distributed computing that can be made available to the general public. Electronic mail is, therefore, often used to justify substantial investments in computer networking equipment.

These two forces may sound somewhat at odds with each other in that both are competing for control of the wide-area networking market. To a large extent, vendors are pushing large private networks, whereas service providers are pushing public services similar in tariffing and administration to telephone networks. This contrast can best be likened to that which already exists between PBX vendors which provide private PBX switches and the telephone companies which provide the backbone telephony services, but also allow end users to tie directly into their backbone networks.

In reality, however, electronic mail represents a major new business opportunity for both the computer industry and the PTTs. Regardless of where the boundary in service is drawn between public and private networks, the PTTs will rely on computer vendors to provide the hardware and software they will use for their messaging services. Vendors will benefit not only from supplying the PTTs, but also from the existence of a worldwide backbone MHS network that will make it easier for them to focus on developing products for the very lucrative end-user market.

The conflicting goals of computer vendors and the PTTs, as well as their common objectives, are very much reflected in the work of ISO and CCITT and parallel closely the conflicts and cooperation between the two organizations over the past several years. As mentioned above, ISO is largely made up of the computer manufacturers, and CCITT is made up largely of the PTTs. Each organization has embarked upon the task of standardizing message handling services in a way that is consistent with the underlying business philosophy of its members.

The CCITT vision in developing X.400 has been to define a standard and an architecture that will foster the development of a unified, worldwide electronic messaging service. This vision parallels somewhat what has already occurred in the telephony world, where international agreements were developed to allow the PTTs to develop an integrated set of services that span national boundaries. Just as in telephony, the CCITT administrations (i.e., the PTTs) intend to provide a "backbone" X.400 communication service. Private services can then tie into publicly provided X.400 services in the same way in which PBXs today tie into a unified, worldwide telephony service. National differences in service may exist to reflect differences in local legal and economic policies, but these are smoothed out by the CCITT administrations through specific bilateral agreements that cover service interconnection requirements.

CCITT's primary goal is to provide a set of MHS services that administrations can offer to subscribers to exchange messages on a worldwide basis. These MHS services are intended to subsume existing CCITT Telex and Telematic Services (i.e., the installed base of preexisting services). Therefore, users of MHS must be able to communicate with users of telex and telematic services. In order to do this, functions are provided to perform protocol translations where necessary. In addition, support functions, such as message storage, are provided to supplement the services of the connected terminals and ensure a consistent level of service across message handling, telex, and telematic services.

Message handling services for Teletex terminals are defined by X.400 in recommendation X.430, while Teletex and other telematic services are left for future study. Videotex is viewed in X.400 simply as a device type that can attach to the network in order to either send or receive mail. However, the X.400 permits the inclusion of videotex graphics in the content of messages exchanged.

The CCITT vision of worldwide interconnected MHS services is as ambitious and powerful as telephony was several decades ago. If successfully implemented, it will lead to fully interconnected public and private messaging services linking individual users and businesses across the world. It will also complement current telephony services with an additional means of interpersonal communication that supports the exchange of a multitude of diverse kinds of information.

ISO's vision of electronic mail does not conflict with that of CCITT but has a slightly different orientation. The ISO standards are written from the perspective of promoting interoperability among electronic mail systems irrespective of whether they are private or public. In this view, X.400 becomes the common method of mail interchange among all electronic mail systems. ISO, therefore, openly discusses the interconnection of private systems to each other directly (i.e., without going through a public service provider), whereas CCITT deals exclusively with the attachment of private systems to public services.

It is important to note that it is largely the ISO view of private networks attaching directly to each other that has been adopted as the basis for the work of NIST and the other major functional standards groups. The result is that most of the GOSIP specifications that are or will be published by national governments will deal primarily with the direct interconnection of private MHS systems, as well as of course the interconnection of private to public MHS systems.

1.5 About This Book

This book looks at the prevalent protocols and architectures in use today to support electronic mail. It describes how electronic mail technologies have evolved in recent years and discusses some of the complex interoperability issues that implementors and system designers are grappling with today. The book focuses extensively on the X.400 Message Handling Standards (MHS), both the 1984 and 1988 versions of the international standards. This is not intended to suggest that X.400 is the only valid example of electronic mail. However, because X.400 MHS is an international standard, it represents a good summation of all the technological knowledge and experimental experiences accumulated to date in the research and development of distributed electronic mail systems. X.400 represents by far the most complex, most complete electronic messaging architecture defined today. Not surprisingly, many parts of the X.400 standards have not even been fully implemented and tested yet. Nevertheless, X.400 provides a basic model of electronic messaging that much of the industry is embracing to implement and deploy in government and commercial electronic mail systems. It represents, therefore, even in its more esoteric pieces of functionality, a major statement of direction and a blueprint for future research.

Chapter 1 of the book provides an introduction to the overall concept of electronic mail: What electronic mail is, what it does, what its advantages are, and how it came about. It also introduces the reader to the standards development process and the major organizations that are developing electronic mail standards today. It describes the economic background against which electronic mail standards are being developed and discusses what commercial impact is likely to derive from the development of electronic mail standards.

Chapter 2 introduces the reader to some of the basic concepts of computer networking. It describes the two vendor independent networking architectures that predominate in the industry today: TCP/IP and OSI. It also begins to introduce the reader to some of the basic architectural notions common to all electronic messaging systems.

Chapter 3 deals specifically with electronic mail in the context of the TCP/IP architecture. It discusses the early development of electronic messaging in the Internet and provides a thorough overview of the Internet mail protocols in use today based on the Simple Mail Transport Protocol (SMTP) and RFC-822. This set of protocols represents a much simpler approach to electronic messaging than X.400 MHS and yet represents an equally popular standard for electronic mail in use today.

Chapter 4 begins to address in detail the architecture of the X.400

Message Handling standards. It does so from a protocol layering perspective by showing how and where X.400 fits into the overall OSI architectural model. It describes in detail the differences between the 1984 and 1988 MHS protocol stacks and introduces some of the basic underlying protocols such as ROS and RTS upon which X.400 is defined. It also provides a brief introduction to the ASN.1 notation which is used to define the X.400 protocols and data structures. Excerpts of ASN.1 from the actual standards definitions are shown throughout the remainder of the book, although they are not essential to understanding the basic architectural topics being presented.

Chapters 5 and 6 describe in detail the 1984 version of X.400. 1984 X.400 is still extremely important today since most of the commercial implementations of X.400 mail are based largely on the 1984 version of the standards. Also it is much easier to comprehend 1988 X.400 in terms of "deltas" to the 1984 standards. Chapter 6 is heavily technical and will be of interest primarily to readers who are looking to implement X.400-based systems. It also serves to provide a sound foundation for those who will need to understand the 1988 protocols in detail.

Chapter 7 describes the architecture of 1988 X.400. It does so by emphasizing what has been added since 1984 and by explaining the functional relationships between its various architectural components. Chapter 8 is devoted entirely to the topic of the message store, which is one of the principal architectural changes introduced in the 1988 standards. Chapter 9 introduces the reader to the complex yet very important topic of security in MHS systems.

Chapter 10 provides an introduction to some of the topics of greatest current impact in the industry: interoperability between 1984 and 1988, interoperability and gatewaying between X.400 systems and RFC 822 systems, development of standard application programming interfaces (APIs) for MHS, and the use of X.400 to support Electronic Data Interchange (EDI) transactions. Finally, Chap. 10 provides a brief overview of ongoing standardization work in the area of X.400 MHS.

References and for Further Study

The evolution of the ARPANET and its impact on computing research in the 1980s are described in DARPA report no. 4799 (DARPA 1981) and Perry et al. (1988). Watson (RFC 196) describes an early protocol for electronic messaging. Tanenbaum (1988) provides a detailed overview of the international standards development process. The U.S. government requirements for the procurement of OSI network computing equipment are defined in GOSIP (1989).

Chapter

2

Basic Concepts of Electronic Mail

Over the past two decades, research in computer communications has led to the development of a multitude of networking technologies and architectures to support the interconnection of distributed computer systems. The emergence of technologies such as Ethernet and Token Ring has fostered the evolution of local area networks (LANs) where computer systems interact at fairly high speeds (e.g., 10 Mbits/s) over relatively short distances (i.e., 1 to 2 miles). As local networks have grown in popularity and size, they have, in turn, created a need for technologies and protocols that can support the interconnection of disparate LANs into larger wide area networks (WANs). This growing need for computer networking has led to the development of numerous protocol architectures to support the interconnection of computer systems across both LAN and WAN environments.

This chapter gives an overview of the two principal networking architectures that are shaping the computer industry today: TCP/IP and OSI. It also provides a "generic" overview of the major architecture and design concepts common to all messaging systems. This serves as an introduction to the more detailed description which follows in later chapters of the electronic messaging protocols currently in use in the context of TCP/IP and OSI.

2.1 Basic Networking Principles

A protocol architecture is a family of protocols that together provide a desired level of functionality allowing application programs that execute on distinct computer systems to interoperate effectively with each other. When talking about architectures, it is useful to distinguish between *proprietary* and *standards-based* architectures. Traditionally, computer vendors have developed protocol architectures specific to their own computer equipment. These are called proprietary architectures for two reasons:

1. The technical details of the protocols are not made available to the general public, thus making it difficult for others to implement the same protocols.
2. The protocol specifications often make explicit assumptions regarding the type of computer hardware and software that will be used to implement the protocols. This makes it difficult to duplicate most proprietary architectures on another vendor's equipment.

Standards-based architectures have become increasingly relevant over the past few years because of the increasing need to interconnect computer equipment from different vendors. Two standards-based architectures dominate the computer industry today: TCP/IP and OSI. TCP/IP has grown out of the experimental work done with the Internet, whereas OSI represents an effort by the international standards bodies to formalize a set of protocol specifications and technologies that will enable full interoperability among heterogenous computer systems. Most computer vendors today are integrating either TCP/IP or OSI, or both, with their own proprietary architectures. Both TCP/IP and OSI strive to maximize the level of interoperability between heterogenous end systems. However, they arrive at it through a very different process. TCP/IP has grown out of the day-to-day experimentation by many researchers over the past two decades with the development of the Internet. OSI, on the other hand, represents an attempt to collect all the research and knowledge that exists to date about networking architectures and to formalize it within a series of standards specifications that can provide a framework for the construction of interoperable network systems.

One of the most prevalent design principles adopted by all network architectures has been that of protocol layering. Protocol layering allows the various networking functions to be logically segmented into well-defined "layers" of functionality. Each layer relies on the services and functions provided to it by the layer below it and does not concern itself with the details of how these functions are implemented at the lower layer. Layers within the same end system interact with each other via well-defined *interfaces* that make all the services provided by the layer available to the next higher layer. Protocol layering offers several major benefits:

1. It allows functionality that is common to a number of protocols to be packaged in a single layer which can provide a set of common services to multiple higher layer protocols.
2. It allows each layer in the architecture to be designed and tested independently of each other.

While all network architectures rely on protocol layering, they usually vary in the number of layers they define, the semantics they attach to each layer, and how they apportion functionality over different layers. Nevertheless, three distinct levels of functionality are always present in any protocol architecture:

1. *Transmission media level:* This is a set of physical and electrical specifications that enable the correct flow of bits of information across a physical connection between two end systems. Ethernet, FDDI, and EIA-232D are all examples of different physical media. Protocols operating at this level in the architecture deal primarily with interfacing the computer system to the underlying physical communication media.
2. *Transport level:* The transport layer handles the transfer of blocks of information across the physical media. The transport layer is independent of any of the details of interfacing to the underlying physical media, and most transport layer protocols are designed to operate over a wide range of physical layer protocols. Transport level protocols typically fit into either of two categories: *reliable,* that is, they provide end-to-end transmission reliability through packet acknowledgment schemes; or *unreliable,* where they rely on datagram (i.e., unidirectional) data exchanges, which are typically faster but also less reliable. TCP and OSI transport class 4 are examples of reliable transport level protocols. UDP, on the other hand, is an example of an unreliable, datagram-based transport protocol.
3. *Application level:* The application layer is the level in the architecture where the value-added distributed computing functions lie. Application layer protocols can be designed to operate over either reliable or unreliable transport mechanisms. Filing programs, virtual terminal programs, and especially electronic mail are all examples of application layer functions.

Figure 2.1 provides a diagram of the three distinct levels of functionality that can be identified within any two communicating end systems. Each level in the architecture communicates with a corresponding entity at the same level in the other end system through a

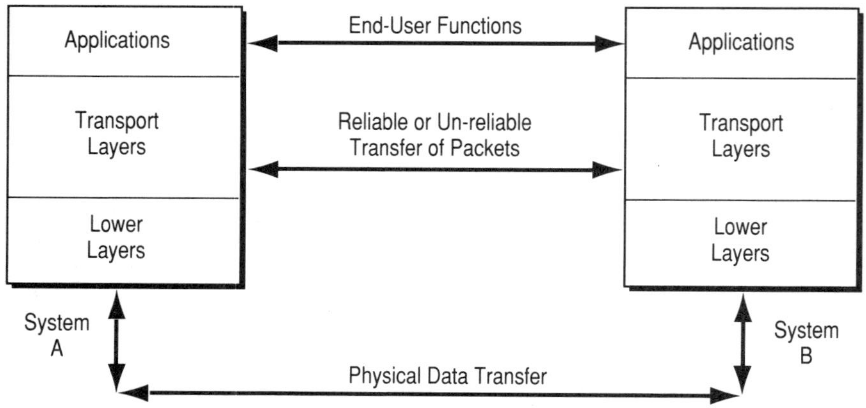

Figure 2.1 Protocol layering principles.

protocol (or possibly a set of protocols) specific to that level. Information originating within system A is therefore progressively "pushed down" through the layers within system A. At each stage, it may be fragmented and encapsulated in a format understandable by the corresponding layer in the other end system. The fully encapsulated and fragmented information is then transferred from system A to system B, as a series of bits, according to the data transfer characteristics of the underlying physical media. As the information is received at system B, it moves up through the layers of system B where it is progressively reassembled and de-packetized until it can finally be passed on to the application layer of system B in a format that it is able to understand. In this manner, application programs within system A and system B can cooperate to execute complex distributed computing functions that straddle both systems.

Electronic mail programs are application layer entities. Regardless of the architecture, electronic mail protocols are typically designed to assume that the problems of end-system to end-system communication have already been solved by the underlying layers in the architecture. Electronic mail therefore focuses on the need to provide value-added services to the end user by relaying end-user messages between a sender and a recipient.

2.2 The TCP/IP Architecture

TCP/IP is a far simpler architecture than OSI. It supports only four distinct protocol layers:

1. *The network interface layer:* This is responsible for interfacing with the underlying physical communication media.
2. *The internet layer:* This handles the correct routing of packets across a wide range of diverse communication media and network topologies.
3. *The transport layer:* This currently supports two protocols: the Transmission Control Protocol (TCP), which provides a reliable packet transport service, and the User Datagram Protocol (UDP), which, as the name implies, provides an unreliable transport service.
4. *The application layer:* The application layer of TCP/IP consists of a collection of programs and applications that have been developed over time to address the specific needs of researchers working on the Internet. New Internet applications are continuously coming into use within the Internet.

The electronic mail application in use within the Internet today is called the Simple Mail Transport Protocol (SMTP). Other popular applications are the File Transfer Protocol (FTP); Telnet (a virtual terminal protocol); Domain Name, which provides distributed naming and addressing services to the Internet; and a number of less familiar protocols such as the Boot Protocol (BootP) and Trivial File Transfer Protocol (TFTP).

Figure 2.2 depicts the layering of the TCP/IP architecture and the choice of protocols that may be employed at each layer to support end-

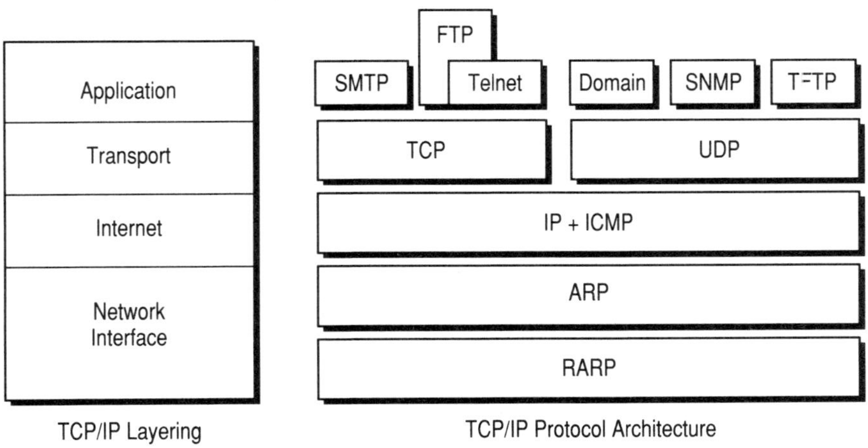

Figure 2.2 TCP/IP architecture.

system to end-system communication. The diagram shows clearly how SMTP, FTP, and Telnet rely on the reliable TCP transport protocol, while Domain Name, BootP, and TFTP (among others) rely on the datagram-based UDP protocol. Both TCP and UDP rely on IP for network routing. Finally, IP relies on ARP and RARP for network access.

2.3 The OSI Reference Model

OSI stands for Open Systems Interconnection. Work on the OSI reference model began within ISO in the early 1980s. The intent in developing the OSI reference model was to develop an architectural framework that would support the specification of a family of networking protocols that would be truly independent of computer hardware platforms or operating systems. OSI encompasses several important goals:

1. It strives to specify and publish an architecture and a set of protocols that taken together, will allow the establishment a unified, interoperable computer networking environment.
2. It strives to define these protocols and architecture in a way that is free of references to specific implementation aspects of any particular hardware or software platform. In this respect, OSI has had to develop a set of abstract concepts, as well as a terminology, that allows its protocols to be specified independently of any references to actual hardware or software implementation details. At times, this can make OSI protocol standards more difficult to read than the corresponding TCP/IP protocol specifications; however, it also makes them more universal in nature.

The OSI reference model defines a seven-layer model of networking, as depicted in Fig. 2.3. Each layer provides the following functions:

1. *Physical layer:* The physical layer defines the electrical characteristics necessary to transfer bits of information over a physical medium, e.g., Ethernet, EIA-232D lines, etc. It specifies in detail the signaling characteristics that need to be employed in order to properly interface to the physical medium.

2. *Data link layer:* The data link layer is responsible for framing data correctly over the underlying physical layer. It is also concerned with the correct sequencing and reliable transmission of the individual data frames.

3. *Network layer:* The network layer supports the protocols necessary to route information correctly within the network. As such it deals with fully formed packets of information that must be appropriately directed from a source system to a destination system. In order

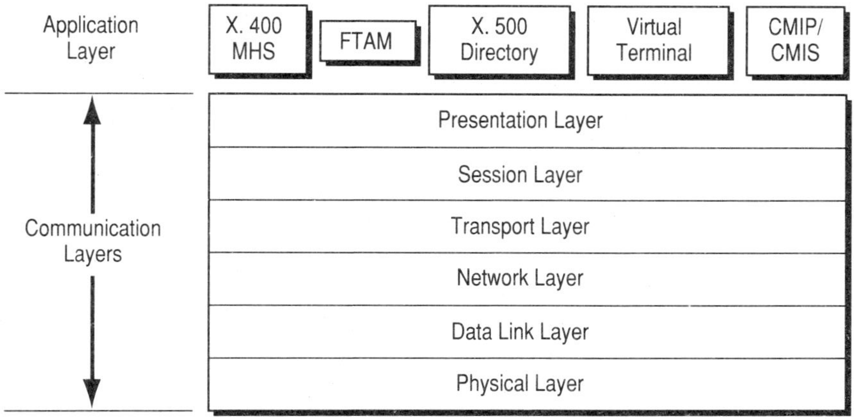

Figure 2.3 OSI protocol architecture.

to reach a particular destination, packets may have to be routed through a number of intermediate nodes in the network.

4. *Transport layer:* The transport layer provides the facilities for the reliable or unreliable transfer of streams of information. The transport layer is the first end-to-end layer of the OSI architecture. It is responsible for ensuring that a stream of information is correctly transferred from a source to a destination.

5. *The session layer:* The session layer provides facilities to manage associations between two end systems. In particular, the session layer is responsible for managing the dialogue between two end systems, that is, allowing data to flow in one direction or the other, as well as setting what are called synchronization points in the dialogue. Synchronization points serve as check points for denoting the successful completion of an information exchange. In the event that one of the two end systems involved in the dialogue crashes, the synchronization point is used to denote the point from which the information transfer exchange should be resumed. Note that no equivalent to the session layer exists in the TCP/IP architecture. Rather, each application implements whatever dialogue and session management facilities it needs in order to get its job done.

6. *The presentation layer:* The presentation layer provides facilities to translate between different data formats used on different computers. It provides facilities for two end systems to negotiate what data transfer syntax they will use in exchanging information. This is very important because it allows computers that normally employ dissimilar data representations to agree on a common data syntax.

7. *The application layer:* The application layer provides all the end-user services typical of distributed computing, such as Filing, Mail, Directories, and Virtual Terminal services. The electronic mail application in OSI is provided by the X.400 Message Handling Services. Other principal OSI application layer protocols are File Transfer Access And Management (FTAM), X.500 Directory Services (which provides a distributed naming service analogous to Domain Name service in TCP/IP), and Virtual Terminal.

From the perspective of the OSI application layer all the protocols and functions provided by layers 1 through 6 can be viewed simply as "communication layers," which provide the basic underlying communication function. Not surprisingly, the application layer is typically where most of the complexity in distributed computing resides. In fact, the application layer is often subdivided into a number of sublayers proper to each particular application.

2.4 Electronic Mail: Basic Functions

Electronic mail systems generally comprise several distinct functions, including

1. Protocols to reliably transport messages from one end system to another.
2. Facilities to create messages.
3. Facilities to display and manage messages locally.

Electronic mail protocols are application layer protocols that typically operate in a store-and-forward manner to reliably transport electronic messages from one end system to another. They are said to be store-and-forward, because messages are not transferred instantaneously from one end system to another. Rather, they are held in the originating end system or one or more intermediate systems until they can be reliably delivered to the intended recipient. The messaging application, which resides within the application layer, is responsible for establishing and managing the underlying communication connection required to transfer messages across a network. The recipient information contained in the envelope of the message is typically used to correctly route messages within the network environment.

Increasingly, electronic mail systems are being designed to accommodate much more than just the transfer of text messages. Most electronic mail systems differentiate clearly between the message tranporting function and the use of that function by different applications to transfer different kinds of information. Such information may include whole electronic documents, spreadsheets, graphics, images, and even voice. Research is under way to experiment with the use of messaging protocols to transfer voice messages in a store-and-forward manner. Experimental systems have been implemented as part of Internet research activities, and standardization work is currently underway within CCITT to include voice messaging as part of the 1992 X.400 MHS recommendations. The basic electronic messaging function is also being used to construct more complex information management applications, such as Electronic Data Interchange (EDI). EDI implements a set of services to support the automated movement of commercial financial transactions.

In order for electronic mail to become widespread not only among computer researchers but also with the general public, it is extremely important that electronic mail systems provide user-friendly facilities to create electronic mail messages. These facilities will typically include text editors that allow information to be changed easily and sophisticated techniques for helping users specify the appropriate message addressing information, as well as request any special messaging delivery options that may be provided by the underlying messaging system.

From the perspective of the message recipient, features must be available locally to display electronic mail messages in various formats as well as organize them according to various criteria, e.g., by time of arrival, by sender in alphabetical order, and so on. Most mail systems, for example, allow mail messages to be retained in some sort of stable storage area organized according to some search criteria selected by the recipient. These kinds of facilities add considerable value to the mail transfer function, and also allow the electronic messaging function to be more closely integrated with a number of other information manipulation facilities, which may already be available on the host computer. For example, users may be able to add whole electronic documents to be sent as attachments to a text-only electronic mail message.

Figure 2.4 shows how the various electronic mail functions relate to each other. At the topmost level the end user sees only the mail creation and display functions. These are typically built upon a set of message management functions that may vary from fairly complex database-like message repository facilities to more simple minded stable storage facilities. Finally, both the message display and management functions rely on the messaging application functionality to actually transport the mail messages between two end systems. The messaging application relies on some sort of communication stack that handles all the specifics of reliably moving data across a network connection.

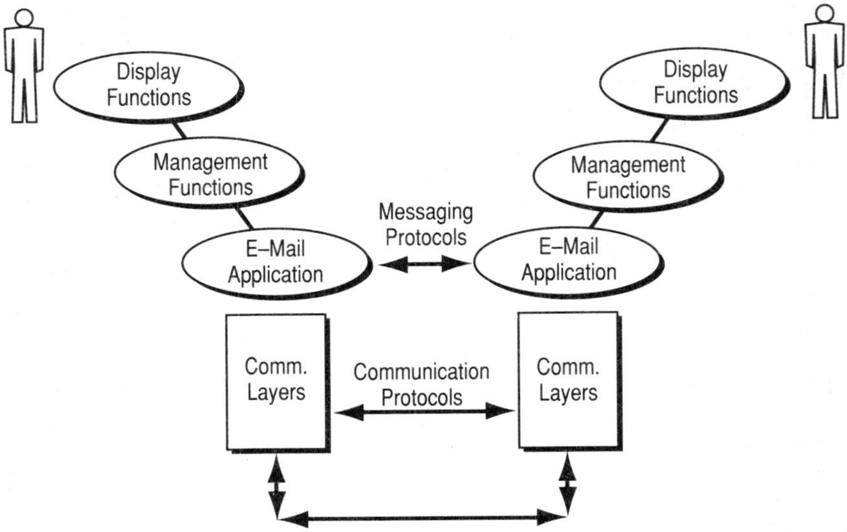

Figure 2.4 Electronic mail functions.

In the future, most of the popularity of electronic mail within the office workplace will derive from its ability to provide significant value-added features. These will include features to help users organize the information they send and receive, as well as more easily move information from a variety of applications into and out of electronic mail messages.

2.5 Mail Forwarding and Relaying

As mentioned earlier, relaying messages within an electronic messaging environment relies almost entirely on the addressing information contained within the header (or "envelope") of the message. Messages are transferred from the host system of the sender to that of the recipient (or recipients if a message is addressed to multiple users) by potentially going through a number of different hosts. Each host uses its local routing information to decide which host to forward the message to next. In making this kind of decision, the host typically relies on routing information previously entered within its routing database by a network administrator. Message routing, therefore, takes place in an incremental fashion that avoids the complexity of having to establish the full path for message transfer at the sender's host system.

Figure 2.5 shows the simplest possible model of store-and-forward message delivery, where the sender and receiver both share the same mail server. Figure 2.6, on the other hand, shows a slightly more com-

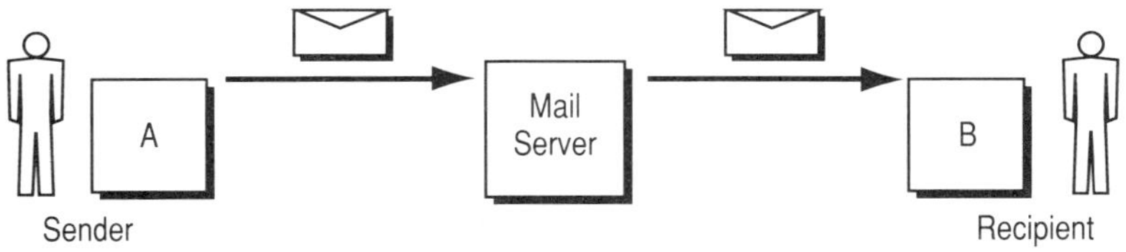

Figure 2.5 Mail server model.

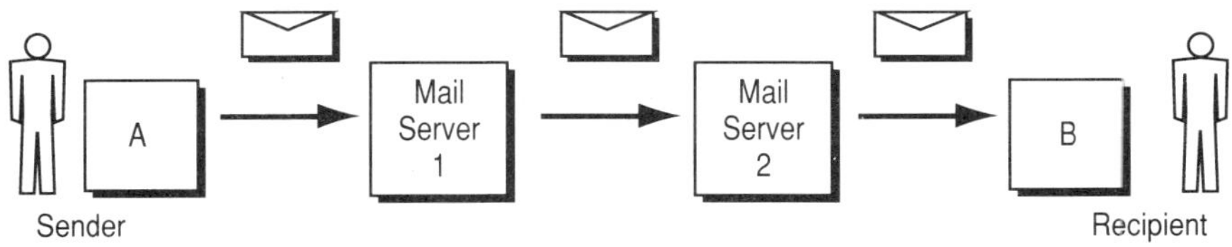

Figure 2.6 Electronic mail being relayed between two Mail Servers.

plex scenario where the message is relayed from the mail server of the sender to that of the recipient. Note that the mail server functionality may be physically colocated with the end user's message display and creation station or it may be separated out as a stand-alone system dedicated to serving as a mail server (as shown in the two figures).

When messages are addressed to multiple recipients, special care must be exercised to avoid the looping of messages in complex networks. This is typically accomplished by maintaining a significant level of trace information, which enables hosts to discern when a message is being forwarded repeatedly through the same path without reaching its intended destination. Some errors can contribute to message looping, such as incorrectly specified routing table information in one of the hosts involved in the routing process.

2.6 Electronic Mail Messages

Electronic mail messages are normally composed of

1. A *header,* which contains all the information necessary to address the message to a set of intended recipients.
2. And a *body,* which contains the actual information that is to be transmitted in the message between two or more end users.

In some electronic mail systems, like X.400 MHS, additional information, called the envelope, is added to the message by the messaging transport protocols to enable the appropriate routing of the message within the network. The envelope information is obtained largely by parsing the header information provided by the sender of the message. In X.400, the header is included with the body of the message and contains user-level addressing information. Throughout the rest of this chapter we will simply distinguish between a generic header, which contains all the necessary message routing information, and the body of the message, which contains the information that the user wishes to have transferred.

Figure 2.7 depicts a typical interoffice memo that may be sent from one employee to another. Most of the typical header information that may be found in a paper message has direct equivalents within an electronic mail message. The header of the interoffice memo corresponds in essence to the header of the electronic mail message, while the text of the message constitutes the body of the electronic mail message.

2.6.1 Message headers

In many of the early mail systems, messages were nothing more than a series of text strings with special delimiters that denoted what portion of the text constituted the "header" portion of the message and what portion constituted the actual end-user message. The function of the header in many early electronic mail messages is, thus, analogous to that of the TO: and CC: fields in physical interoffice memos. X.400 extends the electronic mail analogy to resemble more closely how mail is handled in the real-life postal mail system. In X.400, messages are

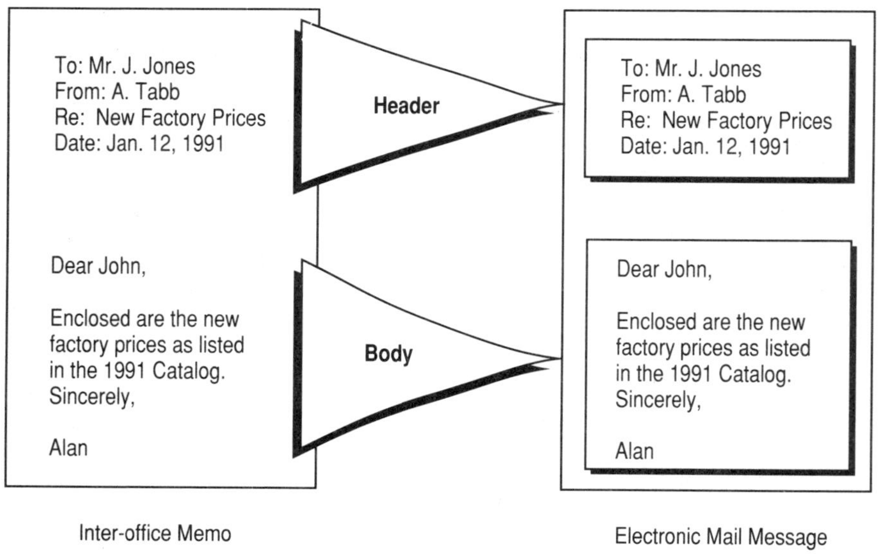

Figure 2.7 Typical office memo.

encapsulated within an "envelope" that contains all the addressing information needed to appropriately route the message within the system. The body of the message contains the header of the message as constructed by its originator and is displayed as such to the recipient upon arrival.

The information contained in the message header, or envelope, is what is used to "route" the message to its intended recipient. In the early mail systems where both sender and recipient shared the same host, the header served simply to indicate which user's mailbox the message was intended for. With the development of geographically dispersed computer networks, however, the role of the message header has expanded to provide enough addressing information to allow the message potentially to be routed through several intermediate hosts until it reaches its final destination.

The address of the message recipients must contain enough information to allow any host in the network to appropriately direct the message. Typically, the address will contain the name of the mailbox (or user) to which the message is addressed, what host the mailbox resides on, and possibly what network the host is connected to.

The header of the message contains all the relevant addressing information, as well as any additional information on status or expected response to the message. It will typically contain information such as

1. *To whom the message is addressed:* This may be the name of another mail user or it may be the name of a group (see Sec. 2.8, "Distribution Lists").
2. *Who is sending the message:* Some electronic mail systems differentiate between two kinds of senders: the name of the user who actually sent the message, and optionally the name of another user who has authorized the sending of the message.
3. *Any additional recipients who should receive a copy of the message:* This is a secondary set of recipients to whom the message is not being directly addressed but rather who are to receive copies of the message for informational purposes only. This field is equivalent to a "cc:" list on an interoffice memorandum.
4. *A time stamp:* This indicates either the time of sending or receipt of the message, or both.
5. *A privacy level:* This may denote the level of confidentiality of the message.
6. *"A reply to:" indication:* Most mail systems carry this as a way of indicating to the recipient of the message who they should address a reply to. This piece of information is supplied within the header of the message by the message originator at the time the message is created.

2.6.2 Message Bodies

The content of a message typically contains a body of text that corresponds to the information being conveyed between two or more end users. In the more sophisticated electronic mail systems, the body of the message may take on many different content types beyond just text. By making the body of the message a logically separate entity from the header information, it becomes easier for messaging systems to transport messages of very different content types transparently. This allows different types of information such as graphics, images, or even voice to be conveyed without changing the basic message transfer protocols. X.400, for example, defines an extensive number of body types of various formats that may be conveyed transparently within the body of a message.

By separating the header information from the body of the message, it also becomes possible for a message to contain a number of different body components, possibly of different types. The real-life analogy is that of a letter containing multiple pages and other kinds of information such as photographs or checks.

Figure 2.8 illustrates a typical office memo made up of text, finan-

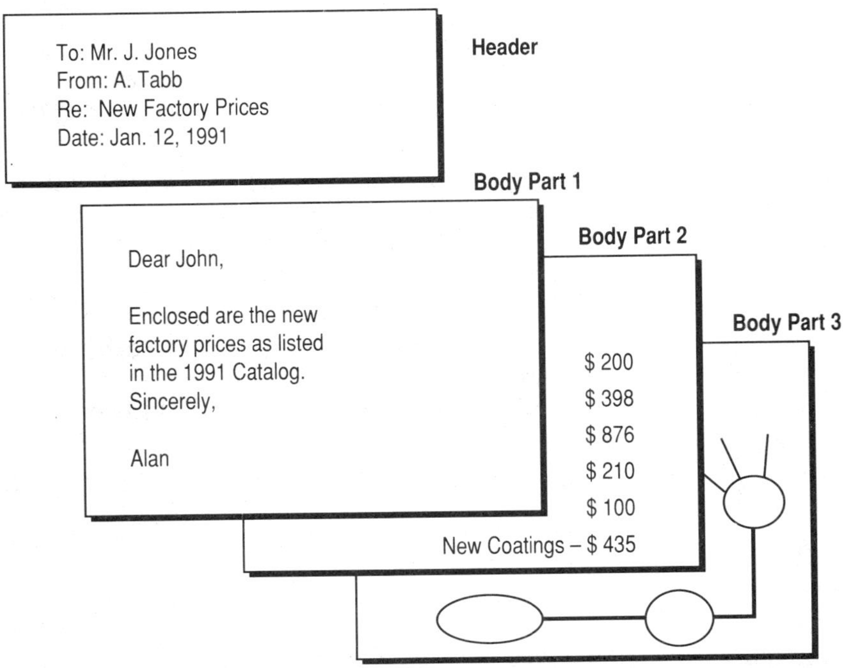

Figure 2.8 Multiple part electronic mail message.

cial figures, and some graphics. Such a memo can be conveyed via electronic mail as a message comprising three distinct body parts: a first body part containing the text of the message, a second body part containing a spreadsheet with the financial information, and a third body part containing the graphic illustration.

2.7 Double Enveloping

The analogy with the real-life postal system is extended in some electronic mail systems, including X.400, to support the concept of double enveloping of messages. (Fig. 2.9). That is, it is possible to embed a complete message composed of a header and potentially multiple body parts within the body of another message. In this case, the underlying messaging protocols system sees only the outer envelope, and the message is routed only according to the information contained in the outer envelope.

Double enveloping of messages is a very simple yet powerful technique that eases the transfer of messages among messaging systems with dissimilar addressing syntaxes and conventions. The use of double enveloping makes it easier to construct gateways among diverse messaging environments (see Sec. 2.9, "Messaging Gateways").

2.8 Distribution Lists

Distribution lists are one of the most powerful concepts in electronic mail. Distribution lists allow messages to be sent to a group of users with the same ease as to a single individual by simply specifying the

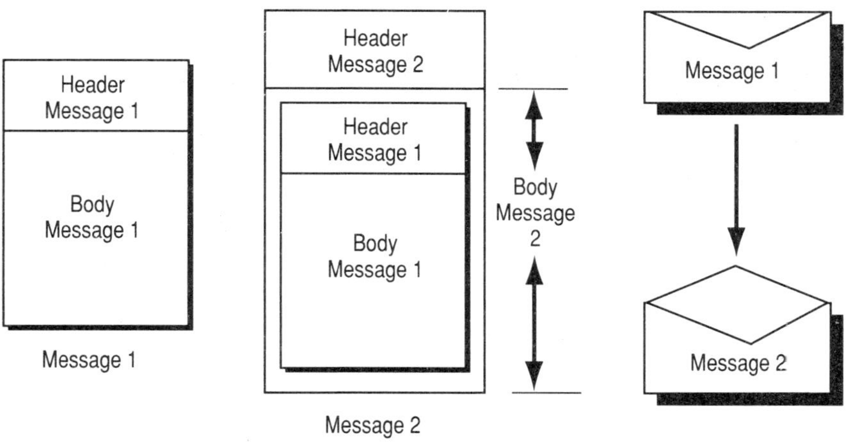

Figure 2.9 Double enveloping of electronic mail messages.

name of the group as one of the recipients of the message. In more advanced systems, distribution lists may also be nested indefinitely. That is, a distribution list can contain other distribution lists as its members.

For example, a network administrator may set up a distribution list containing the names of all the employees of the accounting department, called "Accounting." Thereafter, simply specifying "Accounting" in the list of recipients of the message will cause the message to be delivered to all the members of the accounting department. This avoids the need to type out the name of each member of the accounting department individually. If nesting of distribution lists is allowed, the network administrator may also place the "Accounting" distribution list as a member of a larger distribution list containing all the employees at a particular location, e.g., Headquarters. By specifying "Headquarters" as one of the intended recipients of a message, it is then possible to send electronic mail to all the employees at the headquarters building, including the members of the accounting department.

This kind of functionality offers two very powerful advantages; it frees the sender of a message from having to type potentially very long lists of recipients, and it also avoids the need for the sender to know explicitly all the members of a particular group. This makes it easy to address electronic mail messages to potentially very large groups of recipients without having to remember each individual recipient's name.

Although distribution lists sound like a very simple concept, their implementation can be fairly complex. This is because mechanisms need to be put in place to enable the mail servers to automatically expand distribution lists into their constituent members, as well as recognizing possible message relaying loops caused by misconstructed lists. Due to these complexities, distribution lists are not yet supported by all messaging systems. Even in X.400 MHS, distribution lists are a relatively new concept, which was introduced only in the 1988 version of the standard.

Two issues in particular contribute to make distribution lists difficult to implement:

1. *The need for an underlying distributed directory system:* In a large distributed network environment, it is practically impossible to store the full expansion of large distribution lists composed of many sublists within a single place. Rather, the distribution list information must be stored in an information database, which can be readily accessed by any mail server on the network. This kind of network-wide database is called a directory. Directories are designed to maintain the name-to-address binding of all addressable network entities; as

such, they are an ideal place in which to store distribution list information. More information on directories and their role in supporting distribution lists is provided in Chap. 6.

2. *The potential they introduce for routing loops:* One of the great concerns in the design and implementation of electronic mail systems is the avoidance of messages looping indefinitely from one mail server to another. Because distribution lists can be nested indefinitely, they inherently increase the likelihood that a message will be repeatedly routed through the same mail server. This likelihood, which is part of the normal operation of the system, makes it more difficult for a mail server to detect when a message is being repeated because of a legitimate distribution list expansion or because of an error in routing. Again, this topic is dealt with more extensively in Chap. 6 where the implementation of distribution lists in 1988 X.400 MHS is described.

Figure 2.10 shows an example of how a distribution list may be expanded in a distributed system involving several mail servers. A message addressed to the accounting distribution list is submitted for delivery to mail server 1. Mail server 1 begins to expand the accounting distribution list and finds that it is composed of three members: Mike, Joe, and a nested distribution list called Payroll. Since Mike and Joe have mailboxes on mail server 2, mail server 1 forwards a copy of the message to mail server 2 for delivery to Mike and Joe. It also finds that it does not hold the list of members for the Payroll distribution list, so it forwards the message to mail server 2 for further expansion. Upon receipt of the message, mail server 2 delivers a copy of it to users

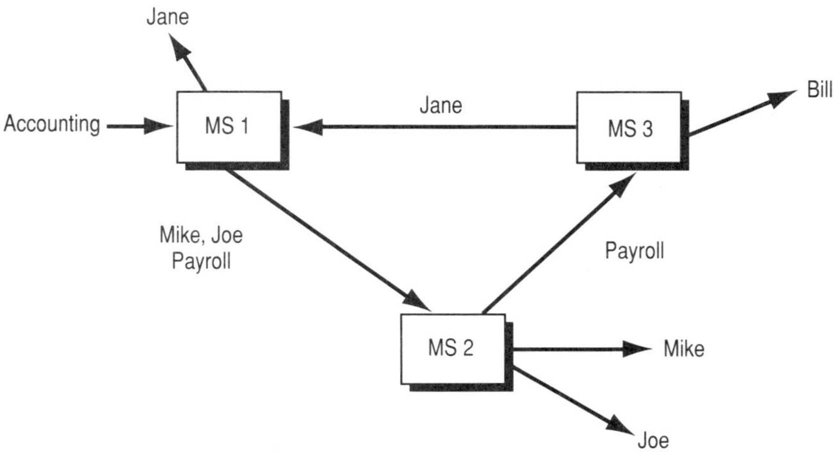

Figure 2.10 Example of distribution list expansion.

Mike and Joe, and also attempts to expand the Payroll distribution list. Again, it finds that it does not have the membership information necessary to expand Payroll, so it forwards a copy of the message to mail server 3 for further expansion. Mail server 3 is able to expand Payroll and discovers that it consists of two members: Bill and Jane. Since Bill has his mailbox on mail server 3, it simply delivers the message to Bill's mailbox. Since Jane has her mailbox on mail server 1, mail server 3 forwards a copy of the message to mail server 1 for delivery to Jane's mailbox. In this manner the distribution list is progressively expanded until all its constituent members have received a copy of the message as intended. Also, the example shows how the message can return to mail server (in this case, mail server 1) after all the nested distribution lists been fully expanded.

2.9 Messaging Gateways

In large networks it is often likely that different parts of the network are being managed by different administrative organizations. This means that the network is effectively partitioned into different administrative domains (or simply "domains" as they are called) which may be following somewhat different rules for handling electronic mail within their environments. In the simplest case, all domains have implemented the same basic mail protocols and architecture but may still vary in setting security policies or other locally definable administrative concerns. In more complex cases, different domains may have implemented very different mail protocols and messaging architectures. In either case, a special effort is required to transfer electronic mail across domains with different messaging characteristics. This task is accomplished through the use of what are called messaging gateways.

Messaging gateways are a very important concept in electronic mail as they enable messages to traverse messaging domains that may require very different message syntaxes. Typically, a gateway encapsulates the message it has received into a new message, which has a new header constructed mostly out of information contained in the old one, but formatted according to the syntax rules required by the new domain.

One of the major benefits of gatewaying in messaging systems is that it allows electronic messaging environments with very dissimilar characteristics to communicate with each other. As the push to interconnect users among disparate electronic mail systems increases, it is usually possible to do so through the use of gatewaying techniques rather than forcing everyone to migrate over to the same messaging system. This is important since many existing proprietary messaging

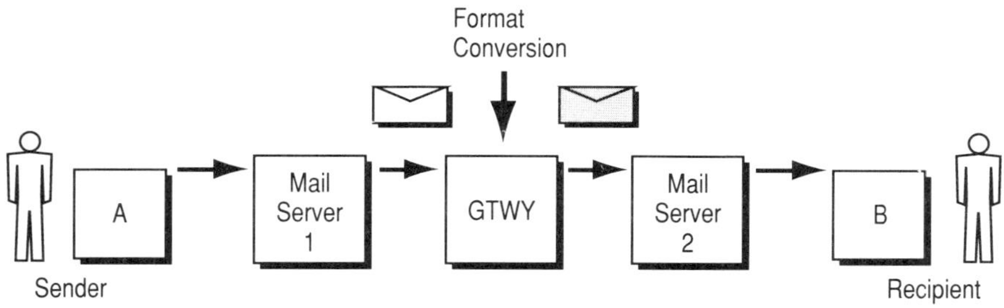

Figure 2.11 The use of gateways in message delivery.

systems provide extensive value-added features, which users have typically become accustomed to. By gatewaying, often much of the value-added functionality is lost; however, the basic information can effectively be transferred from one environment to the other.

Figure 2.11 shows a mail message that is being transferred from a user in one administrative domain to a user in a different administrative domain requiring a different message encapsulation syntax. A mail gateway is required between mail server 1 and mail server 2 to allow the electronic mail message to be forwarded correctly from the sender's environment to that of the recipient. The mail gateway performs any header translation or message encapsulation that may be required to transform the original message into one that will be understandable by the new domain. Note that while the diagram above depicts the mail gateway as a stand-alone network entity, in reality, it is usually physically coresident with one of the mail servers involved in the message transfer (i.e., either mail server 1 or mail server 2).

References and for Further Study

Tanenbaum (1988) gives an in-depth introduction to computer networking. Comer (1988) gives an in-depth description of the Internet protocols and architecture. The OSI reference model is fully defined in ISO 7498 [ISO 7498].

Chapter

3

A Brief Survey

This chapter provides an introduction to some of the electronic mail system designs that preceded X.400 MHS. In particular, it provides a detailed overview of the Simple Mail Transport Protocol (SMTP), which is widely in use in the Internet today. SMTP is a simple, elegant, yet very powerful technique for electronic messaging which is becoming increasingly popular as a result of the widespread use of the TCP/IP protocol suite as a de facto standard for both commercial and research network environments.

3.1 Mail in the Internet

Electronic mail in the ARPANET was initially implemented as two File Transfer Protocol (FTP) commands MAIL and MLFL. These commands permitted an FTP user process to deliver a file, or a string of text, to an FTP server process. The information transferred in this manner was designated as mail for delivery to a specified user or set of users. Users were identified simply by a local name in their host (see RFC 524).

Gradually, three major tasks became clearly delineated within the ARPANET messaging system:

1. The transport of mail messages.
2. The relaying of messages among various intermediate hosts to route them from an original sender to the intended recipient.
3. Addressing, which is the task of naming the intended recipient in such a way that mail can be routed to that recipient, potentially across a variety of disparate intermediate systems, or gateways.

Today, mail in the Internet has evolved into an application that can operate on top of a generic message transfer system and is implemented according to two RFCs:

1. RFC-822 is the standard for the format of ARPA Internet text messages, developed by D. Crocker, which specifies the format of mail messages exchanged.
2. RFC-821, or Simple Mail Transfer Protocol (SMTP), as it is more commonly called, which specifies the protocol interactions required to transfer mail messages between two computers.

Keeping the messaging format separate from the protocol mechanisms that transfer the mail messages between host computers has several advantages. First of all, it makes it possible to add new or additional message formats without forcing the entire messaging system to change. Second, it makes it easier to design messaging gateways, since the message formatting aspects are cleanly separated from the message forwarding mechanisms. RFC-822 can operate over a number of diverse message transfer environments which include

1. *SMTP:* This is the predominant mail transfer protocol used in the Internet. It is often used in conjunction with RFC 1034, which specifies a distributed name service for use in the Internet environment.
2. *UUCP:* This is the UNIX-to-UNIX copy protocol used over dial-up phone lines. When RFC-822 is used in UUCP networks, it carries some addressing extensions.
3. *Csnet:* While some portions of Csnet use the Internet protocols, the dial-up portion of Csnet uses the Phonenet protocols rather than SMTP.
4. *Bitnet:* Some portions of Bitnet use RFC-822 with EBCDIC encoding.
5. *JNT Mail:* JNT stands for joint team network. A number of X.25 networks, particularly those of the U.K. academic community, use a sort of "home brew" mail protocol called the "Greybook" over JNT networks.

Messages formatted according to RFC-822 consist simply of lines of text. No provisions are provided to support the exchange of graphic drawings, facsimile, speech, or even structured text (i.e., documents). An RFC-822 message consists essentially of a header and a body, much in the same way as an interoffice memo or a letter does. The header and body are both contiguous streams of text and are separated only by a NULL line (i.e., two contiguous carriage linefeeds) which denotes the end of the header portion.

Addressing in RFC-822 relies on hierarchical, logical name-domains, which provides greater flexibility in large geographical environments. It also means that while in most cases domain names will correspond to the names of hosts, that dependency is no longer a strict requirement.

Addresses in RFC-822 take the following form:

```
<user @ domain1.domain2.domain3>
```

for example,

```
jsmith@alpha.novell.com
```

Where domain3 is called the top-level domain, and domains 2 and 1 are considered subdomains. Some examples of top-level domains are COM for commercial networks (e.g., private companies), EDU for educational institutions (e.g., university networks), GOV for government networks, MIL for military networks, and ORG for nonprofit organizations (e.g., ISO).

RFC-822 supports source routing, where the full transfer path is specified by the originator posting the message. The use of source routing is highly discouraged, particularly because it makes gatewaying to other messaging environments more difficult. However, when using RFC-822 it may sometimes become necessary to use source routing to send a message to a destination node that serves as a gateway to another network. Two source routing syntaxes are defined to support this:

1. <mailbox % domain3 % domain2 % domain1>

This syntax causes a message to be routed first to domain1, and subsequently to domain2 and domain3, where it will finally attempt to match a recipient's mailbox. While this syntax is not officially documented in RFC-822, it has become generally accepted in every electronic mail system in the Internet. The second kind of permissible syntax is

2. <@ domain1, @ domain2:mailbox @ domain3>

Using this second kind of source routing, messages are first addressed to domain1, then domain2, and finally to domain3, where the intended recipient's mailbox is located.

RFC-822 supports addressing of messages to groups (i.e., distribution lists), but not to nested groups (i.e., groups within groups). This considerably simplifies concerns over looping of messages. RFC-822 also supports forwarding of messages, that is, the resending of a message by adding some new fields to its header information. When a field is preceded by the string "Resent-", the field is treated as more recent than the equivalent original field. For example, "Resent-from" denotes the person that forwarded the message, while the "From" field denotes the original author of the message.

Trace fields are used to provide an audit trail of message handling. This is important in detecting potential message forwarding loops, while at the same time providing valuable information about the state of the network.

User-definable extension fields are also supported. These are fields that a user may define to carry some semantics particular to a specific user application. Extension fields are recognized by prepending them with an "X-" string. Users are encouraged to register such fields with the Network Information Center (NIC), at SRI International, Menlo Park, California. We will see in Chap. 10, "Advanced Topics," how this capability plays a major role in enabling the implementation of gateways between RFC-822–based systems and X.400-based systems.

RFC-822 also allows for the specification of a special "Postmaster" address. This is a mailbox that can be set aside to catch undeliverable mail, that is, mail for which a valid recipient could not be found will be posted at the Postmaster address, and eventually returned to the originator of the message along with an indication of nondelivery.

3.1.1 SMTP

SMTP replaces an earlier, more complex mail protocol called MTP (Mail Transfer Protocol). SMTP defines the protocol interactions required by a sender machine to deposit mail messages into the work storage of the recipient's mail server machine. The sender contacts the recipient's mail server directly in order to deliver the mail message. This is very reliable and efficient because the messages are deposited directly from the working space of the sending machine into that of the recipient machine. There is therefore no need to rely on intermediate mail routers which can potentially introduce delays in the transfer, as well as lose messages in transit. Figure 3.1 summarizes SMTP's simple interactions model where messages and commands are exchanged between a sender and a receiver process operating on different hosts. Each process manages the interaction with the local file system and reacts to messaging requests initiated by a user at the sending host. An SMTP user may be either a human user or another application program.

All the protocol messages exchanged between the client (i.e., sender) and the mail server (i.e., recipient) are human readable text

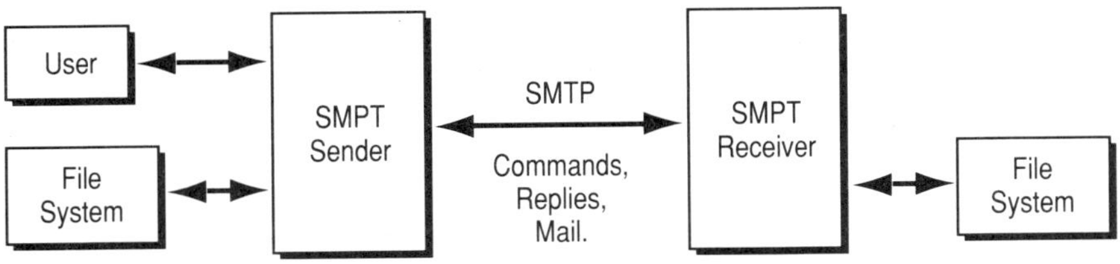

Figure 3.1 SMTP model of interactions.

messages. This makes SMTP a truly simple tool for message transfer. All SMTP commands start with a number, which also makes them easy to parse.

SMTP is defined independently of a particular underlying transmission subsystem; it requires only a reliable, ordered data stream upon which to operate. It relies on the concept of an interprocess communication environment (IPCE) that can cover one or more networks. Mail can be relayed between hosts on different transport systems by a host that operates on both transports.

The process for sending mail via SMTP is as follows:

1. A sender-SMTP establishes a two-way channel to a receiver-SMTP.
2. The receiver-SMTP may be either the intended end destination of the message or an intermediary.
3. The SMTP-sender sends a MAIL command, indicating who the sender is. The SMTP-receiver can either accept or reject the proposed mail transfer. If it accepts, it responds with an OK reply message.
4. The SMTP-sender then sends a RCPT command for each intended recipient. The receiver replies with an OK reply for each recipient. It can choose to reject a particular recipient without rejecting the entire exchange.
5. The sender then sends the mail message, or messages, it wishes to send and terminates with a special sequence denoting the end of the message transfer.

The argument of the MAIL command is a reverse-path list indicating from whom the mail is being sent. Incorporated in the reverse path are all the hosts that may have been traversed to date in the message delivery process. The reverse-path can be used as a return route in order to return the message to its sender when an error occurs. The first host in the list is the one sending the command. The argument of the RCPT command is a forward-path stating who the mail message is for. The forward path is a source route; the first host in the list is the one receiving the command, while the last one is the final intended destination. Both SMTP commands and replies are composed uniquely of ASCII characters.

3.1.1.1 Relaying. The forward path for an RFC-822 message may be a source route of the form:

```
''@ONE, @TWO: Joe@THREE''
```

where ONE, TWO, and THREE are hosts. By using source routing, the SMTP sender can get the SMTP-receiver to relay mail to another SMTP-server. The receiver-SMTP may either accept or reject the task of relaying the message, in the same way that it can accept or reject messages for intended local recipients. Upon receipt of a message to be relayed, the SMTP-receiver moves its own identifier from the "forward-path" to the beginning of the "reverse-path." The receiver-SMTP then becomes a sender-SMTP and sets up a transmission channel to the next SMTP-server in the path.

The forward and reverse path information is only present in the SMTP level command and need not actually be visible in the message header information that is displayed to the end user. Mailboxes represent absolute addresses, whereas routes are relative information that indicates how to reach a particular destination from a given point.

3.1.1.2 Mail forwarding. There are instances where the destination information specified in the forward-path is incorrect. However, the receiver-SMTP may know the correct destination for the message. In this case, two kinds of replies are possible:

1. *"251 User not local; will forward to <forward-path> :* This indicates that the receiver-SMTP accepts the message anyway and will forward it to the correct destination shown in the forward-path. The correct destination information is returned to the sender-SMTP using the forward-path for possible future use.
2. *"551 User not local; please try <forward-path> :* This indicates that the recipient does not accept the message, but the recipient provides the sender-SMTP with the address of the correct destination to which the message should be addressed. In this case, the sender-SMTP can try again to send the message by contacting the correct destination directly.

3.1.1.3 Verifying and expanding. SMTP also provides commands to verify user names and expand distribution lists, called mailing lists in SMTP terminology. The VRFY command allows a character string containing the user name to be passed as an argument, and returns the full name of the user and its mailbox name.

The use of mail aliases also serves as a distribution list mechanism which allows a local site to expand a mail identifier into a set of one or more mail addresses. Using the EXPN command, a character string argument that identifies a mailing list is expanded into the full name and mailbox name of all the users contained in the mailing list.

Both of these commands are considered optional and need not be present in every implementation of SMTP. Also, neither command is expected to work across relays. This is intuitive since the ability to expand naming information across networks requires the presence on the network of some form of distributed naming database. Making this a mandatory requirement would be contrary to the overall simplicity intended for the RFC-822 and SMTP architecture.

3.1.1.4 Sending and mailing. SMTP supports the concept of "mailing" which corresponds to depositing a message in a user's mailbox. It also, however, supports a concept called "sending," in which a message is simply delivered to a user's active terminal. The sending command is not mandatory on all implementations, and users at their terminals may choose to either accept or reject an incoming send request. Sending is a useful concept, however, to force a mail message to the immediate attention of a user logged in at an active terminal.

3.1.1.5 Opening and closing. Two commands are used to open and close the underlying SMTP transmission channel. These are the HELO command followed by the name of the domain that is initiating the request, and the QUIT command that closes the channel.

3.1.1.6 Domains. The concept of domains was introduced only later in the SMTP environment. The introduction of the domain concept modifies the name space from a flat global name space to a hierarchically structured, rooted tree of global addresses. The host name is replaced by a domain and host designator which is a sequence of domain elements. The use of aliases is disallowed in domain names.

3.1.1.7 Transmission channels. SMTP may be used over a variety of transmission environments. It may be used over TCP, NCP (which is the ARPANET host-to-host protocol), or over X.25. However, when it is used over X.25, it is usually coupled with a reliable transport protocol like TCP.

3.1.1.8 Changing roles. SMTP also supports a TURN command that allows an SMTP-sender and SMTP-receiver to exchange roles without having to tear down a connection and reestablish a new one. Again this feature is optional and need not be implemented by all SMTP servers. Also, it is largely unnecessary when the underlying transmission protocol is TCP because of the low overhead TCP carries in opening up a new connection. On the other hand, when operating over transmission channels where the connection set up overhead is high, such as networks running TCP over X.25, this becomes a very desirable feature.

3.1.1.9 SMTP example. A typical SMTP interaction proceeds in the following manner:

1. A client establishes a reliable transport stream connection to the mail server and waits for the server to respond with a "220 READY FOR MAIL" message.
2. Upon receipt of the 220 message, the client sends a "HELO name of mail server" (short for HELLO) command, to which the server responds by identifying itself.
3. At this point the mail session is established, and the sender can send one or more messages, terminate or abort the connection, or exchange sender and receiver roles via a "TURN" command, in order to retrieve mail off the server.
4. The receiver must acknowledge each message. It is also free to abort a particular message transfer or the entire connection.
5. Message transfer transactions begin with a MAIL command that identifies the sender, and a FROM: field that identifies where errors should be reported.
6. The recipient responds to the MAIL command by sending a 250 message, which indicates that everything is OK.
7. After each successful MAIL command, the sender issues a RCPT command for each recipient of the mail message. If a user is not known, it sends back a "550 NO SUCH USER HERE."
8. After going through all the RCPT commands, the sender sends a DATA command. The receiver responds with "354 START MAIL INPUT" and specifies a sequence of characters that must be used to terminate each mail message (e.g., carriage return, linefeed, period, carriage return, linefeed).

3.2 UUCP Mail

UUCP was designed at Bell Laboratories for use on hardwired communication links or dial-up lines ranging from 300 to 9600 baud between UNIX systems. Two programs are used to realize the UUCP functionality:

UUCP for file copying

UUX for remote execution

Both rely on a common message transfer program called UUCICO. To connect to a remote host, UUCICO dials up the remote host, logs in, and starts the corresponding UUCICO program. The two UUCICO programs on the connected hosts then begin to exchange user data. Electronic mail is a popular application of this simple dial-up facility. Work is underway to bring the addressing scheme of UUCP mail in line with RFC-822. At the moment, however, compatibility with RFC-822 is achieved largely through host mappings agreed upon offline between network administrators.

3.3 BITNET

The Remote Spooling and Communications Subsystem (RSCS) was released by IBM in 1975 with VM/370 OS. RSCS allows a file transfer to take place between nodes connected with BSC lines and relies on a flat address space that provides a worldwide RSCS-based network addressing scheme.

A principal application built on top of the RSCS facility is BITNET. Two other networks, EARN (Europe) and Netnorth (Canada), are directly connected to BITNET and share the same address space but operate under different administrations.

BITNET has existed since 1981 and was initially developed in cooperation between the City University of New York (CUNY) and Yale University. It is based on hosts directly connected by leased lines operating at either 9.6 kbytes/s or 64 kbytes/s. One of the major advantages of BITNET, which has contributed greatly to its popularity, is that it provides fixed costs rather than volume charging.

BITNET supports store-and-forward message transfer, static routing tables, and gateways to ARPANET.

In 1982 a proposal was made to develop an interactive transaction protocol similar to SMTP for BITNET in order to simulate a real

SMTP hookup. This new protocol was called BSMTP. A major goal of BSMTP has been to ease access to the ARPANET from BITNET by more closely conforming with ARPANET's SMTP. BSMTP is the predominant mail service used in BITNET today.

References and for Further Study

White (RFC 524) gives a perspective on the development of electronic mail in the ARPANET. Bressler and Thomas describe the use of FTP protocols for electronic mail (RFC 458). Postel (RFC 821) defines the Simple Mail Transport Protocol, whereas the text format of Internet messages is defined by Crocker (RFC 822). Comer (1988) gives an in-depth description of electronic messaging development and use in the Internet.

Chapter

4

The X.400 MHS Layer Architecture

This chapter provides an introduction to the OSI protocol layering aspects as they pertain specifically to X.400 MHS. As you will recall from Chap. 2, OSI is primarily a reference model for a family of networking protocols that adhere to some common principles. When actually dealing with a particular OSI application, such as X.400 MHS, many protocol variations are possible within the overall OSI framework. This chapter looks at the protocol layering requirements specific to X.400 MHS. As such, it provides a "vertical" view of X.400. It also examines in detail the protocol layering differences that exist between ISO, CCITT, NIST, as well as 1984 and 1988 X.400 MHS. A number of important supporting application standards that serve as basic "building blocks" for the X.400 MHS protocols are also described.

4.1 The 1984 Layer Architecture

The 1984 MHS protocol stack looks very different from the OSI application layer architecture as we know it today. Figure 4.1 shows the protocol layering mandated by CCITT in the 1984 MHS recommendations. CCITT requires the use of X.25 at layers 1 through 3, the physical, data link, and network layers, respectively, to connect to public data networks. It also mandates the use of unreliable class 0 at the transport layer, with class 1 being defined as optional. The choice of class 0 at the transport layer was not dictated by purely architectural reasons, but rather because most of the public service providers were not yet ready to commit to providing a higher grade of service on very large, commercial networks. Typically in public network environments the use of TP0 implies the use of X.25 at layers 1 through 3.

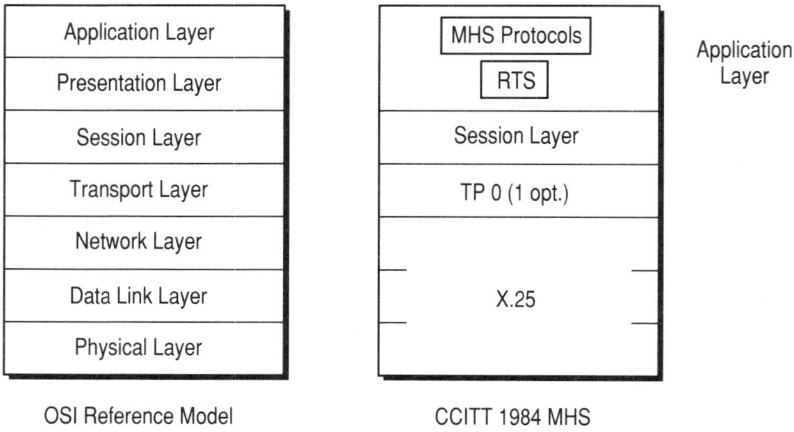

Figure 4.1 1984 CCITT MHS stack.

1984 MHS also defines a protocol called Remote Transfer Service (RTS) which operates directly on top of the session layer. RTS is designed to provide end-to-end reliability when transferring large quantities of data over unreliable network connections. The RTS provides recovery facilities to handle interrupted transfers. The 1984 MHS protocols are designed to operate directly over the RTS protocol.

Work on 1984 MHS also led to the realization that OSI, as defined at the time, lacked some of the basic building blocks necessary for constructing distributed systems. In particular, two functional requirements were identified:

1. The need for a request-reply protocol that can effectively model the interactions of client-server systems.
2. The need for a common data representation language that can straddle data representation differences among different computers.

In order to address these requirements, two new application layer standards were defined: the Remote Operations Service (ROS) and the Abstract Syntax Notation One (ASN.1). A first version of ROS and ASN.1 were approved by CCITT as MHS recommendations X.410 and X.409 respectively at the end of the 1984 study period.

At the time the 1984 MHS standards were being defined, ISO had not yet completed its work on the presentation layer and the OSI upper layer architecture. The presentation layer is, therefore, absent in 1984 MHS, but its functions have been compensated for by the use of ROS and ASN.1. All of the 1984 MHS protocols are defined using ASN.1 notation.

The requirements addressed by ROS and ASN.1 have since been recognized to be common to other OSI distributed applications, besides MHS. They are therefore also employed by other application layer standards, such as X.500 Directories and Network Management.

The 1984 protocol layering is still the predominant architecture used today to attach to PTT-provided MHS services. Most PTTs have offered an initial set of commercial services on the basis of the 1984 MHS. Many PTTs are currently in the process of upgrading their services to the 1988 MHS architecture. However, due to the complexity of 1988 MHS, it is likely this will be a slow process, which will take place gradually over the next few years.

4.2 1984 MHS in Private Networks

ISO MOTIS and NIST chose to specify a protocol architecture which differs slightly from that mandated by CCITT in order to better accommodate the needs of private networks. The NIST agreements differ from the CCITT protocol layering in two major respects:

1. The use of class 4 (i.e., reliable transport) at the transport layer is defined as an option.
2. The use of LAN-based technologies, such as Ethernet, at the lower layers is made optional in addition to X.25.

Figure 4.2 shows the NIST version of the 1984 MHS stack. This is an MHS stack that has been implemented in many computer vendors' products and that is likely to prevail in many private networks, par-

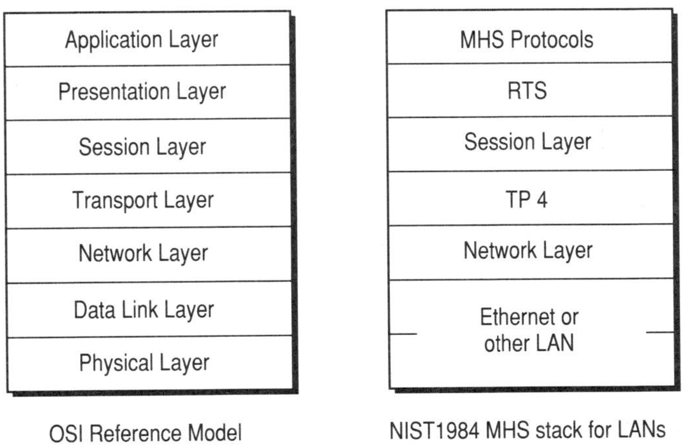

Figure 4.2 NIST 1984 MHS stack for LANs.

ticularly in the United States. When connecting to public services, these private networks must revert back to the use of X.25 and transport class 0. Typically they rely on the use of gateways to convert their operational behavior to comply with CCITT's version of the stack.

While the CCITT, ISO MOTIS, and NIST 1984 architectures may employ slightly different protocol variations at the lower layers, all make similar use of session and RTS at the higher layers. This helps to minimize discrepancies between LAN and WAN environments. By containing the protocol differences to the lower layers, it becomes easier to build gateways between different architectures. Discrepancies at the higher application layers typically require more complex gatewaying functions, which ultimately result in a higher degree of performance degradation.

4.3 The 1988 MHS Layer Architecture

CCITT's work on 1988 MHS coincided well in timing with the completion of ISO's work on OSI upper-layer architecture. This has led both organizations to adopt a common upper-layer architecture at the end of the 1988 study period.

The 1988 upper-layer architecture includes ROS, ASN.1, presentation, and ACSE. As a result, in 1988 MHS, these specifications have been moved out of the MHS recommendations and have been issued as stand-alone documents that are now part of the X.200 series recommendations. This makes it easier for these standards to be referenced by other OSI application layer standards, such as X.500 and Network Management.

An additional conceptual refinement that grew out of ISO work on upper-layer architectures is the notion of an Application Service Element (ASE). ASEs are application layer entities that provide a particular set of services, for instance, a request-reply style of interaction. In the 1988 OSI standards the terminology changes to refer to ROS as a Remote Operation Service Element (ROSE) and RTS as a Remote Transfer Service Element (RTSE). Application Service Elements may be "bound" together in many different ways to yield what are called Application Contexts (ACs). "Application context" is a fancy term for application layer protocol. So, while OSI disallows sublayering at the application layer, the use of ASEs and ACs makes it possible to mix and match functionality at the application layer to fit specific application requirements.

One of the advantages that derives from defining protocols as comprising different application contexts rather than simply relying on different classes of service is that it does away with the need for protocol negotiation at the application layer. Some of the earlier OSI pro-

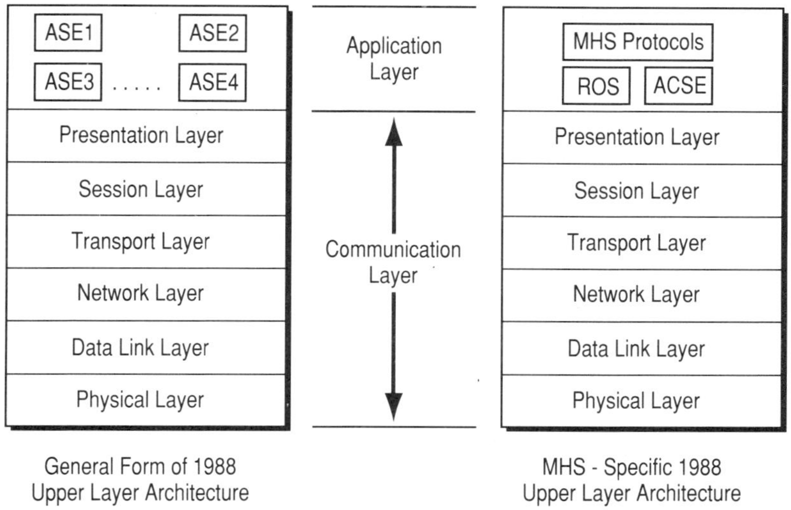

Figure 4.3 1988 OSI upper-layer architecture.

tocols such as transport and session defined very lengthy and complex negotiation interactions which allowed two parties to agree on a common class of service. With the use of application contexts, two application entities will simply attempt to establish an association with an application context and will either succeed or fail in doing so. If the request fails, the application will simply attempt to connect using a different application context, and so on until a suitable common application context is found. This process is considerably simpler and more straightforward than performing class and parameter negotiations.

Figure 4.3 shows the OSI upper-layer architecture as we know it today. The stack on the left shows the general form of the architecture where the application layer is composed of a number of potential ASEs, each of which implements a particular service. The stack on the right illustrates more specifically some of the ASEs that make up a 1988 MHS stack.

Figures 4.4 and 4.5 show the 1988 version of MHS. Again one can differentiate between a CCITT version of 1988 (Fig. 4.4), which utilizes X.25 and transport class 0 at the lower layers, and the ISO MOTIS version (Fig. 4.5), which may also support transport class 4 and a variety of LAN technologies at the lower layers.

The topics of interoperability between 1984 and 1988 systems, as well as conversion between private and public data networks, are discussed in greater detail in Chap. 10, "Advanced Topics."

In order to understand the MHS standards it is necessary to gain

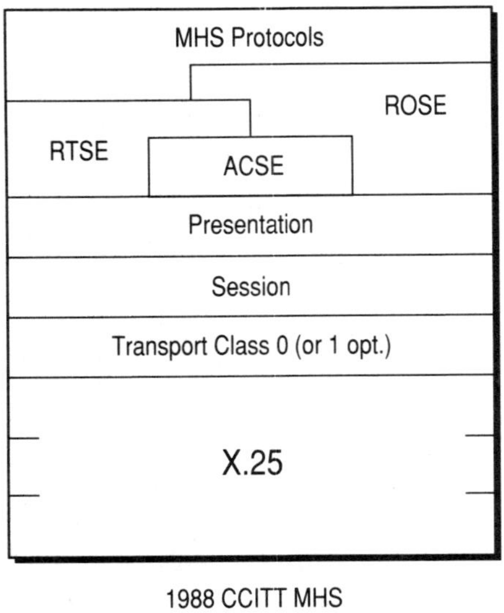

Figure 4.4 1988 CCITT MHS stack.

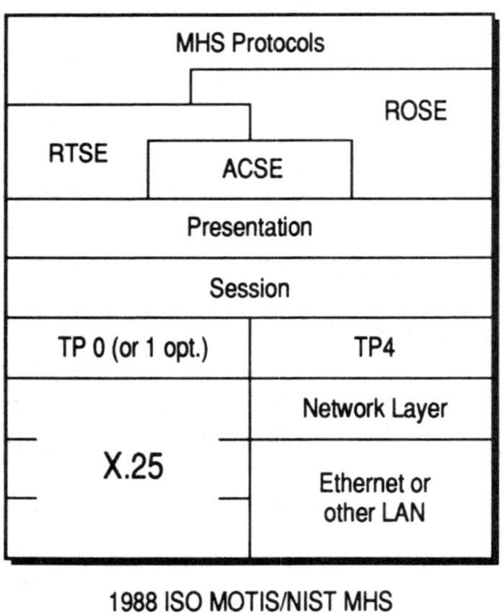

Figure 4.5 1988 NIST MHS stack.

familiarity with four underlying protocol standards that serve as the supporting foundation for the MHS protocols. These standards include ROS, RTS, and ASN.1 for 1984 and 1988 MHS, as well as what is called the Association Control Service Element (ACSE) for 1988 MHS. The following sections provide a very brief overview of these four supporting standards. It is recommended that readers who need to gain a detailed understanding of the MHS protocols, particularly implementors, study these underlying standards documents in detail before approaching the MHS standards themselves.

4.4 The Association Control Service Element (ACSE)

ACSE provides services to control the establishment and release of associations between OSI application entities. Application layer associations are simply logical connections between two application layer entities that are engaged in carrying out some end-user action. The ACSE protocol exchange is used to trigger the establishment, release, and aborting of all the underlying communication mechanisms necessary to manage an association between two end systems. Once an association has been set up using ACSE, it can be used by any number of protocols (e.g., ROS) to actually exchange application level information.

ACSE is also used to support the transparent exchange of security credentials (e.g., password information) between two end systems at the time an association is established. The exchange is considered to be transparent because ACSE does not enter into the semantics of the security credentials exchanged but merely transfers them unchanged across the network.

4.5 The Reliable Transfer Service (RTS)

RTS is designed to reliably transfer what are called Application Protocol Data Units (APDUs) between two end systems. Each APDU corresponds to an MHS message that needs to be delivered from a source to a destination. The RTS layer is responsible for breaking up the message into data units that match the capabilities of the underlying session layer and for sequencing the information correctly. Since the encoding of the ADPUs transferred in 1984 MHS is dependent on the ASN.1 syntax, the lack of a formal presentation layer is not a problem to the correct interpretation of the data between different end systems.

In 1988 MHS, RTS changes its name to RTSE mostly as cosmetic change to bring it in line with the OSI model for upper-layer standards, which define various protocols operating at the upper layer as "service elements." Also, in 1988 MHS when it is operating in 1984 compatibility mode, RTSE uses the presentation layer in what is called a *pass-through mode.* Effectively this means that while a presentation layer is conceptually present in each end system, it is not used to add value to the communication exchanged. The RTS-level information that is exchanged, however, is encoded as Presentation Service Data Units (PSDUs) for consistency with the overall OSI upper-layer model. RTS is accessed directly by the message transfer service of X.400.

While there is a one-to-one correspondence between session connections, transport connections, and network connections, the termination of a session connection does not necessarily imply the termination of the underlying transport connection.

RTS may be thought of as comprising three distinct phases: a session establishment phase, a data transfer phase, and a session release phase. Thus, when the message transfer layer needs to send a message, it first establishes an RTS association through the use of the OPEN.Request primitive. This maps directly to the corresponding session layer primitive to establish an association with the remote application layer entity.

While the association is active, several messages may be sent over it, and each message is confirmed before another one is sent. For long messages, minor synchronization points are used to reduce the amount of retransmissions needed in the event of a recovery. If the association breaks for any reason, such as the crashing of one of the two partners, the session layer recovery mechanisms are used to restart the activity.

1984 X.400 defines five distinct RTS primitives:

1. *OPEN.Request:* This establishes an association between two application layer entities. Open is a confirmed request and returns an OPEN.Confirmation indication. Various association parameters may be negotiated, such as who has the initial turn to send, the message size, and the frequency of acknowledgments to be returned on messages being sent over the association.
2. *CLOSE.Request:* This serves to orderly release an association between two entities. Close is also a confirmed request and returns a CLOSE.Confirmation indication.
3. *TRANSFER Request:* This is used by the message transfer layer to transfer one message.

4. *TURN-PLEASE.Request:* This is used by one application layer entity to request the turn to send messages from the other.
5. *TURN-GIVE.Request:* This is used by an application layer entity to hand the turn to send to the other.

An EXCEPTION.Indication may be generated by the RTS layer if it cannot transfer an APDU (Application Protocol Data Unit) successfully. In addition, the message transfer layer must deal with two session layer primitives directly for aborting associations: U-ABORT and P-ABORT. Associations may be aborted by the user (i.e., the message transfer layer) via the direct use of session's U-ABORT primitive or by the session layer itself via the P-ABORT session layer primitive. The session layer may provide a P-ABORT indication if it detects some inconsistency in service.

The above description resembles some of the activities typically provided by a reliable transport protocol service. In essence, the 1984 X.400 architecture is ensuring a reliable data transfer function above the session layer through the use of the RTS protocol.

In 1988 RTSE, the EXCEPTION.Indication has been replaced by a TRANSFER.Confirm primitive, which is a positive confirmation, vs. the EXCEPTION, which was a negative type of confirmation.

The 1988 version of the X.400 MHS standards is evolving to phase out RTS in favor of the more traditional OSI architecture, which mandates the use of presentation directly above the session layer.

4.6 The Remote Operation Service (ROS)

ROS is a request-reply protocol intended for interactive applications. It resembles closely a remote procedure call protocol in that it may be used to define procedures that can then be executed remotely. It supports four basic kinds of information exchanges, or Operation Protocol Data Units (OPDUs) as they are called:

1. *Invoke:* This takes an invokeID, an operation name, and some arguments. Invoke causes the specified operation to be executed remotely.
2. *ReturnResult:* This takes an invokeID and a set of results. ReturnResult returns the results of the invoked operation upon its completion.

3. *ReturnError:* This takes an invokeID, an error name, and an error parameter. It returns any errors that may arise during the execution of the remote operation.
4. *Reject:* This takes an invokeID and a problem name. It is returned to indicate that the operation has been rejected by the remote system (i.e., that the remote system refuses to execute the specified operation). Typically this will occur if the remote system does not support the specified operation or if it supports an incompatible version of it.

The invokeID is a unique operation identifier that is used to distinguish one instance of an operation from another.

ROS is used between two application entities residing in the application layer (see Fig. 4.3). On the basis of an Invoke OPDU, a receiving entity may return either one of a ReturnResult, ReturnError or Reject OPDUs. If the operation requested by the Invoke operation completes successfully, the ReturnResult indication is returned; if an error is generated, the ReturnError is returned. Reject is returned if the remote application process does not even accept the operation for execution (possibly because of a version mismatch). Figure 4.6 summarizes the ROS request-reply interactions which are defined to occur between two application layer entities.

All X.400 protocol interactions are described as ROS procedure calls. This requires a little bit of overhead in gaining familiarity with the language but allows for a very compact modeling of the protocol interactions. Even though ROS was originally specified in conjunction with X.400, it has now been adopted by numerous OSI application layer standards as a useful technique for designing protocols that require a request-reply style of interaction.

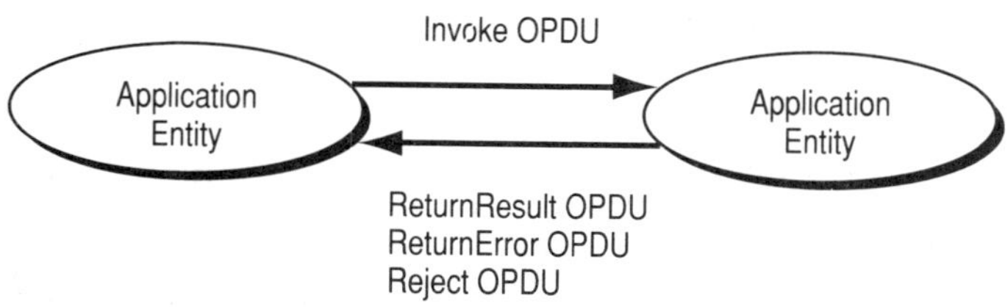

Figure 4.6 ROS request-reply interactions.

4.7 The Abstract Syntax Notation One (ASN.1)

ASN.1 was defined to obviate differences in the way in which different computer systems store and transmit information. It provides a common "abstract" language that can be used to describe any data structure which may be transferred between two systems. As such, ASN.1 solves the typical computer incompatibility problems such as most significant bit first vs. least significant bit first.

ASN.1 is the formal syntax definition language that is typically used in conjunction with ROS. Where ROS is used to specify interactions between application entities in terms of procedure calls, ASN.1 is used to model the parameters being exchanged between application entities. It thus provides a common language for use by application layer entities in system-to-system communications.

All information exchanged in ASN.1 notation is described in terms of a type and value (or set of values). ASN.1 types are formally defined using Backus-Naur Form (BNF) notation. Identifiers are used to uniquely distinguish one type from another.

4.7.1 Primitive language constructs

ASN.1 defines the following built-in primitive language constructs:

BOOLEAN used to represent logical data (i.e., TRUE or FALSE).

INTEGER is used to represent numeric data.

BIT STRING is used to represent binary data (i.e., sequences of 0's and 1's).

OCTET STRING is used to represent textual data or any other type of data that lends itself to be represented as a sequence of bytes.

NULL is used to represent the null value; it is essentially a placeholder.

SEQUENCE is used to denote an ordered collection of data.

SET is used to denote an unordered collection of data.

TAGGED is used to denote data that are semantically tagged for identification.

CHOICE is used to model data whose type may be chosen from a collection of types which are listed.

ANY is used to represent an unrestricted type of data (i.e., it could be used to represent anything).

4.7.2 Primitive syntax definitions

In addition to the above primitive language constructs, ASN.1 also defines a set of primitive syntax definitions that can be used to represent any of the above types of information. These include the following syntax definitions:

IA5String is used to represent textual data conforming to international alphabet no. 5.

Numeric String is used to represent the encoding of numeric data into textual form such as can be done from a telephone handset.

Printable String is used to represent data that can be entered from Telex terminals.

T.61 String is used to represent data that are suitable for processing by Teletex terminals.

T.100 serves to represent textual and graphic data for processing by Videotex terminals.

Generalized Time models the date and local or UTC (universal time coordinated) time.

UTC Time is a more constrained form of Generalized Time.

The 1988 version of ASN.1 defines a number of additional language constructs and syntaxes. However, the set described above is typically sufficient to gain a working knowledge of both the 1984 and the 1988 recommendations for X.400 as well as related standards such as X.500 and OSI Network Management.

4.7.3 Macros (1988 version only)

The 1988 version of ASN.1 also provides the concept of *Macros,* which may be used to define new, nonstandard types. Thus, the above constructs and syntaxes become the basic building blocks of what is an endless possibility of definitions. Macros are identified by a reference name that is assigned to them. They consist of a series of type and value constructs and any nonterminal definitions that may be recursively built up. An example of a Macro definition is as follows:

```
ATTRIBUTE-SYNTAX MACRO ::=
BEGIN
     TYPENOTATION    ::= Syntax MatchTypes | empty
     VALUENOTATION   ::= value (VALUE OBJECT IDENTIFIER)
     Syntax          ::= type
     MatchTypes      ::= ''MATCHES FOR'' Matches | empty
     Matches         ::= Match Matches | Match
     Match               ::= ''EQUALITY'' | ''SUBSTRINGS'' |
                         ''ORDERING''
END
```

4.7.4 Modules

The concept of a module allows related type, value, and macro definitions to be grouped together. Just as with Macros, they are identified by a reference name. Most of the X.400 protocol definitions are examples of Modules. Modules may be imported as a way of bringing definitions from one another. An example of a Module is as follows:

```
DirectoryAccessProtocol {}
DEFINITIONS ::=
BEGIN
EXPORTS....
IMPORTS....
......
END
```

Both Modules and Macros are concepts very similar to those by similar names which already exist in many computer languages such as C and Pascal. They allow for recursive definitions as well as a modular approach to the definition of complex interrelated data structures and groupings of definitions.

4.7.5 Example

The following example illustrates the use of ASN.1 in the definition of a file structure:

```
File ::= SEQUENCE {
         Owner,
         fileName [0] PrintableString,
         createDate [1] UTCTime,
         contents [2] ANY }

Owner ::= SEQUENCE {
     personalName [0] IA5String,
     organizationName [1] IA5String }
```

The above example illustrates a file that is defined to contain a sequence of an owner name, a file name which is defined to be of type

Printable String, a create date which is defined to be of type UTCTime, and a contents field defined to contain any syntax type. The owner field is then further specified to be composed of a sequence of a personal name which is of type IA5String and an organization name which is of type IA5String.

References and for Further Study

The X.400 MHS 1984 and 1988 protocol layering requirements are specified in the Red Book (CCITT X.400, 1984) and Blue Book (CCITT X.400, 1988), respectively. The ASN.1 notation is fully defined in recommendations X.208 and X.209 (CCITT X208, X.209). ACSE is defined in recommendation X.217 (CCITT X.217). The 1984 version of RTS is defined in the Red Book, whereas 1988 RTSE is defined in recommendation X.218 (CCITT X.218). The 1984 version of ROS is also defined in the Red Book, and the 1988 version of ROS is defined in recommendation X.219 (CCITT X.219).

Chapter

5

The 1984 Message Handling Services

This chapter describes the message handling services (MHS) model as seen by the application layer of the OSI architecture. It describes in detail the basic functional components that make up an X.400 MHS environment and discusses how these components can be physically and organizationally deployed within a network environment. While this chapter focuses only on the 1984 MHS architecture, most of the concepts it presents remain valid in 1988 MHS. Message routing, as well as naming and addressing, in X.400 MHS networks is also discussed.

5.1 Structure of the 1984 Recommendations

The CCITT 1984 MHS standards, also known as the "Red Book," comprise eight recommendations that include the following documents:

MHS: System Model-Service Elements	X.400
MHS: Basic Service Elements and Optional User Facilities	X.401
MHS: Encoded Information Type Conversion Rules	X.408
MHS: Presentation Transfer Syntax and Notation	X.409
MHS: Remote Operations and Reliable Transfer Server	X.410
MHS: Message Transfer Layer	X.411
MHS: Interpersonal Messaging User Agent Layer	X.420
MHS: Access Protocol for Teletex Terminals	X.430

5.2 The MHS Model

Message handling systems consist of two principal components:

1. User Agents (UAs)
2. Message Transfer Agents (MTAs)

UAs act on behalf of users, which may be either actual persons or application programs, to carry out specific messaging functions. Application programs may be users of MHS, in the sense that they may rely on messaging services as a subset of some broader functionality which they implement. For example, a distributed calendaring application may rely on electronic messaging to send out periodic reminders to particular groups of users to inform them of the occurrence of some event.

MTAs handle the forwarding and relaying of electronic mail messages in the network. As such, they implement the mail server function described earlier in Chap. 2. Figure 5.1 summarizes the basic relationship between UAs and MTAs. MTAs implement the message transport function in X.400 MHS by handling the routing and relaying of mail messages from a sending UA to a recipient UA. UAs interact with MTAs to submit and receive messages, thus accomplishing the successful end-to-end transfer of messages from an originator to one or more recipients. In summary, UAs correspond to the "client-side" in client-server systems, while MTAs correspond to the "server-side."

UAs may also carry out a number of message formatting functions, as well as message conversion and display actions on behalf of the user. In fact, UAs may include a number of local functions for creating, displaying, sending, receiving, and manipulating electronic mail messages. These local functions are not described in the MHS standards. The design of these kinds of services is left up to individual implementations of X.400 MHS. Adding functionality at the interface between the UA and the user does not affect the end-to-end interoperability between UAs. Therefore, this kind of local function-

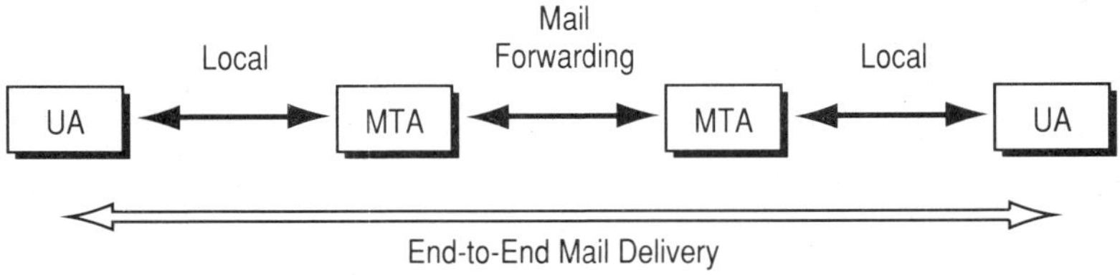

Figure 5.1 Basic MHS functions.

ality does not need to be specified in the international standards. Much of the value-added functionality that will be offered by vendors of X.400-based MHS systems and services in the near future will be provided at this level in the architecture.

MTAs do not operate on the contents of the messages they are transferring, with the exception of the envelope information, which is used to route messages throughout the network. A collection of MTAs comprises what is called a Message Transfer Service (MTS). The MTS provides the basic message transporting function in an MHS system. The MTS plus a set of UAs comprise what is called the Message Handling Service (MHS).

Figure 5.2 shows two MTAs that make up an MTS and a collection of UAs, which in conjunction with the MTS make up the whole MHS environment. From a logical perspective, each UA corresponds to a single user, but in actuality implementations may choose to physically combine the UA functionality for a set of users onto a single computing device, as well as combining UA and MTA functions into a single process.

5.2.1 The MHS protocols

1984 MHS defines three message handling protocols:

1. *An MTA-to-MTA protocol, commonly referred to as P1:* P1 is defined in recommendation X.411. It sets out the rules and procedures for reliably relaying messages between MTAs. P1 defines the envelope structure that is appended to messages prepared by the UA in order to allow MTA entities to properly route the message through the network.
2. *A UA-to-MTA protocol, referred to as P3:* P3 is also defined in recommendation X.411. It allows a message submission or delivery entity contained within the UA to access the services of the message transfer layer.

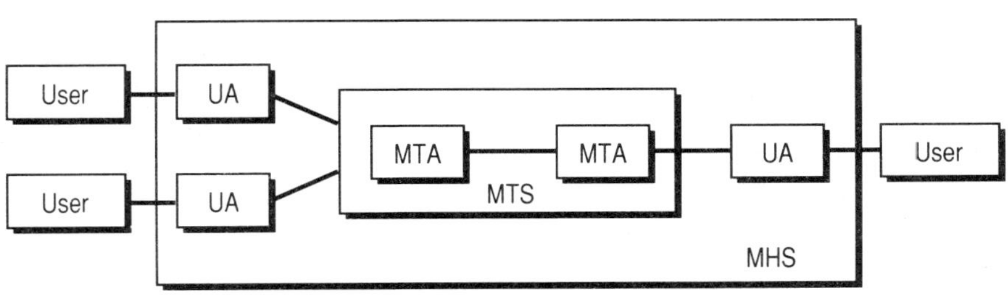

Figure 5.2 MHS systems overview.

3. *A UA-to-UA protocol, referred to as P2:* P2 is defined in recommendation X.420. P2 is the first instance of a range of protocols that will be defined to specify the syntax and semantics of the message contents being transferred between two UAs (e.g., voice, graphics, etc.). P2 specifies the exact message syntax for humanly-readable electronic mail messages, or interpersonal messages as they are called.

Figure 5.3 shows how the three protocols relate to each other and how they are deployed among the MHS functional components. P1 is used strictly among MTAs to transport messages. P3 is used between UAs and MTAs to submit and accept delivery of messages. P2 is end-to-end in scope, in that it conveys information that enables the recipient to parse and display the contents of the message correctly. Note, however, that UAs never communicate directly on a point-to-point basis. Rather, they exchange P2 messages that are relayed from the originating UA to the recipient UA via MTAs.

The P2 and P1 protocols specify the structure of messages exchanged at the MTA and UA levels, and the set of services that correspond to each field contained in the message header. P3 is the submission and delivery envelope that encapsulates messages exchanged between UAs and MTAs.

5.2.2 A layered view of the MHS functionality

The functions provided by UAs and MTAs may also be thought of as providing two distinct layers of service:

1. *A Message Transfer Service (MTS):* This is provided by the MTAs.
2. *An Interpersonal Messaging Service (IPMS):* This is provided by the UAs.

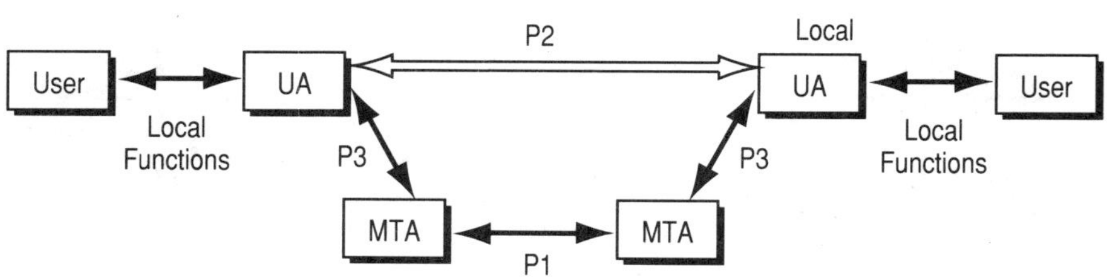

Figure 5.3 Protocol relationships.

The MTS is intended to function as a general, application-independent message transfer service. It is also referred to as the Message Transfer Layer (MTL). The IPMS supports the requirements for interpersonal communication between end users. It represents a layer of functionality that is also referred to as the User Agent Layer (UAL).

The IPMS assists individuals in communicating with other individuals. An IPMS comprises the Message Transfer Service (MTS), a class of cooperating UAs, that is, UAs which share common characteristics, and access to telex and CCITT telematic services. The users of an IPMS constitute a community of users who share similar characteristics. There may be UAs which are outside of a particular IPMS community; however, they can still tie into the overall message transfer service. Also, preexisting CCITT services such as telex and telematics services may be partially "brought in" by IPMS services.

Figure 5.4 illustrates an IPMS environment. It shows UAs that are within the IPMS community because they speak the same protocol, e.g., P2. It also shows UAs that are outside the IPMS because they handle different information messaging conventions such as proprietary, pre-X.400 electronic mail formats. Telex services can be considered to be partially within the IPMS because there are provisions in X.400 MHS for addressing information to and from them.

The interpersonal messaging function within a UA is implemented by an entity called an Interpersonal Messaging User Agent Entity

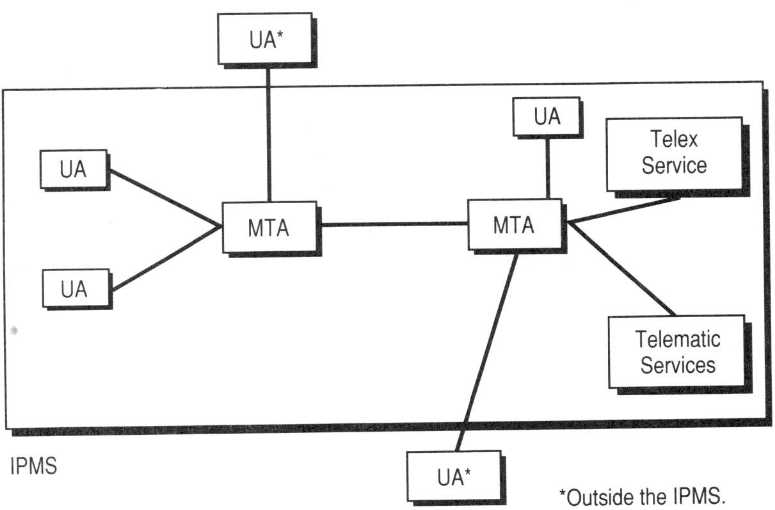

Figure 5.4 IPMS services.

(IPM-UAE). IPM-UAEs must generally be able to carry out the following functions:

1. Support the preparation of messages.
2. Handle the submission of messages to the message transfer service.
3. Handle the delivery of messages from the message transfer service.
4. Perform functions to present messages to the user.
5. Provide functions to cooperate with other UAs.
6. Perform additional message preparation and manipulation functions, such as correlating a message with another that it may have been received in reply to.

The user agent layer contains all of the UA functionality that enables it to deal with message contents, such as message formatting and conversions facilities. The MTL provides the basic message transfer and transport capabilities.

Figure 5.5 illustrates how the boundary between the two layers constitutes a common interface that is activated by entities on either side through what are called "service primitives." These service primitives represent internal procedural actions that do not necessarily translate into protocol actions which can be seen externally to the end system.

An instance of an application layer program implementing the UA functionality is called a User Agent Entity (UAE), while an instance of an application program implementing the MTA functionality is called a Message Transfer Agent Entity (MTAE). An additional MTL-level entity called a Submission and Delivery Entity (SDE) is defined to allow User Agent Entities to interact with MTAEs. The SDE interacts via the P3 protocols with peer-level Message Transfer Agent Entities (MTAEs) and by means of internal interface service primitives with the UAE.

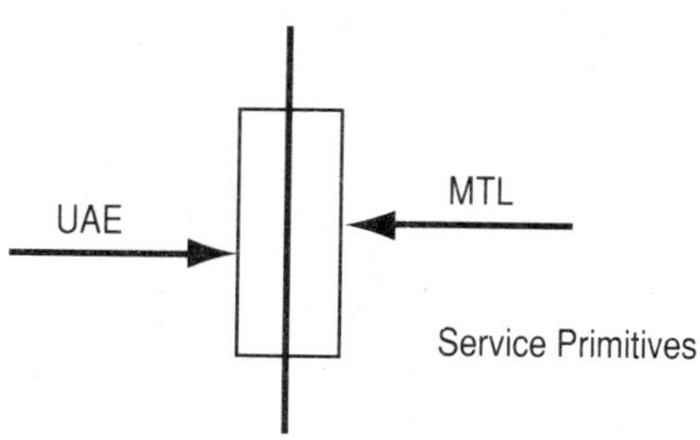

Figure 5.5 Interface relationships.

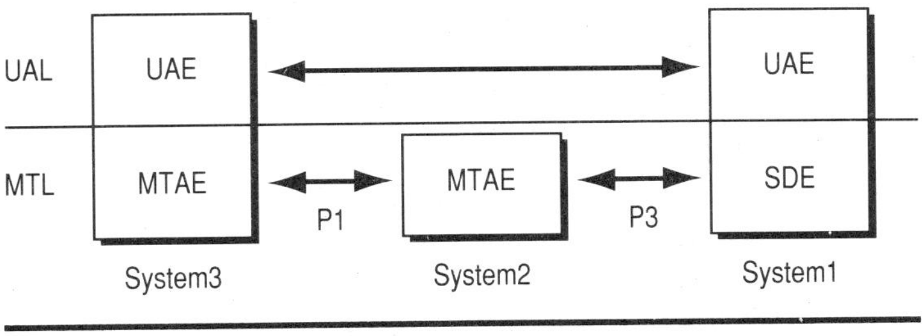

Figure 5.6 The layered functional model.

Figure 5.6 provides a good visual summary of how messaging entities at various levels in the MHS architecture relate with each other. It shows three kinds of systems that may exist: System3, which contains both MTA and UA functionality; System2, which contains only MTA functionality; and System1, which contains only UA functionality and interacts with MTAs through an SDE component. MTAs and SDEs represent MTL levels of functionality.

X.400 MHS also defines a class of protocols that allow remote users to interact with their UAs as though they were locally attached. These protocols are called interactive terminal to system protocols and are generically referred to as "Pt." X.29 is an example of a Pt type protocol. Users may connect via a terminal that speaks a Pt class protocol to their local UA, which may in turn be coresident with either the user agent entity or the message transfer agent entity.

Figure 5.7 shows a remote terminal interfacing to a set of locally defined messaging functions available on a host via a Pt class protocol. The host may support only the UAE and SDE functionality, in which case it implements the P2 and P3 protocol, or it may support the UAE and MTAE functionality, in which case it will implement the P2 and P1 protocols.

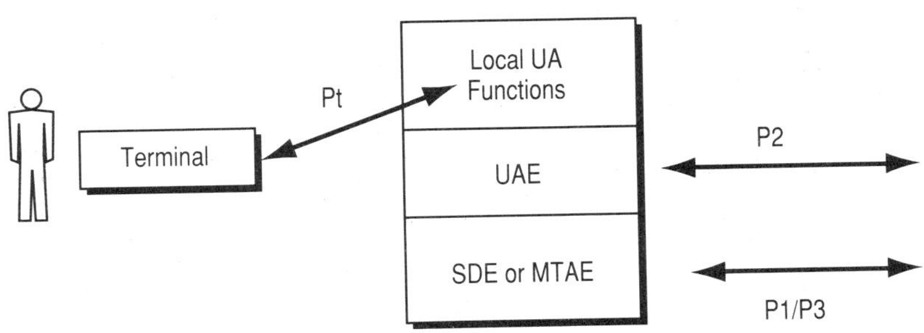

Figure 5.7 Layering of functions within the user agent.

5.3 Message Structure

X.400 messages are made up of two basic parts:

1. *An envelope:* This contains information necessary to correctly transfer the message.
2. *A content:* This is the information the originating UA intends to have delivered to one or more recipient UAs.

The envelope of the message is supplied by the message transfer layer and contains all the information necessary to route the message in the MHS environment. The content of the message contains the information that one UA is addressing to one or more recipient UAs. As such, it contains an interpersonal message composed of both a header and a body. Figure 5.8 shows how an ordinary interoffice memo can be mapped into an X.400 interpersonal message.

Interpersonal messages may be of two types:

1. *IP messages:* These carry information generated by and transferred between users of the IPMS.
2. *IPM status reports:* These carry information generated by one IPM-UAE (such as a receipt notification) for another IPM-UAE. The information contained in the report is used by the IPM-UAE and is not passed to the user (although it may of course trigger various kinds of status notifications to be made visible to the end user).

The actual contents of IP messages may comprise information such as voice, text, facsimile, and graphics. Recommendation X.420 specifies the valid permissible IPM content types. Recommendation X.408 specifies the procedures for converting between different types of IPM encoded information.

Figure 5.9 gives a layered view of the structure of an IP message. It

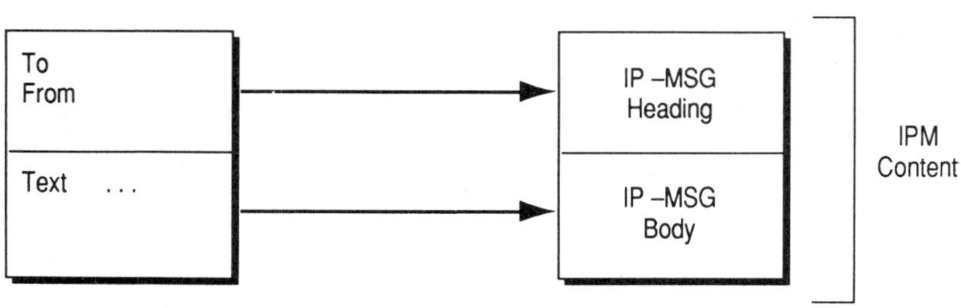

Figure 5.8 IP message structure.

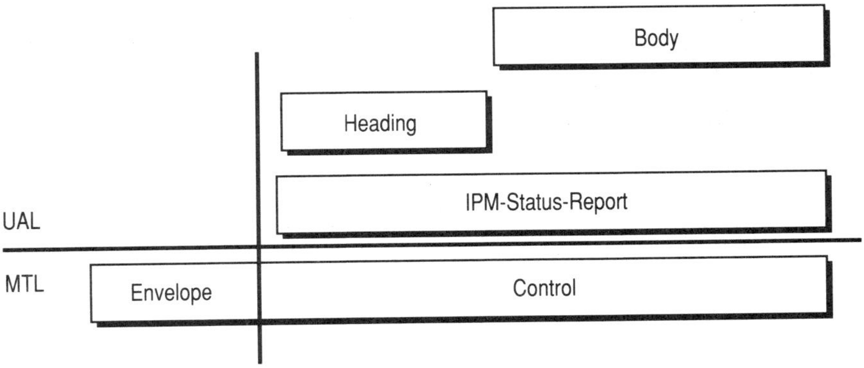

Figure 5.9 Layered view of the IP message structure.

shows how at the MTL level the message is comprised of an envelope plus a content field which transported transparently by the MTL, except for possible format conversions that may have been requested by the sender. At the UAL level, however, the contents comprise either an IPM-level status message, or an IP message generated by one end user for another and composed of both a header and a body.

Figure 5.10 shows an even more complex scenario where the IP message may in fact contain multiple body parts, one or more of which

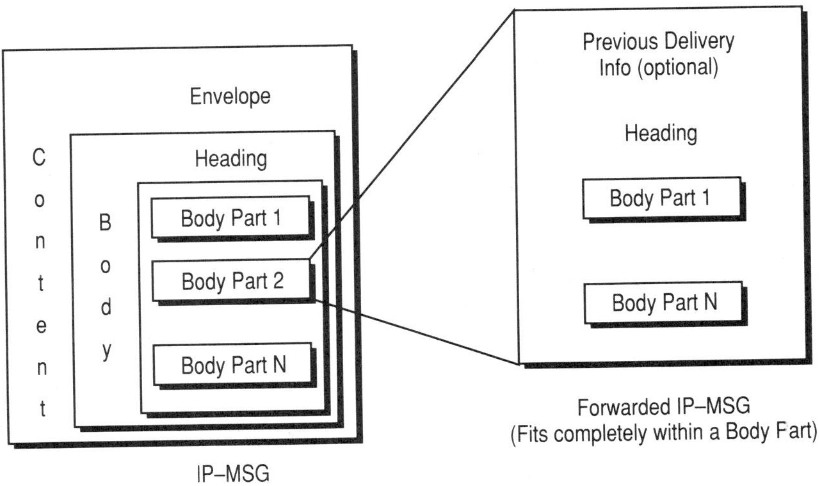

Figure 5.10 Message encapsulation.

may be a fully formed IP message that is being reforwarded fully encapsulated within another IP message.

5.4 Physical Mapping of Functions

The functional model described thus far may be deployed in a number of ways in actual computer systems by combining or partitioning the services of UAs and MTAs in a variety of ways. Three possible scenarios exist:

1. Stand-alone UAs, which contain only UA functions, where the UA communicates with the MTA via the P3 protocol.
2. Stand-alone MTAs, which contain only the MTA function.
3. Systems that contain both the UA and MTA functions.

In all cases, the different kinds of systems may be interconnected with each other via either dedicated, or switched, network connections.

Figure 5.11 gives an example of a mail server that contains the MTA function and two colocated UAs that serve two different end users. The users communicate with their respective UAs through the services of a terminal device which interfaces to the UA functionality on the mail server. The use of the word terminal in this case does not imply necessarily a dumb terminal; rather, any kind of interactive device may be used in this case ranging from personal computers to workstations, etc.

Figure 5.12 shows a scenario involving two mail servers. In one case the mail server provides both the MTA and the UA functionality (as in Fig. 5.11 above), while in the other the mail server provides a stand-alone MTA functionality. The stand-alone MTA is accessed via a UA, which is also a stand-alone system. In this case, the UA is probably colocated with a set of message creation and display facilities that allow the user to interface directly to it.

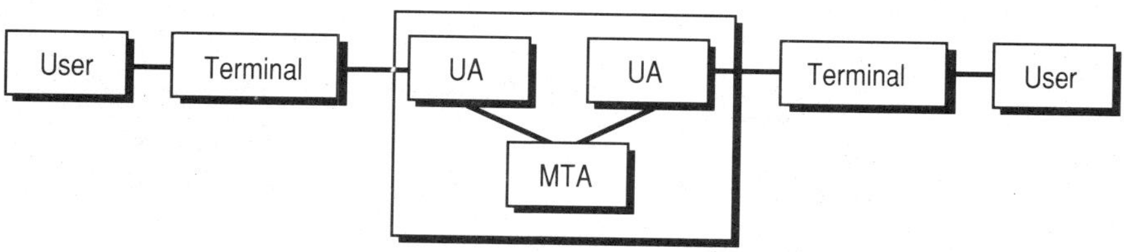

Figure 5.11 Colocated MTA and UA functions.

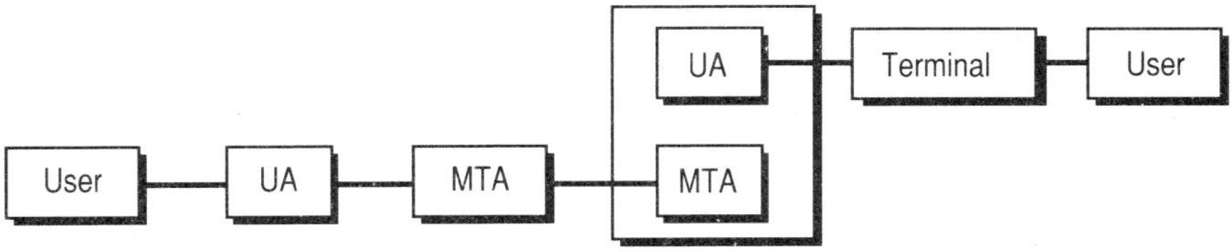

Figure 5.12 Separate and colocated UA and MTA functions.

Figure 5.13 shows the most complex scenario thus far, where a number of UAs are coresident on the same system that provides only the UA functionality to a set of users, each of which accesses its respective UA through the use of some terminal device. There is a single mail server in the diagram, which holds a colocated UA capability that is accessed via an external terminal device. The MTA capability on the mail server is accessed directly by another MTA which contains both UA and terminal display capabilities and can thus interface directly with the end user.

Colocating the UA with the terminal capabilities is equivalent to having a PC, workstation, or some other kind of computing device that has implemented the UA function on the same system which handles the message display and creation functions. While this is a straightforward scenario, it places a considerable amount of processing on the end-user system. In particular, some of the typical UA functions, as we will see in Chap. 6 (the 1984 MHS protocols), require that the UA be on-line at all times to receive messages. This is usually impractical in most systems. It is therefore more common to find the UA functionality packaged directly with the mail server (i.e., coresident with the MTA). This has the additional advantage of placing most of the burden for processing mail on the mail server. This is the scenario

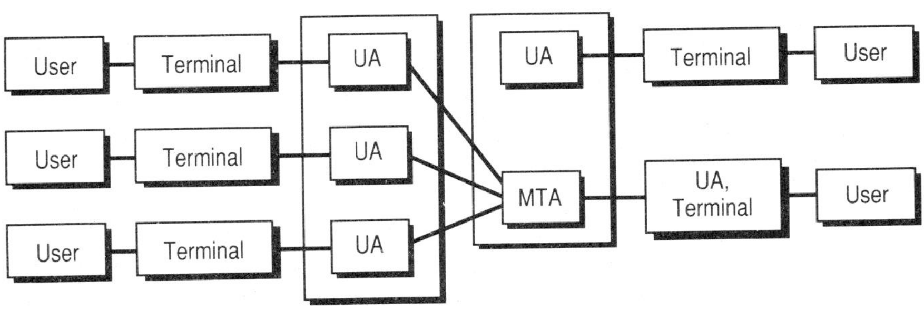

Figure 5.13 Colocated UAs.

that has been most widely adopted in commercial systems to date, since it cleanly separates out the mail functions from other computing functions that users may need to perform on their end system.

5.5 The Organizational View

There is an organizational view of X.400 which attempts to fit the configuration of MHS systems to the needs of administrative boundaries, called Management Domains (MDs). MDs represent portions of the MHS that are managed by a particular administrative authority. An MD is usually defined as consisting of at least one MTA, plus zero or more UAs.

X.400 MHS distinguishes between two kinds of administrative authorities:

1. Administrative Management Domains (ADMDs)
2. Private Management Domains (PRMDs)

ADMD is the term used to refer to messaging systems managed by public service providers (i.e., PTTs) such as ATT or British Telecom. PRMDs, on the other hand, refer to private networks which a company may purchase for its own internal use from any of the major computer vendors. Using a telephony-oriented analogy, PRMDs may be thought of as attaching to ADMD services in the same way in which PBXs attach to the public telephone services. The analogy breaks down in that PRMDs, unlike PBXs, may also interface directly with each other.

Three scenarios are defined for how users may interface with either PRMD or ADMD services, as well as for how PRMDs interface with ADMDs.

1. The simplest possible configuration (Fig. 5.14) is that of a user accessing ADMD provided services by interfacing directly to the ADMD. In this case the ADMD owns and manages the UA on behalf of the user.
2. The second scenario (Fig. 5.15) is similar to the first, except that the UA is owned and operated by the user. The user's UA interacts directly with the MTA provided and administered by the ADMD.
3. The third scenario (Fig. 5.16) envisions a PRMD that attaches to an ADMD on behalf of a group of users. The PRMD is essentially a private network that comprises both UAs and MTAs. At least one MTA in the PRMD interfaces directly with an MTA in the ADMD to transfer messages across the boundary between the two domains.

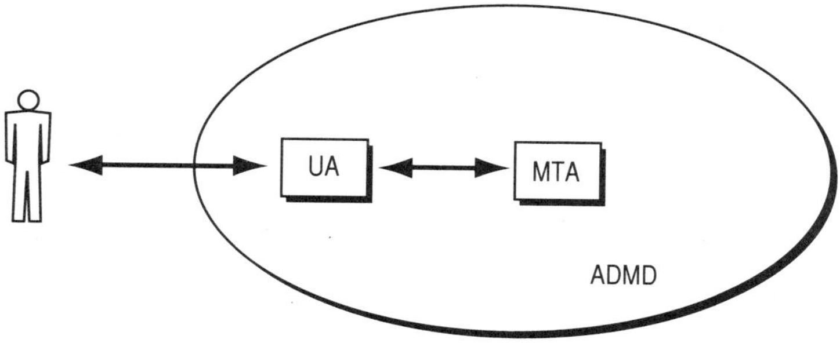

Figure 5.14 ADMD-owned UA and MTA.

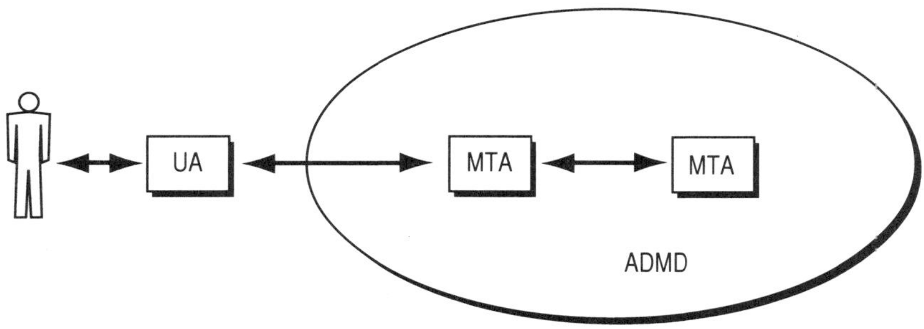

Figure 5.15 Private UA interfacing to an ADMD.

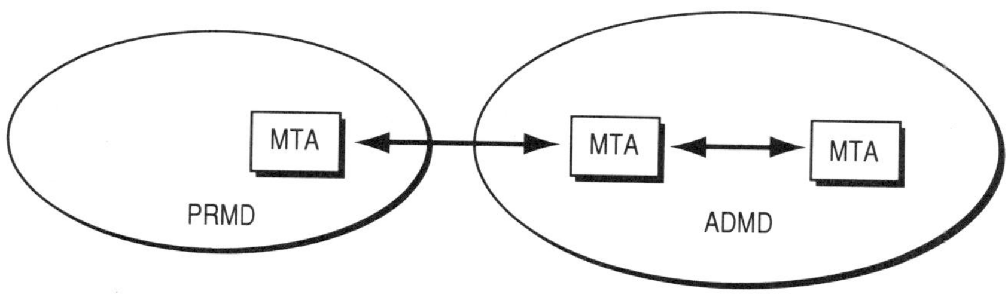

Figure 5.16 PRMD to ADMD interconnection.

Each of the above scenarios corresponds to a different economic requirement. In the first case the service provider is in control and offers a uniform level of service to a potentially very large installed base of users. The advantage to the user of this type of arrangement is that they merely purchase the service and along with it everything they need from the service provider. The analogy with telephony again applies, in that telephones in people's homes attach directly to the public telephone network.

The second scenario gives users the freedom to provide their own UAs. This allows users to select UAs with different local characteristics. For example, UAs that may provide more sophisticated features for the creation and management of local messages than those offered by ADMD-provided UAs.

In the third scenario (Fig. 5.16) the user owns an entire self-contained network (again analogous to a private PBX). The private network, or PRMD, is largely self-sufficient but attaches to the service provider's network occasionally to send or receive mail from the ADMD. In this way it can exchange mail with other PRMDs or stand-alone UAs, which also attach to the same ADMD.

The CCITT X.400 standards focus primarily on the needs of ADMD-to-ADMD connections and PRMD-to-ADMD connections. PRMD-to-PRMD connections are permitted by the ISO/MOTIS version of the standards, and the resulting interoperability requirements have been addressed primarily by functional standards groups such as NIST.

In the event that a PRMD needs to attach to more than one national ADMD, it will use a different name depending on which ADMD it is linked to (i.e., PRMDs may be named relative to the ADMD they are attaching to). Also, PRMDs are restricted, at least in the CCITT view, to be wholly self-contained within a national boundary. This restriction is invalidated by ISO and the functional standards bodies that permit PRMDs to interconnect directly to each other. This means that a PRMD can appear as local in scope at the national level, but nevertheless interconnect directly with other PRMDs across national boundaries. This allows private corporations to provide their users a worldwide unified, global interconnection service. Pragmatic administrative reasons make it desirable to segment multinational PRMDs into national-level components, while allowing the national-level domains to interact directly with each other without having to go through an ADMD.

While it is likely that messages will pass through several different MDs in their path from a sender to a recipient, PRMDs are explicitly prohibited from relaying messages between two ADMDs according to CCITT (ISO takes a different view). PRMDs may exchange messages directly with each other but may not act as intermediaries relaying mail between ADMDs, or they would be constituting themselves as an ADMD service. Figure 5.17 summarizes the valid and invalid ADMD-to-PRMD relaying possibilities.

Figure 5.18 illustrates the case of two PRMDs attaching directly to each other across national boundaries. This kind of interconnection is

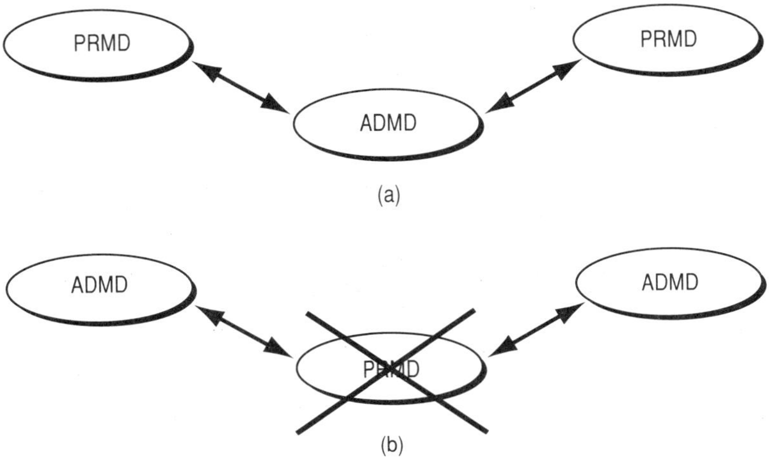

Figure 5.17 Valid vs. invalid ADMD-to-PRMD connections (per the CCITT recommendations).

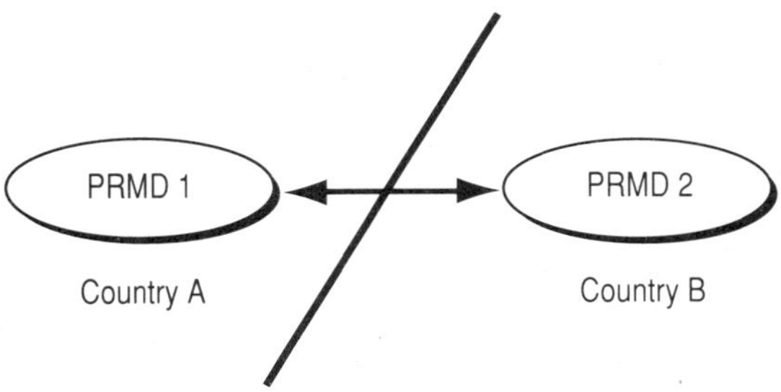

Figure 5.18 PRMDs connecting across national boundaries.

explicitly prohibited by the CCITT recommendations but is permitted by the ISO MOTIS version of the standards.

Figure 5.19 gives CCITT's view of how PRMDs should interconnect with each other only by going through their national ADMDs. ADMDs are the only kind of domains that may interconnect with each other across international boundaries.

Figure 5.20 depicts the interconnection scenario that is most likely to prevail commercially over the next few years. PRMDs serving private corporations will exist within national boundaries and may attach directly to other private MHS services in other countries. The PRMDs they attach to may belong either to the same corporation or

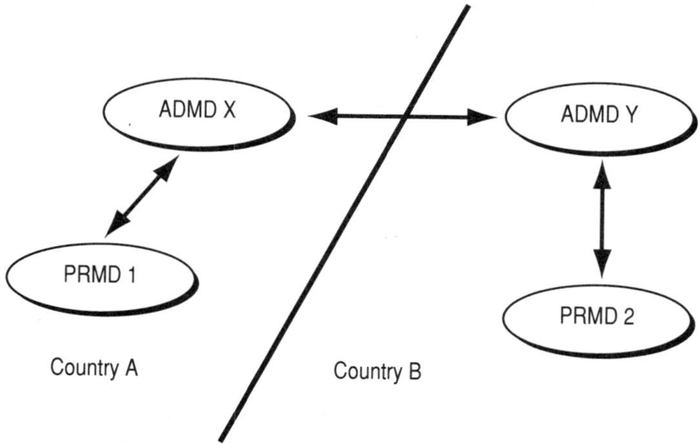

Figure 5.19 CCITT View: PRMDs communicating across international boundaries only through ADMDs.

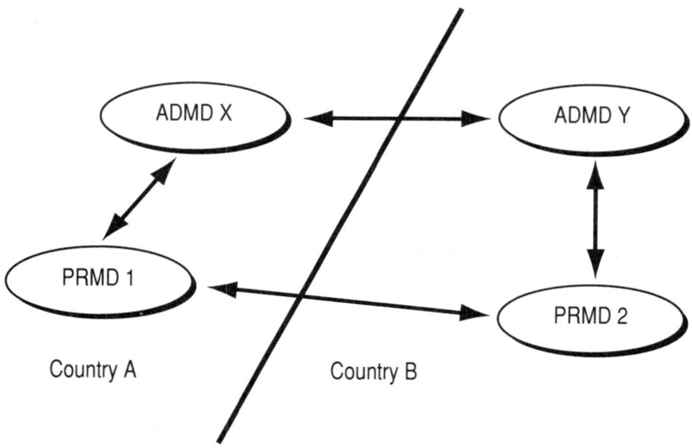

Figure 5.20 ISO view: PRMDs attached directly across national boundaries as well as through national ADMDs.

possibly with other companies with which business exchanges take place on a regular basis. At the same time, PRMDs may also attach to national ADMD services offered within their own countries. PRMDs in different countries will thus have the option of exchanging mail with each other either via publicly provided ADMD services, or through direct PRMD-to-PRMD connections.

5.6 Naming and Addressing

X.400 distinguishes between primitive names that are intended to be unambiguous within a limited context, for example, a single MD, and descriptive names that identify an entity through its relationship to other entities in the system. Originator/recipient names, or O/R names as they are called for short, are descriptive names that consist of a list of attributes. Attributes in the list may be multivalued, which means that a particular type may have more than one value associated with it.

Users are addressed through the use of descriptive names that are associated with their corresponding UA. In principle, users and other entities in the MHS environment possess both an O/R name and an O/R address. The name is intended to be user-friendly in nature and easy to remember, whereas the address contains information specific to the configuration of the network and is intended to be used primarily for routing messages.

In the 1984 X.400, however, the use of O/R names and addresses was considerably simplified by requiring that O/R addresses also be used in lieu of O/R names. This allows O/R names to be used both to identify entities in the MHS, as well as to correctly route messages. In general, every O/R address constitutes a valid O/R name, but every O/R name need not be an O/R address.

5.6.1 O/R addresses

O/R addresses are essentially descriptive names that help the message transfer service locate a UA's point of attachment. The restriction that O/R names be used as addresses makes it possible for the 1984 X.400 to operate in the absence of a distributed naming service. This results in a simpler overall system architecture as well as a reduced cost and delay per each message delivery. On the other hand, it represents a limitation in that it makes names more difficult to use and remember, as well as more subject to change.

5.6.2 Constructing O/R names

X.400 specifies a set of standard attributes that can be used to construct valid O/R names. Individual management domains are responsible for ensuring that each UA, within their domain, possesses at least one name. O/R names may be composed of both mandatory and optional attributes.

X.400 also supports what are called domain-defined attributes whose types are not specified by CCITT. These attributes permit the inclusion of preexisting naming conventions within MHS. When domain-specific attributes are used to address MHS entities, it must also be possible for users in other domains to learn about these attributes and to use them in creating appropriate names.

The MHS attributes defined for constructing O/R names can be categorized into four different groups:

1. Personal attributes, such as a personal name
2. Geographical attributes, such as a country name
3. Organizational attributes, such as an organization name or an organizational unit name (e.g., the name of a department within a company)
4. Architectural attributes, such as an X.121 address or a unique UA id

X.400 defines two basic forms of O/R names:

1. Form 1, which is used primarily by MHS users
2. Form 2, which is used for Teletex and other telematic services

Chapter 7 (1988 MHS) describes how O/R names evolve in 1988 MHS to include X.500 Distinguished Names. Messages relayed between MDs must support addresses of either one of the two types listed above. The domain of the recipient UA must be identified by at least one base attribute set chosen by the UA's domain.

5.6.2.1 O/R names: Form 1. Form 1 specifies Originator or Recipient by means of the country and ADMD to which it belongs plus some other attributes. In the case of private UAs, the name of the ADMD to which the PRMD is also associated is required. Three possible variants of form 1 exist:

Variant 1 contains:

Country Name

ADMD Name

PRMD Name (optional)

Personal Name (optional)

OrgName (optional)

OrgUnitNames (optional)

Domain-defined attributes (optional)

The Country Name represents the name of the country where the ADMD is located. The ADMD is the name of the ADMD that serves the intended recipient. Most countries will correspond to a single ADMD, since they are served by a single PTT. In the United States, several service providers will offer ADMD services just as they do for telephone services. The PRMD name is the name of the PRMD to which the intended recipient is attached. Personal Name is the personal name of the intended recipient. OrgName is the name of the organization to which the intended recipient belongs. OrgUnitNames, of which there may be more than one, are the names of the organizational unit to which the intended recipient belongs. The Domain-defined attributes represent any preexisting naming attributes of the recipient MD. At least one of the last five optional attributes must be present for the name to be valid.

Example:

CountryName = UK

ADMD Name = BT

PRMD Name = WidgetNet

OrgName = Widget

OrgUnitName = Marketing

PersonalName = Jim Smith

Indicates that the originator or recipient of the message is located in the UK and is connected to BT, which is the public service provider for the UK. WidgetNet is the hypothetical name of the private network for Widget corporation. The organization name is Widget, and it is further subdivided into an organizational unit for the marketing department. Finally, the name of the person sending or receiving the message is Jim Smith, as shown in the personal name field.

Variant 2 contains:

Country Name

ADMD Name

UA unique numeric ID

Domain-defined attributes (optional)

The Country Name and ADMD Name have the same meanings as above. The UA ID is a numeric identifier for the intended recipient's UA. The Domain-defined attributes are the only optional field in this case.

Example:

CountryName = UK

ADMD Name = BT

UA id = *a unique numeric identifier*

Variant 3 contains:

Country Name

ADMD Name

X.121 Address

Domain-defined attributes (optional)

Variant 3 resembles closely variant 2 except that the UA is identified by an X.121 address.

Example:

CountryName = UK

ADMD Name = BT

X.121 Address = *a terminal address*

5.6.2.2 O/R names: Form 2. Form 2 is for use only by teletex and telematic services and contains only the following two fields:

X.121 Address

Telematic Terminal ID (optional)

The X.121 address uniquely identifies the intended recipient teletex or telematic entity. The Telematic Terminal ID may be a telex answer back string or a Telex Terminal ID.

5.7 Message Routing

X.400 supports only what is called incremental routing. That is, each domain determines the next MTA to which to send the message in an adjoining MD but does not attempt to establish a full route to the final MD. The base attribute set in the O/R address provides the information necessary to perform this kind of routing. Messages are relayed to an MTA in the recipient MD or to an MTA in an intermediate MD which is closer to the recipient MD. The choice of which MD to forward to depends on local policy, and technical as well as economic concerns. Once a message reaches a destination MTA, it is routed to the appropriate UA attached to that MTA. Messages with less than a complete attribute set are rejected. Once a message reaches the recipient MD, the user attributes may be used to determine the recipient UA. If the message is transferred to a PRMD, the base attribute set gets the message only as far as the ADMD associated with the PRMD. The ADMD then uses the user attributes in the base attribute set to deliver the message to the correct PRMD. The standard does not define a way to designate UAs that are attached to PRMDs. Messages addressed to these private UAs are routed to the PRMD itself, which then internally identifies the specified UA. In order to support this kind of routing, ADMDs require that the PRMD name or some other user attribute (e.g., the organizational name) which identifies the recipient PRMD be included as part of the O/R name.

In the case of telematic terminals (i.e., X.121 addresses), messages are transferred to the ADMD that serves the terminal, or directly to the terminal if it is not served by an ADMD.

Note that the entire mechanism relies on network administrators having successfully interconnected various MDs such that a valid path exists between all possible senders and recipients. The standard specifies no particular mechanism for accomplishing this; rather it is up to the network administrators to set up common naming procedures that will enable them to ensure the full connectivity of their networks.

References and for Further Study

The 1984 X.400 messaging architecture and naming and addressing conventions are fully specified in the Red Book (CCITT X.400, 1984). Tanenbaum (1988) gives a good brief overview of X.400 MHS concepts in the overall context of computer networking in general.

Chapter

6

The 1984 MHS Protocols

The 1984 MHS standards are described in terms of a set of services which the MTS or the IPMS provide to their users. These services are typically implemented via specific fields in the envelope or header of the mail messages exchanged. Since the MHS protocols are primarily defined in terms of the structure of the messages exchanged, each message field which provides a particular service is called a Service Element. Service elements are often also referred to as Protocol Elements since they represent visible pieces of protocol information exchanged between two entities.

This chapter looks in detail at the 1984 MHS protocols. Although ISO and CCITT have already published an updated 1988 version of the MHS protocols there are still a number of very important reasons for taking the time to study the 1984 MHS protocols in detail. First of all, most of the commercial systems in use today are still based predominantly on 1984 MHS. In fact, many vendors and service providers are still in the process of releasing 1984 based products and services. Given the challenges service providers face in establishing worldwide interoperable electronic mail services, 1984 MHS will be around for a long time. The second reason to still study the 1984 MHS protocols in detail, is that they are simpler and therefore somewhat easier to understand than the 1988 MHS protocols. Also, the 1988 MHS protocols are more easily understood if one has a good grasp of the 1984 protocols.

6.1 The P1 Protocol

P1 is the protocol which is used to transfer messages between MTAs. It can be used to transfer messages across ADMD to ADMD boundaries, PRMD to PRMD boundaries, as well as PRMD to ADMD boundaries.

The units of information exchanged by the P1 protocol are called Message Protocol Data Units (MPDUs). Two kinds of MPDUs exist:

1. User MPDUs (UMPDUs), and
2. Service MPDUs (SMPDUs).

User MPDUs carry user-level information, i.e., the message which an end user wishes to send to another end user. Service MPDUs are used within the Message Transfer Layer to carry status information about the delivery of other messages. Service MPDUs are further subdivided into 2 kinds of MPDUs:

1. DeliveryReport MPDUs, and
2. Probe MPDUs.

DeliveryReport MPDUs provide information about the successful or unsuccessful delivery of a message. Probe MPDUs, on the other hand, provide information about the state of health of the Message Transfer Layer. Probe messages are used to test whether a message with a particular set of header information can be successfully delivered through the Message Transfer Layer.

The P1 protocol thus comprises the specification of three kinds of MPDUs:

1. UserMPDUs—which serve to transfer end-user messages.
2. DeliveryReportMPDUs—which convey information about previously submitted messages.
3. ProbeMPDUs—which test the state of the Message Transfer Layer.

This can be summarized in ASN.1 as follows:

```
MPDU ::= CHOICE {[0] IMPLICIT UserMPDU, Service MPDU }

ServiceMPDU ::= CHOICE {
                [1] IMPLICIT DeliveryReportMPDU,
                [2] IMPLICIT ProbeMPDU }
```

6.1.1 Common data types

All P1 MPDUs share a number of data types that are used in constructing the header information specific to each type of MPDU. Many of these data types are also common to the P2 and P3 protocols.

6.1.1.1 ORNames. The ORName is a sequence of naming attributes that is used to specify the intended recipient of a message. As discussed in Chap. 5, ORNames provide not only naming information, but also the information necessary to route the message. An ORName is defined in ASN.1 as a list of standard attributes plus a list of domain-defined attributes. The domain-defined attributes are optional and are permitted for backward compatibility reasons only. They allow preexisting nonstandard naming conventions to be used in conjunction with the X.400 naming structure. It is intended that these preexisting naming structures will eventually be phased out in favor of the structure defined in X.400. The list of standard attributes consists of a sequence of information that includes a country name, an administrative domain name, an X.121 address, a terminal ID, a private domain name, an organizational name, a unique UA identifier, a personal name, and possibly a sequence of organizational unit names. The following ASN.1 summarizes the definition of ORNames:

```
ORName ::= [APPLICATION 0] IMPLICIT SEQUENCE {
                StandardAttributeList,
                DomainDefinedAttributeList OPTIONAL }

Standard Attribute List ::= SEQUENCE {
            CountryName OPTIONAL,
            AdministrationDomainName OPTIONAL,
            [0]  IMPLICIT X121Address OPTIONAL,
            [1]  IMPLICIT TerminalID OPTIONAL,
            [2]  PrivateDomainName OPTIONAL,
            [3]  IMPLICIT OrganizationName OPTIONAL,
            [4]  IMPLICIT Unique UAIdentifier OPTIONAL,
            [5]  IMPLICIT PersonalName OPTIONAL,
            [6]  IMPLICIT SEQUENCE OF OrganizationalUnit OPTIONAL }
```

The standard attribute list may be used to construct any one of the O/R name forms described earlier in Chap. 5 for MHS users or telematic addresses:

1. The ASN.1 definition of telematic addresses is given by

```
TelematicAddress ::= { x121 Address,
                       TerminalID OPTIONAL }
```

2. The ASN.1 definition of message handling addresses is given by

a.
```
MHSAddress ::= { CountryName,
                 ADMDName,
                 UniqueUAIdentifier,
                 DomainDefinedAttributes OPTIONAL }
```

b.
```
MHSAddress ::= { CountryName,
                 ADMDName,
                 x121Address,
                 DomainDefinedAttributes OPTIONAL }
```

c.
```
MHSAddress ::= { CountryName,
                 ADMDName,
                 PersonalName,
                 PRMDName,
                 OrganizationalName,
                 OrganizationalUnit (s),
                 DomainDefinedAttributes OPTIONAL }
```

6.1.1.2 Extension identifier. The extension identifier is an integer value that provides a shorthand way of identifying an individual recipient within a particular message. It is used in combination with the MPDU identifier to unambiguously identify a copy of the original user or probe MPDU more reliably than by simply using O/R names.

6.1.1.3 Global domain identifier. The global domain identifier serves to unambiguously identify a domain within the MHS. This serves to identify the source of trace information and report MPDUs. It is defined in ASN.1 as

```
GlobalDomainIdentifier ::= [APPLICATION 3] IMPLICIT SEQUENCE {
                               CountryName,
                               AdministrationDomainName,
                               PrivateDomainIdentifier OPTIONAL}
```

Only a CountryName and AdministrationDomainName are needed to identify an ADMD. When identifying PRMDs, the AdministrationDomainName denotes the ADMD to which the PRMD is attached, and an additional PrivateDomainIdentifier parameter is used to identify the PRMD itself.

6.1.1.4 Encoded information types. The EncodedInformationType identifies the type of information that is being carried in the MPDU content field. It consists of a bit string, which depending upon its value, will denote a particular content type from a set of predefined types. The string may take on values for undefined, telex, teleprinter-type, IA5Text, Group3Facsimile, TextInterchangeFormat 0, Teletex, Videotex, SimpleFormattableDocument, or TextInterchangeFormat. The EncodedInformationType is defined in ASN.1 as

```
EncodedInformationTypes ::= [APPLICATION 5] IMPLICIT SET {
                   [0]  IMPLICIT BIT STRING { undefined(0), tLX(1),
                            iA5text(2), g3Fax(3), tIFO(4), tTX(5),
                            videotex(6), voice(7), sFD(8), tIF1(9)},
                   [1]  IMPLICIT G3NonBasicParams OPTIONAL,
                   [2]  IMPLICIT TeletexNonBasicParams OPTIONAL,
                   [3]  IMPLICIT PresentationCapabilities OPTIONAL }
```

6.1.1.5 Trace information. A trace information field is carried along with every MPDU to provide Domains and MTAs in the MHS with status information on how processing of the message is progressing. The TraceInformation field consists of the following information:

```
TraceInformation ::= { GlobalDomainIdentifier,
                       DomainSuppliedInfo}
```

The GlobalDomainId identifies the Domain which is supplying the trace information. The DomainSuppliedInfo field may consist of: a time of arrival, a deferred delivery time (if this option was selected), an action indicator denoting whether the message was relayed or re-routed, a series of encoded information types indicating what conversions have taken place (if any), and the GlobalDomainIdentifier of the previous Domain which the message went through.

6.1.1.6 The MPDU identifier. The originating MTA assigns a string identifier to each MPDU it creates. The MPDU identifier serves to distinguish one MPDU from another in the message transfer service. This allows MTAs to later unambiguously distinguish between the following events:

1. The submission of a message
2. The submission of a probe
3. The generation of a delivery report

When a copy of a user or probe MPDU is generated during message routing, each copy bears the MPDU identifier of the original event. The MPDU identifier consists of the GlobalDomainIdentifier (see sect. 6.1.1.5) plus an IA5String. The addition of the IA5String ensures that the MPDU identifier will be unique.

6.1.1.7 Content type. The content type field denotes how the contents of the MPDU are structured. The only structure available in '84 X.400 is that given by the P2 protocol (i.e., the Interpersonal Messaging protocol defined in X.420). It is intended, however, that new kinds of UA to UA protocols will be defined in the future (i.e., for example PEDI is currently being defined within the 1992 study period, see Chap. 10).

6.1.1.8 UA content identifier. The UA content identifier consists of a printable string that is generated by the originating UA, and is carried back to the originator by the Message Transfer Layer in the Delivery Report MPDU.

6.1.1.9 Time. Time is a time stamp in UTCTime that is conveyed in the protocol between two messaging entities. A universal time protocol does not exist in OSI; UTCTime is therefore used with the understanding that it will not reliably distinguish events that occur very close to each other.

6.1.2 User MPDU structure

A UserMPDU is made up of an envelope plus a content field. It is formally defined in ASN.1 as

```
UserMPDU ::= SEQUENCE { UMPDUEnvelope, UMPDUContent }

UMPDUEnvelope ::= SET {
                 MPDUIdentifier,
                 originator ORName,
                 original EncodedInformationTypes OPTIONAL,
                 ContentType,
                 UAContentID OPTIONAL,
                 Priority DEFAULT normal,
                 PerMessageFlag DEFAULT {},
                 deferredDelivery [0] IMPLICIT Time OPTIONAL,
                 [1] IMPLICIT SEQUENCE OF
                 PerDomainBilateralInfo OPTIONAL,
                 [2] IMPLICIT SEQUENCE OF RecipientInfo,
                 TraceInformation}

UMPDUContent ::= OCTET STRING
```

The content field of the UserMPDU is defined simply as an octet string. It is passed transparently by the message transfer layer and can contain any number of data types as denoted in the message envelope.

The envelope of the UMPDU, on the other hand, consists of the following fields:

1. An MPDUidentifier, which distinguishes the submission event that produced this MPDU from other submissions.
2. An originator, which specifies the originator of the message being transported by the MPDU.
3. The original EncodedInformationTypes, which is the value of the encoded information types parameter upon submission of the UserMPDU. If it is absent, the content types of the message are undefined.
4. The contentType, which denotes the content type of the message.
5. The UAContentID, which allows the originating UA to supply a printable content identifier. This identifier is not delivered, but it is returned to the originator with any Delivery Report MPDU relating to the status of the message.
6. The Priority of the message is carried by the MPDU. Allowed priority settings are normal, nonUrgent, or urgent. This service is not mapped to lower layer services in that it does not truly result in a faster message delivery. However, it is carried in the protocol primarily as an indicator to the receiving entity of the level of urgency that the originator of the message intended. This indication can be used by the recipient UA to display the message more rapidly or perhaps to indicate the level of urgency of the message when displaying it.
7. The perMessageFlag field is a bit string which indicates what op-

tions apply to all the recipients of the message. It may take on the following possible settings:

a. disclose recipients, which indicates whether all the O/R names of the recipients should be disclosed upon delivery of the message.

b. conversionProhibited, which indicates whether conversions were requested by the originator when the MPDU was submitted. If it is not set, conversions may be carried out implicitly by any MTA along the path of the message that deems it necessary.

c. alternateRecipientAllowed, which indicates whether the message may be delivered to an alternate recipient, in the event that the originally intended recipient is not available. This feature allows network administrators to set up an entity on the network that serves as a default message collection point.

d. contentReturnRequest, which denotes whether the content of the message should be returned when a nondelivery notification is generated.

8. The PerDomainBilateralInfo field carries information that is supplied by the originating domain for one of the domains on the way through the MTS. More than one of these may be present in the same message. The nature of the information transferred in this field is outside the scope of the standard and is agreed upon independently between two cooperating domains. Typically this field will be used to append billing and accounting information.
9. deferredDelivery, which is the time at which deferred delivery by an MTAE other than the originating MTAE has been requested.
10. The RecipientInfo field contains information that is recipient-specific such as the recipient's ORName, an ExtensionIdentifier, a PerRecipientFlag, and an optional ExplicitConversion indication. The UserMPDU's envelope will carry one such block of information per each intended message recipient. ExplicitConversion denotes the type of conversion requested by the originator of the message. The only conversions defined in 1984 X.400 are IA5Text to Teletex and Teletex to Telex. By setting the PerRecipientFlag, the originating MTA can request one of three kinds of reports for each intended message recipient:

a. Basic requests a delivery report to be generated only in the case of nondelivery. It contains the last item of the trace information field.

b. Confirmed requests a delivery report to be generated regardless of successful or unsuccessful delivery. It contains only the last item of the trace information field.

c. Audit and Confirmed requests a delivery report to be returned in every case, regardless of successful or unsuccessful delivery of the message. It contains the full trace information field.

6.1.3 Delivery report MPDU

At the originator's request, a delivery report MPDU is returned to an originating MTA to indicate the successful or unsuccessful delivery of a message. The Delivery Report MPDU is composed of a DeliveryReportEnvelope and a DeliveryReportContent, as follows:

```
DeliveryReportMPDU ::= SEQUENCE {
                   DeliveryReportEnvelope,
                   DeliveryReportContent }

DeliveryReportEnvelope ::= SET {
                  report MPDUIdentifier,
                  originator ORName,
                  TraceInformation }

DeliveryReportContent ::= SET {
                  original MPDUIdentifier,
                  intermediate TraceInformation OPTIONAL,
                  UAContentId OPTIONAL,
                  [0] IMPLICIT SEQUENCE OF
                  ReportedRecipientInfo,
                  returned [1] IMPLICIT UMPDUContent OPTIONAL,
                  billingInformation [2] ANY OPTIONAL}

ReportedRecipientInfo ::= SET {
      recipient [0] IMPLICIT ORName,
     [1] IMPLICIT ExtensionIdentifier,
     [2] IMPLICIT PerRecipientFlag,
     [3] IMPLICIT LastTraceInformation, intendedRecipient
     [4] IMPLICIT ORName OPTIONAL,
     [5] IMPLICIT SupplementaryInformation OPTIONAL }
```

The delivery report envelope contains an MPDUIdentifier which identifies the report that is being generated, the ORName of the originator of the subject message, and a set of TraceInformation.

The content of a delivery report contains the MPDUIdentifier of the original message, an optional TraceInformation field, an optional UAContentId, and a sequence of ReportedRecipientInfo fields per each message recipient. In addition, it may carry the content field of any previously nondelivered User MPDU, as well as a set of optional billing information.

The ReportedRecipientInfo field contains information that may vary from one recipient to another and includes

1. The ORName of the intended recipient and an ExtensionIdentifier, which identifies the recipient to whom the rest of the information applies.
2. A PerRecipientFlag, which is the report requested by the originator.

3. The LastTraceInfo, which indicates the fate of the subject message. It contains a set of information including the arrivalTime at which the subject UMPDU entered the MD making the report, and the results of any conversion that may have taken place. Depending on whether or not delivery succeeded, the Delivery Report content field carries either a DeliveredInfo or a non-DeliveredInfo field.

The following ASN.1 summarizes the structure of the report content field:

```
Report :: CHOICE {
             [0]  IMPLICIT DeliveredInfo,
             [1]  IMPLICIT NonDeliveredInfo }

DeliveredInfo ::= SET {
                delivery [0] IMPLICIT Time,
                typeOfUA [1] IMPLICIT INTEGER {public(0), private(1)}
                DEFAULT public}

NonDeliveredInfo ::= SET {
             [0]  IMPLICIT ReasonCode,
             [1]  IMPLICIT DiagnosticCode OPTIONAL }
```

If delivery succeeded, the report field carries the time the message was delivered to the UA and whether the UA to which it was delivered is public or private. If delivery failed, it returns a reason for the failure plus some diagnostic information.

The reason for failure may involve any one of the following conditions:

1. transferFailure indicates that a communication failure prevented the relaying or delivery of a message.
2. unableToTransfer indicates that, due to some problem with the message itself, the MTA could not relay or deliver the message.
3. conversionNotPerformed indicates that a conversion necessary for delivery of the message could not be performed.

In the event of nondelivery, the DiagnosticCode will indicate any one of the following situations: unrecognizedORName, ambiguousORName, mtaCongestion, loopDetected, uaUnavailable, maximumTimeExpired, encodedInfoTypesUnsupported, contentTooLong, ConversionImpractical, conversionProhibited, implicitConversionNotRegistered, invalidParameters.

6.1.4 Probe MPDU

A probe MPDU can be generated by an MTA to verify that a message with an intended header can be successfully delivered through the message transfer service. The probe message is designed to test the viability of the MTS. A probe MPDU is carried only as far as the recipient MTA but is not delivered to the addressee. Instead, an indication is returned to the sending MTA via the delivery report MPDU of whether the probe message was successfully or unsuccessfully delivered to the recipient MTA. A successful delivery of a probe MPDU denotes that a user MPDU containing similar characteristics and addressed to the same recipient will be delivered successfully. A probe MPDU consists merely of a message envelope; its structure is summarized in ASN.1 as

```
ProbeMPDU ::= ProbeEnvelope

ProbeEnvelope ::= SET {
      probe MPDUIdentifier,
      originator ORName,
      ContentType,
      UAContentID OPTIONAL,
      original EncodedInformationTypes OPTIONAL,
      TraceInformation,
      PerMessageFlag DEFAULT {},
      contentLength [0] IMPLICIT INTEGER OPTIONAL,
      [1] IMPLICIT SEQUENCE OF PerDomainBilateralInfo OPTIONAL,
      [2] IMPLICIT SEQUENCE OF RecipientInfo }
```

The information contained in the probe envelope may change as it makes its way through the message transfer layer. The ProbeEnvelope carries the same set of parameters as the user MPDU, with two exceptions:

1. It does not have a deferred delivery parameter, since it is intended that the viability of the system be tested now, rather than at a later time.
2. It has an additional content length field to allow the testing of the recipient's ability to accept messages of a certain size even in the absence of the actual message content field.

All the other fields of the probe MPDU are identical to the user MPDU and are interpreted in the same manner by all the MTAs involved in its transfer through the MTS. Figure 6.1 summarizes the possible sequence of MPDU exchanges defined by the P1 protocol.

6.1.5 The message transfer agent model

The 1984 standard models in great depth the internals of the MTA operation and tries to clearly define what actions an MTA must perform in relaying messages within the message transfer layer. The MTA is modeled as a message transfer agent entity (MTAE) that comprises the RTS layer functionality for reliable message transfer, plus two ad-

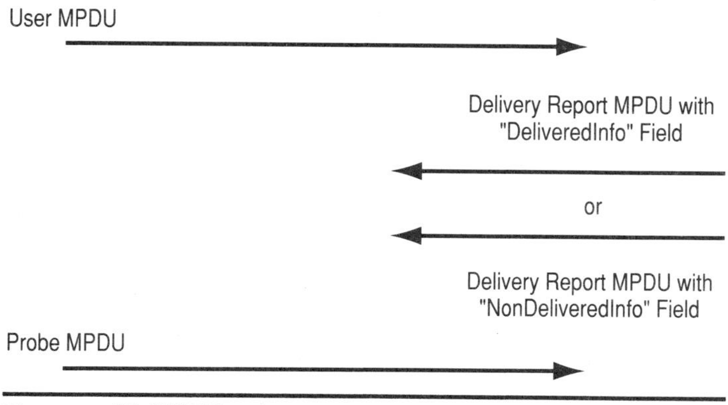

Figure 6.1 P1 MPDU exchanges.

ditional functional elements that are useful in describing the MTAE behavior but are largely conceptual in nature:

- An association manager
- A message dispatcher

The association manager is responsible for controlling and releasing the underlying RTS associations. The message dispatcher, on the other hand, is responsible for constructing and decoding MPDU envelope structures and executing the P1 protocol itself. The role of the message dispatcher can be summarized as

1. Relaying messages in the MTL
2. Generating delivery reports
3. Providing content conversion

Figure 6.2 shows the internal architecture of an MTA. One or more user agent entities may be using the services of each MTA entity to submit or receive messages.

6.1.5.1 Relaying messages in the MTL. The MPDU envelope contains a recipient information parameter that carries a Responsibility Flag which allows an MTAE to decide what recipients have yet to receive the message. The Responsibility Flag indicates to the MTAE that it is not to take responsibility for delivering the message to a listed recipient because that recipient has already been serviced by a previous MTAE. Alternatively, the MTAE may choose to remove the name of

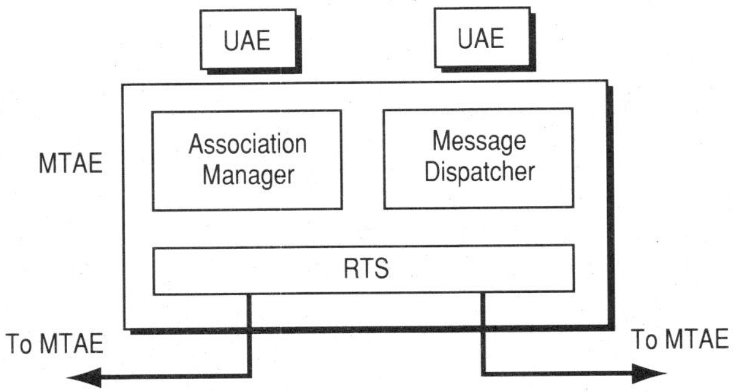

Figure 6.2 MTA internal model.

any intended recipients it has already serviced from the MPDU envelope.

Figure 6.3 shows conceptually how messages are relayed from one MTA to another. A message is submitted to MTAE 1 by the UA. A copy of the message is relayed to MTAE 2 and MTAE 3. Each MTAE in the sequence is responsible for delivering the message to its locally attached UAs and for relaying a copy of the message to any adjoining MTAEs, which may be responsible for servicing additional recipients.

6.1.5.2 Generating delivery reports. The MTL notifies user agent entities of the successful or unsuccessful delivery of messages. The mes-

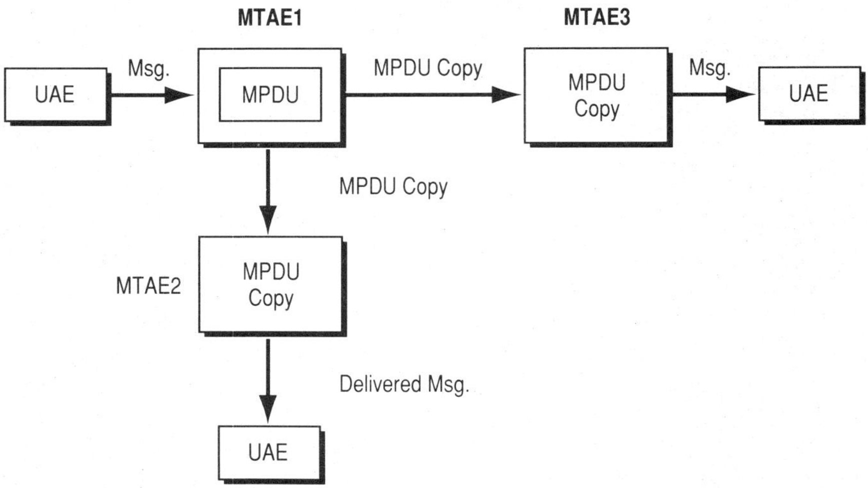

Figure 6.3 Message relaying.

sage dispatcher generates a positive delivery report when it successfully delivers a message to a UA.

6.1.5.3 Content conversion. Any MTAE may perform some format conversion on the contents of the user MPDU. The possible conversions allowed in 1984 X.400 are described in X.408. In order to know what content conversion is required, the MTAE must first know what information types the recipient UAE is willing to receive. It can obtain this information through any of the following means:

1. The UAE tells the MD, at subscription time, what information types it supports.
2. The MTAE may deduce the conversions from the name of the MD of the recipient.
3. The recipient ORName may contain some attributes from which the encoded information types of the recipient UAE are deduced.

6.1.6 Management of associations

Associations between two MTAEs are created according to bilateral agreements between two MDs that cover

1. The maximum number of associations that can exist simultaneously.
2. Whether one-way or two-way alternate associations should be used.
3. Which MTA is responsible for establishing the association.
4. Whether the association is permanent or will be set up on a need-to basis.

If associations are set up on a need basis, the decision to set up an association is made locally on the basis of some local pragmatics such as time of day, number of MPDUs waiting, etc.

Associations are established by invoking the RTS OPEN.Request. The underlying RTS layer responds by returning an OPEN.Response. Associations are released by issuing an RTS CLOSE.Request primitive. Once an association is established, MPDUs are transferred using the RTS TRANSFER.Request primitive. In two-way alternate associations, the message dispatcher can change the turn by sending a TURN-PLEASE.Request. The message dispatcher that has the turn will respond by issuing a TURN-GIVE.Request.

MPDUs are assigned to associations on a priority basis, according to the type of MPDU. Higher priority MPDUs are sent first, while messages of the same priority are sent first-in first-out. Service MPDUs are always sent with a priority setting of URGENT.

The message dispatcher is activated by a SUBMIT.Request, and a PROBE.Request at the user agent layer, or by a TRANSFER. Indication, and an EXCEPTION.Indication at the RTS interface. These primitives are carried from the UA to the MTAE via the P3 protocol.

6.1.6.1 Action on SUBMIT.Request. Upon receipt of a SUBMIT.-Request from the UAE, the message dispatcher validates the originator of the message as well as the other parameters of the request. A new UMPDU is created with the specified parameters, and a submit-event-id is generated. A SUBMIT.Confirmation is returned to the originating UAE to indicate that these procedures have succeeded. The UMPDU is then passed to the RTS layer via a TRANSFER request, unless deferred delivery was requested, in which case the message is held for delivery until a specified later time. See Fig. 6.4 for the sequence of message submission events.

6.1.6.2 Action on PROBE.Request. The actions carried out in the case of a probe request are similar to those of the SUBMIT.Request, except that a probe MPDU is generated and a PROBE.Confirmation indication is returned to the UAE.

6.1.6.3 Action on TRANSFER.Indication. When the message dispatcher receives a new MPDU from the RTS layer (i.e., via a TRANSFER.Indication), it validates the MPDU envelope. If the enve-

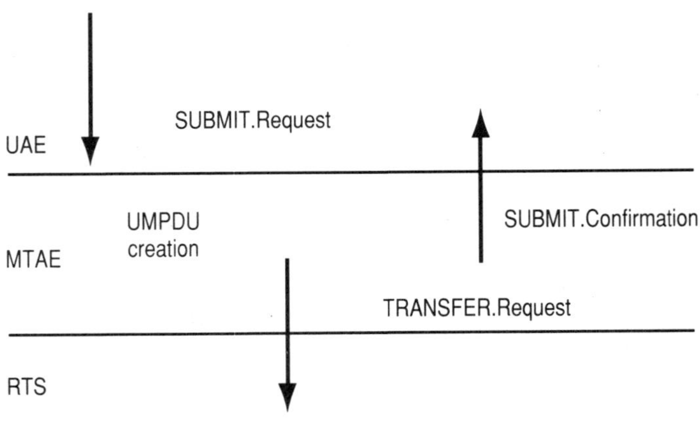

Figure 6.4 Sequence of message submission events.

lope is invalid, a negative Delivery Report MPDU is returned in response to probe and user MPDUs. The global domain identifier of the MD and the arrival time of the MPDU are added to the Trace Information field component of the MPDU. The message dispatcher selects the destination O/R names for which the routing algorithm is to be executed. For each recipient, one of the following three results are possible:

1. The MTA serves the intended recipient, in which case it simply delivers the message.
2. The MPDU must be relayed to another MTA, in which case the MPDU is resubmitted to the RTS layer via a TRANSFER.Request.
3. The routing algorithm detects an error in the ORName.

If the MPDU is a user MPDU or probe MPDU, and the MTA serves the recipient, a time stamp is generated and a DELIVER.Indication is issued. If the message cannot be delivered, a last trace item is generated along with the reason for nondelivery. If the MPDU is a Delivery Report MPDU, the message is correlated to the original user MPDU submission.

In the event of a probe or user MPDU if the MPDU must be relayed to another MTA, the trace information is checked for loops. If the MPDU is a Delivery Report MPDU, the trace information is checked for loops before delivery.

If an error is detected in the ORName once the routing algorithm completes, a check is made to ensure that all necessary delivery report MPDUs have been generated. A TRANSFER.Request is issued for each MPDU that needs to be relayed further. Figure 6.5 summarizes the sequence of events upon receipt of a message.

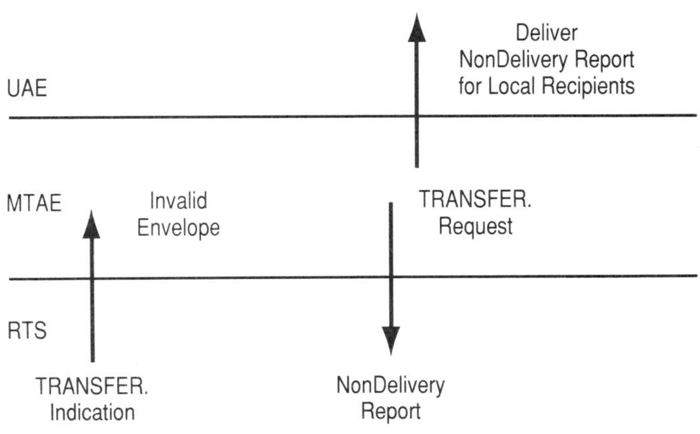

Figure 6.5 Sequence of message receipt events.

6.1.6.4 Action on EXCEPTION.Indication event. An EXCEPTION. Indication denotes the inability to communicate with an intended MTAE. In this case, if the message dispatcher can do alternate routing, the routing algorithm is reexecuted for each recipient. Where there is an alternate route, a copy of the MPDU is made and the responsibility flag is set to TRUE. The trace information is added to all MPDUs which are rerouted. A TRANSFER.Request is issued for each UMPDU. If the MPDU is a user or probe MPDU, a delivery report MPDU is generated. If the MPDU is a delivery report MPDU and no alternate route exists, the MPDU is discarded.

6.2 The P2 Protocol

P2 is the interpersonal messaging service protocol used to exchange information between user agents (UAs). Although a UA may interface with the user in many different ways to present messaging information, it must itself be able to comprehend the information it receives from a remote UA. This requires that there be a standardized UA-to-UA peer-level protocol. UAs that are able to interact via the same interpersonal messaging protocol are called "cooperating UAs." The 1984 X.400 defines a single interpersonal messaging protocol, P2.

6.2.1 Operation of IPM user agent entities

The behavior of a UA is described in terms of the operation of an Interpersonal Messaging User Agent Entity (IPM-UAE, for short) which resides within the UA. An IPM-UAE's actions are described through its interactions with the originating or recipient user of the IPM service, as well as its interactions with the underlying MTL service. The first set of interactions are locally defined and are not subject to standardization, whereas the second set of interactions are fully specified in the MHS standards, as are the semantics of the messages exchanged between two IPM-UAEs.

Figure 6.6 shows how IPM-UAEs relate to the underlying message transfer layer service. Facilities provided between the user and the IPM-UAE are not standardized. These may include options for viewing messages and other message management facilities. Figure 6.1 also shows the internal architecture of a UAE, which consists of a user component that interfaces to the user of the MHS service, an IPM-UAE component that encodes and decodes message information according to the semantics defined in the P2 protocol, and an MTL component that interfaces to the underlying MTL service.

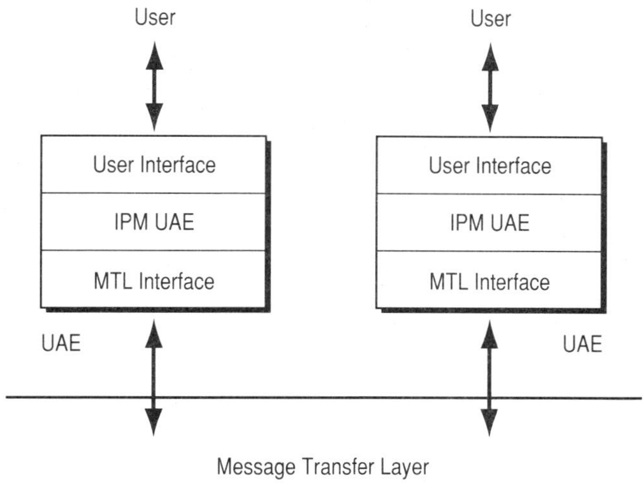

Figure 6.6 UAE internal architecture and how it relates to the MTL.

6.2.2 Sending IP messages

In order to submit a message, the originator's UAE constructs an IM-UAPDU, and issues a SUBMIT.Request to the MTL. If the submission fails (for whatever reason), the UAE notifies the user of the failure. If it succeeds, the MTL returns a set of time and event identification parameters that can later be used by the UAE to correlate notifications regarding the delivery status of the submitted IM-UAPDU. The UAE may, for example, at a later time, receive a NOTIFY.Indication informing it that a previously submitted IM-UAPDU could not be delivered.

The recipient UAE is informed of the arrival of an IM-UAPDU through the receipt of a DELIVER.Indication. All the information carried by the DELIVER indication is made available to the user. In order to correlate a notification with a previously submitted IM-UAPDU, the IPM-UAE relies on the submit-event-id parameters returned by the SUBMIT.Confirmation and the NOTIFY.Indication primitives. Alternatively, the IPMessageId of the IM-UAPDU may be used as the UA-content-id parameter of the SUBMIT.Request, in which case the UA-content-id returned by the NOTIFY.Indication is used to do the correlation.

6.2.3 The protocol information structure

The P2 protocol carries units of information called User Agent Protocol Data Units (UAPDUs). It defines two kinds of UAPDUs:

1. IP-message UAPDUs (IM-UAPDUs), which carry interpersonal messages between an originator and a recipient UAE.
2. Status-report UAPDUs (SR-UAPDUs), which consist of status information generated by one UAE for another UAE.

The status information transported by SR-UAPDU may be used by the peer-level UAE locally, or it may be conveyed to the user. The structure of an UAPDU is defined in ASN.1 as

```
UAPDU ::= CHOICE {
                [0]  IMPLICIT IM-UAPDU,
                [1]  IMPLICIT SR-UAPDU }
```

Figure 6.7 illustrates the structure of a UAPDU. It is composed of an enclosing P1 message envelope and may contain either an IM-UAPDU or an SR-UAPDU in the content field. The IM-UAPDU is in turn composed of a heading and a body, whereas the SR-UAPDU consists only of header information.

6.2.3.1 Common data types. P2 relies on many of the same data types already defined in P1. IP messages are identified by an IP-MessageID, which is unique and unambiguous. It consists of an ORName, plus a printable string as follows:

```
IPMessageId ::= { ORName OPTIONAL,
                  PrintableString }
```

6.2.3.2 Structure of IM-UAPDUs. An IM-UAPDU consists of a header plus a body. The body of the IM-UAPDU carries the message that the

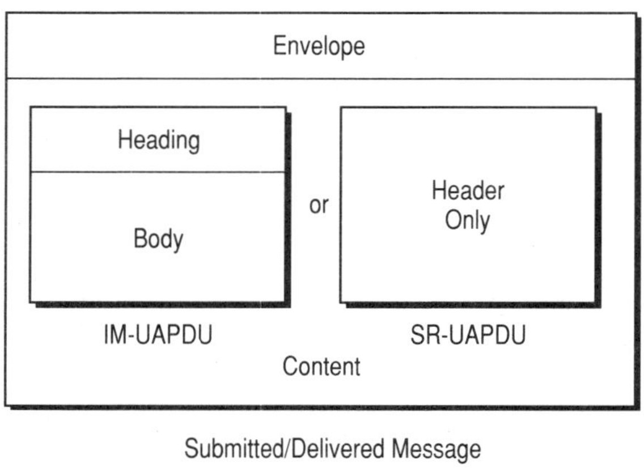

Figure 6.7 UAPDU message structure.

user of the originating UA wishes to convey to the user of the recipient UA:

```
IM-UAPDU ::=  SEQUENCE {Heading, Body}

Heading ::= SET {
  IPMessageId,
  originator          [0] IMPLICIT ORDescriptor OPTIONAL,
  authorizingUsers    [1] IMPLICIT SEQUENCE OF ORDescriptor OPTIONAL,
                          —only if not the originator—
  primaryRecipients   [2] IMPLICIT SEQUENCE OF Recipient OPTIONAL,
  copyRecipients      [3] IMPLICIT SEQUENCE OF Recipient OPTIONAL,
  blindCopyRecipients     [4] IMPLICIT SEQUENCE OF Recipient
                                     OPTIONAL,
  InReplyTo           [5] IMPLICIT IPMessageId OPTIONAL,
                            —omitted if not in reply to a previous message—
  obsoletes           [6] IMPLICIT SEQUENCE OF IPMessageId OPTIONAL,
  crossReferences     [7] IMPLICIT SEQUENCE OF IPMessageId OPTIONAL,
  subject             [8] CHOICE {T61 String} OPTIONAL,
  expiryDate          [9] IMPLICIT Time OPTIONAL,
                            —if omitted expiry date is never—
  replyBy             [10] IMPLICIT Time OPTIONAL,
  replyToUsers        [11] IMPLICIT SEQUENCE OF ORDescriptor
                                 OPTIONAL,—each O/R descriptor must
                                          contain an O/R name—
  Importance          [12] IMPLICIT INTEGER {low(0), normal(1),
                             high(2)} DEFAULT normal,
  sensitivity         [13] IMPLICIT INTEGER {personal(1), private(2),
                             companyConfidential(3)} OPTIONAL,
  autoForwarded       [14] IMPLICIT BOOLEAN DEFAULT FALSE
                      —indicates that the forwarded message body part(s) were
                            autoforwarded— }
```

The heading of an IM-UAPDU consists of the following information:

1. An IPMessageId, which consists of an ORName and a printable string.
2. An originator identifier, which identifies the user who is submitting the IP message.
3. A list of authorizingUsers, which consists of those users who have authorized the sending of the message (i.e., this is in the event that a message is being sent by a user on behalf of another user, e.g., a secretary on behalf of a boss).
4. A list of primaryRecipients is a list of intended primary recipients of the message, i.e., users listed in the To: field of the message.
5. A list of copyRecipients, a list of secondary, or carbon-copy, recipients of the message, i.e., users listed in the cc: field of the message.
6. A list of blindCopyRecipients, which is list of secondary recipients of the message, whose names are not to be disclosed to either the primary or the copy recipients of the message.

All the above recipient lists comprise the name of the recipient, plus for each recipient a reportRequest and a replyRequest indication. The reportRequest indication serves to request that either a receiptNotification or a nonReceiptNotification be returned to the originator to indicate the successful or unsuccessful delivery of the message to that recipient. The sender may also specify whether it wishes a copy of the original IP Message to be returned in the event of nondelivery of the message. The ReplyRequest indication is used to indicate that the recipient of the message should return a reply to the message.

7. The inReplyTo field identifies a previously sent IP message to which the current one is replying.
8. The obsoletes and crossReferences fields identify any previously sent IP messages that are either being obsoleted or are referenced by the current message.
9. The autoforwarded indication indicates whether the body of the IP-message contains an autoforwarded IP message.

The body of an IM-UAPDU consists of a sequence of different possible body parts, as follows:

```
Body ::=   SEQUENCE OF BodyPart

BodyPart ::= CHOICE {
            [0]   IMPLICIT IA5Text,
            [1]   IMPLICIT TLX,
            [2]   IMPLICIT Voice,
            [3]   IMPLICIT G3Fax,
            [4]   IMPLICIT TIF0,
            [5]   IMPLICIT TTX,
            [6]   IMPLICIT Videotex,
            [7]   NationallyDefined,
            [8]   IMPLICIT Encrypted,
            [9]   IMPLICIT ForwardedIPMessage,
            [10]  IMPLICIT SFD,
            [11]  IMPLICIT TIF1}
```

Each body part carries with it an indication of its type and may also include a set of parameters necessary to interpret the body part information. As shown in the above ASN.1 the valid body parts, in 1984 X.400, are a choice of IA5Text, TLX, Voice, G3Fax, TIFO, TTX, VideoTex, NationallyDefined, Encrypted, ForwardedIPMessage, SFD, or TIFI.

6.2.4 Structure of SR-UAPDUs

The SR-UAPDU returns a notification of the successful or unsuccessful receipt of the IP message by its intended recipient. It consists exclusively of header information, as shown in the following ASN.1:

```
SR-UAPDU ::= SET {
            [0] CHOICE {
                nonReceipt     [0] IMPLICIT NonReceiptInformation
                receipt        [1] IMPLICIT ReceiptInformation },
            reported           IPMessageId,
            actualRecipient    [1] IMPLICIT ORDescriptor OPTIONAL,
            intendedRecipient  [2] IMPLICIT ORDescriptor OPTIONAL,
                 —only present if not actual recipient the O/R descriptor must
                 contain an O/R name—
            converted          P1.EncodedInformationTypes OPTIONAL }

NonReceiptInformation ::= SET {
   reason               [0] IMPLICIT INTEGER { uaeInitiatedDiscard(0)
                                               autoForwarded(1)},
   nonReceiptQualifier  [1] IMPLICIT INTEGER {expired(0), obsoleted(1),
                                subscriptionTerminated(2) } OPTIONAL,
   comments             [2] IMPLICIT PrintableString OPTIONAL,
                        —on auto-forward—
   returned             [3] IMPLICIT IM-UAPDU OPTIONAL }

ReceiptInformation ::= SET {
   receipt        [0] IMPLICIT Time,
   typeOfReceipt  [1] IMPLICIT INTEGER {explicit(0), automatic(1)}
                      DEFAULT explicit,
                  [2] IMPLICIT P1.SupplementaryInformation OPTIONAL }
```

If a nonreceipt notification is being conveyed, the SR-UAPDU carries the NonReceiptInformation field. The nonreceipt notification may indicate that the UAE has discarded the IP message for local reasons (uaeInitiatedDiscard), or that the UAE has forwarded the message to another UAE (autoForwarded). If the UAE discards an IP message, it may return any one of the following reasons:

1. Expired, the message was discarded due to the expiration date,
2. Obsoleted, the message was discarded because it was obsoleted by another IP-message,
3. SubscriptionTerminated, the administrative contract between the MTA and the UA has been terminated.

If a message is being autoforwarded, a comments field is used to convey a string of characters on behalf of the UAE which forwarded the message. If requested by the originator of the message, the SR-UAPDU may also convey back the entire originally submitted IP-UAPDU.

If a receipt notification is being conveyed by the SR-UAPDU, the ReceiptInformation field is present. It consists of a receiptTime, which denotes the time at which the IP-UAPDU was received.

An TypeOfReceipt field indicates whether the recipient explicitly authorized sending the notification (explicit), or whether the UAE automatically generated the notification upon receipt of the IP message (automatic).

The supplementaryInfo field is reserved for use by telex and telematic terminals.

The additional fields in the SR-UAPDU indicate

1. reportedIPMessageld is the IP-message to which the status information in the SR-UAPDU refers.
2. actualRecipient is the UAE to which the IM-UAPDU was actually delivered (not necessarily the same as the intended UAE) and which is generating the IPM-status-report.
3. intendedRecipient is returned only if the IM-UAPDU was delivered to an alternate recipient.
4. converted EncodedInfoTypes conveys the new EncodedInfoTypes if the submitted IM-UAPDU underwent some format conversion.

6.3 The P3 Protocol

P3 is the protocol used between Submission and Delivery Entities (SDEs) and Message Transfer Agent Entities (MTAEs) to submit and receive MHS messages. P3 interactions are modeled as ROS procedure calls, and the unit of information exchanged by the P3 protocol is the Operation Protocol Data Unit (OPDU). P3 makes use of RTS (X.410) in order to support reliable associations between an SDE and an MTAE.

P3 is a somewhat controversial protocol, and its 1984 version has not really been implemented in any commercial products (or even experimental networks as far as it is known). There are two reasons for this, a technical one as well as a pragmatic one. The technical reason for not implementing P3 is that it requires the UA (or its SDE component) to be ready on-line to receive mail at all times. This is usually impractical in most real-life implementations where users need to turn their machines off or use them for other tasks besides mail.

The pragmatic reason for not using P3 is that most commercial implementations to date have only built gateways from native mail systems to X.400. A gateway avoids the need for a P3-style protocol in that mail is delivered and submitted on the native side of the gateway via the native mail protocol (rather than via the P3 protocol). Since the gateway normally comprises the MTA functionality, the message is forwarded within the X.400 system via the P1 protocol which operates at the MTA level. Therefore, gateway-based MHS environments have typically implemented P1 and P2, but not P3.

A brief summary of P3 operations is presented here to enable the reader to appreciate its intended role in the architecture and understand how it changed in the 1988 MHS recommendations. The specification of P3 relies on many of the same data-type definitions available in the P1 protocol.

P3 supports three management operations: Register, Control, and Change-Password, and five submission and delivery operations: Submit, Probe, Cancel, Deliver, and Notify.

6.3.1 Register

The register operation allows a UA to set values for its long-term registration parameters. The registration parameters that can be set by the operation are the deliverable EncodedInformationTypes (e.g., EITs), the ORName, the Address, the maximumContentLength, and a set of DefaultControlSettings. P3 does not provide procedures for assigning alternate recipients. Their implementation is left as a local matter for administrations implementing this service.

6.3.2 Control

The control operation allows an MTAE or SDE to temporarily restrict the operations that can be invoked on the other. It allows the following restrictions to be imposed:

1. Deliver or submission permitted.
2. Messages with content length greater than a certain size cannot be transferred.
3. Messages with priority less than a specified value may not be transferred.
4. Only messages with certain Encoded Information Types may be transferred.
5. Notifications or probes may be transferred.

6.3.3 Change password

The Change-Password operation allows either the UAE or the MTAE to change its current password. It takes as parameters the value of the old password and that of the new password.

6.3.4 Submit

The Submit operation transfers both a message envelope and its contents from an SDE to an MTAE. The MTAE may accept or reject the message. The submission envelope contains parameters denoting the originator's ORName, the recipient's ORName, the message content, the content type, the Encoded Information Types, the priority of the message, the deferred delivery time if one was requested, the UA content ID, and any explicit conversions which may have been requested. It returns as results an event ID to identify the particular submission event and the time of submission.

6.3.5 Probe

The probe operation allows SDEs to send abbreviated messages composed simply of an envelope. If it is accepted, the MTAE constructs the probe MPDU. The probe operation may take as parameters the originator's ORName, the recipient's ORName, the content type, the encoded information types, whether explicit conversions are requested, the UA content ID, and the length of the content of the message. It returns as results an event ID to denote the probe event, and the time at which the probe was submitted.

6.3.6 Cancel

The Cancel operation allows the SDE to request that the MTAE stop delivery or transfer of a previously submitted deferred delivery message. The EventID is the submit event ID that was previously supplied by the MTAE in response to the submit operation which requested the deferred delivery of the message. Deferred delivery can be implemented either at the source MTA or at the destination MTA. The cancel operation works only if the deferred delivery is being implemented at the source MTA. No operation is provided to cancel a deferred delivery message at the destination MTA.

6.3.7 Deliver

The Deliver operation is used by the MTAE to initiate delivery of a message it has received to the recipient UA.

6.3.8 Notify

The Notify operation indicates to the SDE the successful or unsuccessful delivery of a message. It carries an event ID that serves to correlate previous submit or probe operations and a sequence of recipient information regarding the success or failure of message delivery for one or more recipients. It may also carry the returned message content.

6.4 What Has Been Implemented

Thus far, relatively few vendors and service providers have chosen to implement the X.400 MHS protocols as their native electronic mail proto-

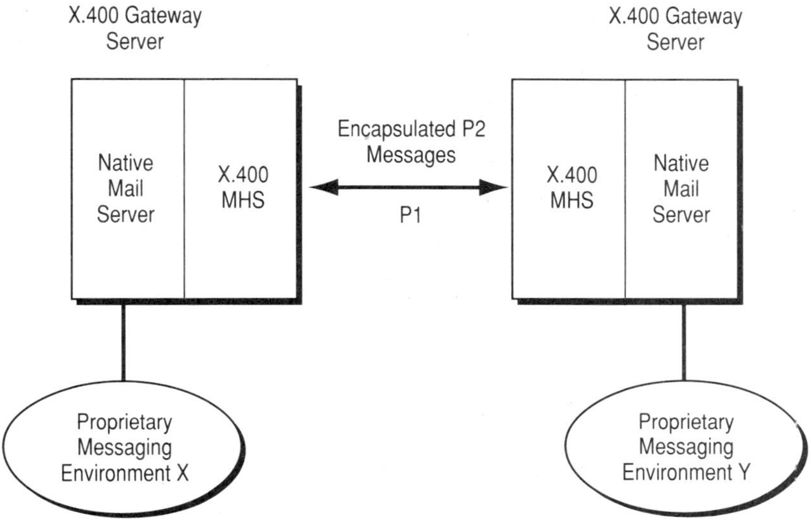

Figure 6.8 X.400 gateway architecture.

cols. The reason for this is the wide market predominance of proprietary electronic mail systems already in operation. This has led most vendors and service providers to build gateways to X.400 as a prelude to full protocol migration later on. This has made X.400 effectively into what could be called a common interchange standard for electronic mail interoperability. Figure 6.8 illustrates the use of X.400 gateways as the interconnection mechanism between different proprietary electronic mail environments. The gateway servers shown in the figure appear as native mail servers on the proprietary side of the gateway and as full-fledged X.400 MTAs on the X.400 side of the gateway. The gateway basically accepts messages in the native format and translates them into P2-compatible messages, which are then transported from one X.400 gateway to another via the P1 MTA to MTA protocol.

One of the side-effects of this type of architecture is that the P3 style protocol is no longer needed. P3 was defined to allow UAs to interact with MTAs. However, in a gateway-based architecture, non-X.400 UAs on the proprietary side of the gateway interact with the X.400-based MTA capability on the gateway server by means of the native messaging protocols in use within the proprietary environment.

References and for Further Study

The 1984 X.400 protocols are fully defined in the Red Book (CCITT X.400, 1984).

Chapter

7

The 1988 MHS Recommendations

Throughout the 1988 study period, ISO and CCITT cooperated extensively to harmonize the MHS architecture and succeeded in producing what is now largely a joint ISO/CCITT specification. However, some differences still remain between the ISO and CCITT texts, as we will see throughout the next two chapters. Fortunately for the most part these differences will not hinder interoperability between ISO- and CCITT-compliant implementations. Functional standards bodies are currently addressing any remaining areas of inconsistencies that might hinder interoperability between private and public networks. The overall MHS service and architecture, however, is exactly the same for the ISO and CCITT versions of the recommendations. Also, both the ISO and CCITT documents summarize at the end of each chapter the differences vis-à-vis the standard published by the other organization.

This chapter looks at the new functionality defined in the 1988 MHS recommendations and the advantages it provides over the 1984 MHS model. It describes how the MHS model changes because of the addition of some major new architectural components, such as the X.500 directories, as well as how the protocols evolve to incorporate both the new 1988 services as well as the 1988 OSI upper layer architecture.

7.1 What's New in 1988 MHS

The 1988 MHS, or the Blue Book as it is called, introduces five major new concepts into the MHS architecture:

1. The Message Store and its associated protocol P7
2. Distribution Lists
3. X.500 Directory Services
4. Support for postal delivery services
5. Security

In addition, in 1988, the MHS protocol layering architecture changes considerably to incorporate the more recent work on OSI upper layers and provide a higher degree of alignment with the design of other OSI applications. Throughout the 1988 study period, ISO and CCITT cooperated extensively to enhance some of the basic OSI application layer building blocks such as ROS, ACSE, ASN.1, and the presentation layer. As a result, ROS and ASN.1 are no longer published as part of the MHS recommendations, but rather they constitute separate documents within the X.200 series recommendations that define the overall OSI reference model. These upper-layer OSI standards serve as the basis for the specification of many of the newer OSI application layer standards, including X.500 and Network Management as well as others which are still under development such as Document Filing and Retrieval (DFR).

7.2 Structure of the 1988 Recommendations

The following chart summarizes the documents that make up the 1988 MHS standards and provides the ISO and CCITT document numbers for each:

	CCITT	ISO	CCITT only
MHS: Service and Overview	X.400	10021-1	
MHS: Overall Architecture	X.402	10021-2	
MHS: Conformance Testing	X.403		
MHS: Abstract Service Definition conventions	X.407	10021-3	
MHS: Encoded Information Types conversion rules	X.408		
MHS: MTS: Abstract Service Definitions and procedures	X.411	10021-4	
MHS: Abstract Service Definition	X.413	10021-5	
MHS: Protocol Specifications	X.419	10021-6	
MHS: Interpersonal messaging system	X.420	10021-7	
Telematic Access to IPMS			T.330

In addition, CCITT has defined a series of recommendations that provide guidance to CCITT administrations for the deployment of MHS services by administrations. These recommendations are known as the F.400 series documents and include the following set of documents:

	CCITT F Series
MHS: System and service overview	F.400
MHS: Naming and Addressing for public MH Services	F.401
MHS: The public message transfer service	F.410
MHS: Intercommunication with public physical delivery services	F.415
MHS: The public IPM service	F.420
MHS: Intercommunication between IPM service and telex	F.421
MHS: Intercommunication between IPM service and telex	F.422

7.2.1 Supporting standards

Both the ISO and CCITT versions of the 1988 MHS rely on the architectural framework provided by the following OSI standards:

	CCITT	ISO
OSI: Basic reference model	X.200	7498
OSI: Specification of abstract syntax notation one (ASN.1)	X.208	8824
OSI: Specification of basic encoding rules for abstract syntax notation one (ASN.1)	X.209	8825
OSI: Association control: service definition	X.217	8649
OSI: Reliable Transfer: model and service definition	X.218	9066-1
OSI: Remote operations: model, notation, and service definition	X.219	9072-1
OSI: Association control: protocol specification	X.227	8650
OSI: Reliable Transfer: protocol specification	X.228	9066-2
OSI: Remote operations: protocol specification	X.229	9072-2

7.2.2 The X.500 standards

The X.500 standards for Directory services were also developed during the 1988 study period. X.500 plays a key role in the architecture of the 1988 MHS. Although X.500 is an application in its own right rather than a supporting layer standard, the functionality it provides is at the heart of the architecture of most other application layer services. The set of documents that make up the X.500 standards are:

	CCITT	ISO
Directory Services: Overview	X.500	9594-1
Directory Services: Models	X.501	9594-2
Directory Services: Authentication Framework	X.509	9594-8
Directory Services: Abstract Service Definition	X.511	9594-3
Directory Services: Distributed Operations	X.518	9594-4
Directory Services: Protocol Specifications	X.519	9594-5
Directory Services: Selected Attribute Types	X.520	9594-6
Directory Services: Selected Object Classes	X.521	9594-7

7.3 The 1988 MHS Functional Model

The MHS functional model evolved considerably in 1988 to include a number of new elements. Among these is the concept of an Access Unit (AU) which serves to denote access to MHS services by what are called *indirect users*. Indirect users are defined to be entities that use the MHS services through some other communication system. An example of an indirect user may be a physical postal delivery system that connects to the MHS services to offer integrated postal and electronic mail services.

A great deal of emphasis was placed in the 1988 recommendations on incorporating the requirements of postal delivery services into the overall MHS architecture. This is not surprising, since the CCITT administrations place a high value on the commercial use of MHS services. Public service providers have a strong desire to provide a unified set of information exchange services that encompass not only electronic mail but also postal mail as we know it today. In order to best support the requirement for physical mail delivery, the standard introduces the notion of physical delivery access units (PDAUs), which are defined to serve as front ends for postal delivery systems. The remainder of this book does not deal with this element in detail, as its implications are largely architectural at this time, and specific to the use of MHS by administrations (i.e., PTTS). The reader should be aware, however, that this type of service is being actively considered by public service providers and that standardization, and planning for it, is proceeding within CCITT.

One of the major new components of the 1988 MHS architecture is the Message Store (MS). The primary purpose of the Message Store is to provide a repository for short-term stable storage of messages received. In doing so the Message Store also provides a greater level of control by UAs on the way in which messages are retrieved on behalf of the user. The specification of the message store functionality is probably the single most significant enhancement over the 1984 MHS architecture. The MS is designed to serve essentially as an intermediary between UAs and MTAs. It supports the submission of messages from UAs and can alert UAs of the occurrence of special message receipt events. Figure 7.1 shows how the Message Store is positioned logically in between the UA and the message transfer service as accessed via a specific MTA. Section 7.3.1 below discusses in greater detail the various possible physical scenarios that can be used to support the Message Store concept.

In the 1984 MHS, the functionality of the message store was largely assumed to be packaged with the UA, and its definition was left as a local matter outside the scope of standardization. By standardizing its behavior and architecture in 1988 MHS, we are in fact raising the level of standardization of electronic messaging systems closer to the user and moving more into the realm of how people and applications interact with the messaging environment. The Message Store architecture and its associated protocol, called P7, are discussed in greater detail in Chapter 8. Some of the practical implications of the Message Store on the development of commercial messaging systems are discussed in Chap. 10.

The other major architectural addition to the 1988 MHS architecture is provided by the Directory services defined in the X.500 standards. The need for X.500 Directories was determined during the definition of the 1984 MHS standards. X.500 is largely a creature of MHS, as the primary impetus behind its definition comes from a desire to provide better support for naming and addressing in large distributed message handling systems. However, MHS-specific use of the directory is specified in X.400. Sections 7.4 and 7.5 below describe extensively the Directory Service and its relationship to MHS services.

Figure 7.2 summarizes the functional components that can make up an 1988 MHS environment. It depicts a set of MTAs that cooperate to provide the core MTS function. Messaging users may gain access to the MTS service via UAs directly connected to MTAs as was the case in 1984, or through the use of a Message Store capability. Postal Delivery Access Units (PDAUs) and other generic Access Units (AUs) are also defined to provide MTS access to postal delivery services and telematic services in general. The 1988 MHS standard does not go into great detail to define what telematic services may be brought into the MHS environment, but it does provide an architectural "placeholder"

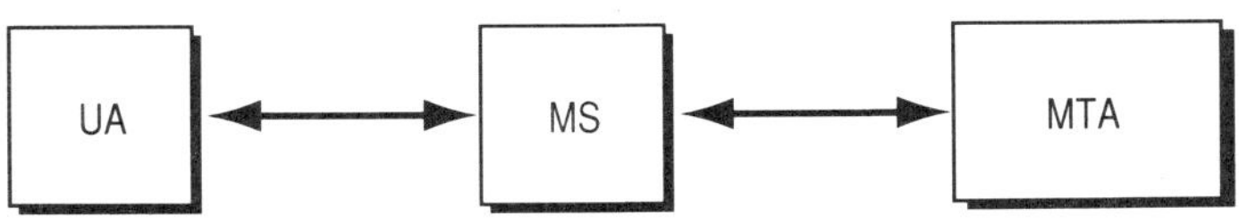

Figure 7.1 The Message Store.

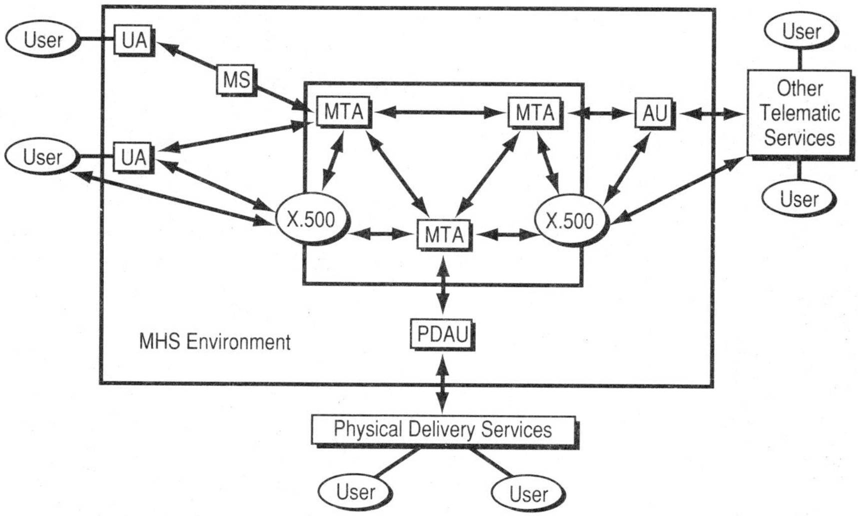

Figure 7.2 1988 MHS environment.

for the later standardization of such services. Figure 7.2 also serves to show how the X.500 Directory Services fit into the MHS architecture. Directory Services may be accessed independently by any number of functional components including MTAs, UAs, AUs, Message Stores, and even directly by the MHS end user. These entities would typically query the Directory to perform name-to-address translation as well as acquire any additional necessary information regarding particular MHS users and resources.

7.3.1 Physical mapping of the 1988 model

With the introduction of the Message Store component, 1988 conformant systems are able to configure MHS systems in many more variations than was previously possible. Message Store services, however, are optional in 1988 systems. When present, they may be colocated with UAs, MTAs, or they may constitute a stand-alone component.

The Message Store may be physically configured in several ways relative to either the UA or the MTA:

1. The Message Store may be physically colocated with the UA, in which case it is functionally equivalent to a stand-alone UA.
2. The Message Store may be a stand-alone entity on a separate system element.
3. The Message Store may be colocated with an MTA.

It is expected that in most implementations the Message Store will be colocated with the MTA, thus in a sense extending the MTA functionality to include a stable storage message repository capability. Figures 7.3 through 7.6 show how Message Store services relate to UAs and MTAs and what protocols would operate between them in each instance.

Figure 7.3 above shows a system element comprising both the UA functionality as well as the Message Store component. In this case the Message Store interacts with an MTA via the P3 protocol, and it interacts with the colocated UA by means of internally defined interfaces. Usually, these interfaces are designed to be totally transparent of the underlying message submission and retrieval protocol.

Figure 7.4 shows separate UAs, Message Store, and MTA systems. In this case the UA communicates the Message Store via the P7 protocol, and the Message Store, in turn, will communicate with the MTA through the P3 protocol.

Figure 7.5 is logically the same as the scenario depicted in Fig. 7.4;

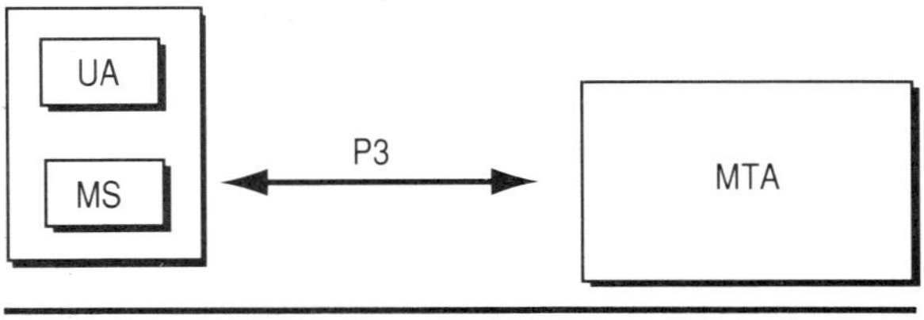

Figure 7.3 Colocated UA and Message Store.

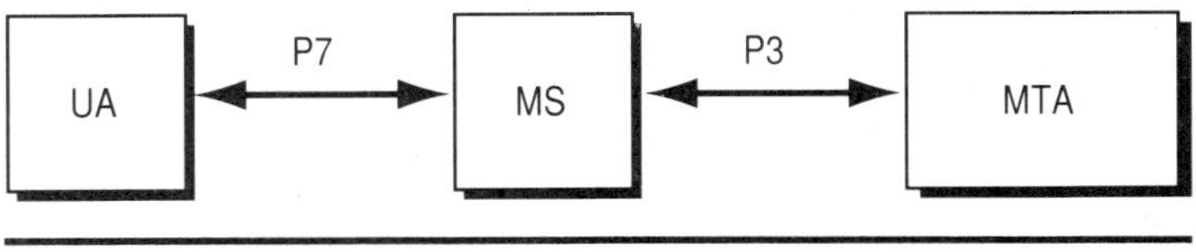

Figure 7.4 Stand-alone UA, MS, and MTA.

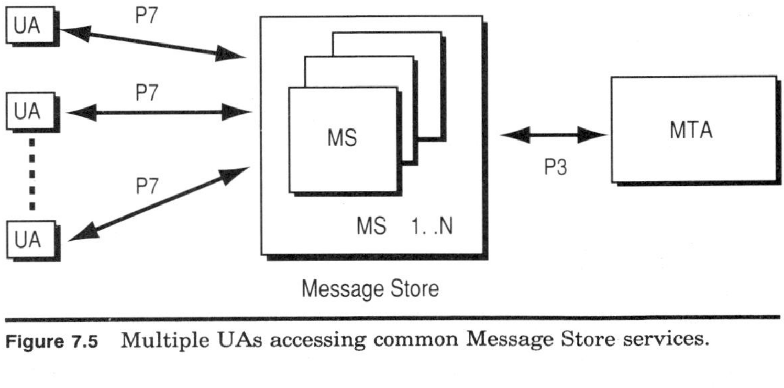

Figure 7.5 Multiple UAs accessing common Message Store services.

however, it shows a number of different UAs accessing the Message Store functionality located on a dedicated server. Logically, the service implementing the Message Store functionality will maintain a separate Message Store for each UA that accesses it, thus giving each UA the impression of dealing with a dedicated Message Store.

Figure 7.6 shows what is likely to be the most common configuration, where the Message Store function is colocated with the MTA function. Again, although the diagram shows a single Message Store service being accessed by multiple UAs, in fact each UA will be accessing a logically distinct and dedicated Message Store repository.

7.4 X.500 Directory Services

The X.500 standards for Directory Services provide the foundation on which much of the 1988 MHS functionality is defined. The Message Store, Distribution Lists, and Security are all based on services provided by X.500 Directory Services. In addition, the technical specifications of 1988 MHS rely on a number of attribute types and object class definitions that are made available by the X.500 standards.

The need for Directory Services was recognized during the 1984 MHS study period. ISO and CCITT began work on a joint directory specification at the onset of the 1988 study period. This led to the ratification by both bodies of a first international standard for X.500 at the end of the 1988 study period coincident with the ratification of the 1988 MHS standards.

The development of the X.500 Directory standards represents to date the most successful example of cooperation between ISO and CCITT. Due to the inherent technical complexity of the subject, however, the 1988 version of the standard is still not complete in certain

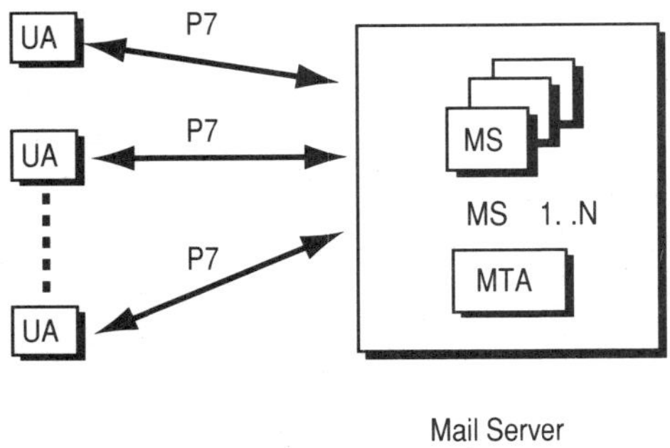

Figure 7.6 Multiple UAs accessing colocated Message Store and MTA services.

important aspects. In particular, it does not yet provide a full set of replication protocols to support the automatic synchronization of remote replicas of the database. Nor does it provide standardized support for access controls. The lack of these two mechanisms makes it more difficult for vendors to realize implementations of interoperable, fully distributed directory systems. Vendors developing directory systems based on 1988 X.500 are often doing so by defining proprietary mechanisms to support access control and replication. Work on replication, access controls, and a number of other enhancements to 1988 X.500 is currently under way as part of the 1992 X.500 work.

The use of X.500 Directory services is, however, optional in 1988 MHS. This is largely due to the fact that the X.500 standards are still immature in some important areas, therefore making its use in MHS mandatory is still premature at this stage. However, where X.500 Directory services are present, they do allow MHS services to become considerably more sophisticated and transparent to the MHS end user.

Figure 7.7 shows how the protocol architecture required to support X.500 is similar to that for 1988 MHS. Like MHS, X.500 relies on ROS and ACSE, as well as ASN.1 and the Presentation layer as the basic application layer building blocks.

7.4.1 What is a Directory?

The Directory Services are designed to provide name-to-address translation within OSI networks. Their primary purpose is to support the

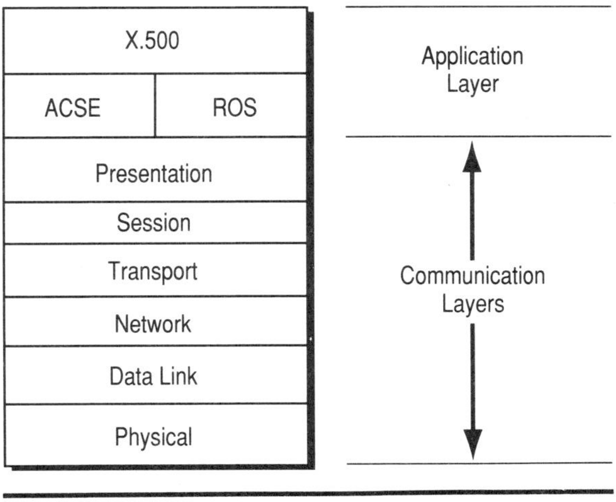

Figure 7.7 The X.500 layer architecture.

mapping of user-friendly names to OSI network addresses. X.500 defines a distributed, replicated database of naming information which is intended to provide a naming service not only to MHS, but also to other OSI application services. The standardization of Directory services was motivated primarily by the need to support name-to-address mapping in the context of message handling services. The presence of a Directory service in an MHS environment allows users to address messages by specifying user-friendly names which are based on a recipient's real name rather than a network address.

Three kinds of access techniques may be used to query X.500 Directory services:

- Whitepage searches (also referred to as name lookups), i.e., find John's network address.
- Yellowpage searches, i.e., find all the printers in building 300.
- Browsing, which is a free-form search through the database usually as a prelude to a white- or yellowpage query.

If a user knows the name of the entity it wants to contact, it can simply query the Directory by providing the entity's name and retrieve its corresponding O/R address. The user can then use the O/R address it obtained from the Directory to set up an association to the specified network entity. Alternatively, a user may do a yellowpage search to, for example, list all the printers located within a specified building before deciding where to print. In some cases, a user will want simply to browse through the Directory to find out what resources are available on the network. Browsing is a particulary useful technique in order to progressively learn enough information about the network environment to be able to formulate a specific yellowpage or name look-up request.

7.4.1.1 Functional components of X.500. The X.500 Directory systems consist of three principal components:

1. A Directory Information Base (DIB)
2. Directory User Agents (DUAs)
3. Directory Service Agents (DSAs)

The DIB contains the collection of information about users, resources, and the network, which is maintained by the directory. It resides physically and is managed by system components called DSAs. As the information contained in Directories grows, it usually becomes necessary to partition the DIB among multiple DSAs.

DUAs represent the "client" side of the Directory service. They are the X.500 equivalent of the UA concept in MHS. DUAs represent the user in accessing the information stored in the directory. DUAs access Directory information through what is called the Directory Access Protocol (DAP).

DSAs interact with each other through a specialized protocol called the Directory System Protocol (DSP). In the 1988 X.500, the DSP provides facilities for locating information in the distributed (i.e., partitioned) Directory environment, but not for automatically updating replicas of information. While it is possible to replicate parts of, or the entire, X.500 DIB, the upkeep and synchronization of the replicated information must be done through proprietary protocols or mechanisms outside the scope of the standards. This makes interoperability between different 1988 DSA implementations rather difficult, because they would be relying on different proprietary protocols to replicate information.

Figure 7.8 shows a Directory environment. Note that a user may be either a person or an application program, such as an MHS entity acting on behalf of a human user.

Figure 7.9 shows a distributed Directory system composed of three DSAs which communicate with each via the Directory System Protocol (DSP). From the perspective of the user of the Directory, or a DUA, the collection of DSAs behave as though they are implementing a single unified database. A Directory query addressed to any one DSA in the system yields the same exact result as is the same query where addressed to any other DSA in the system.

7.4.1.2 Directory names. The DIB is composed of Directory entries. Each entry describes a resource, a user, or a group of users (i.e., a distribution list). The information contained in Directory entries is made up of attributes. Each attribute, in turn, is composed of a type and a set of possible values. Some of the attributes contained in the entry

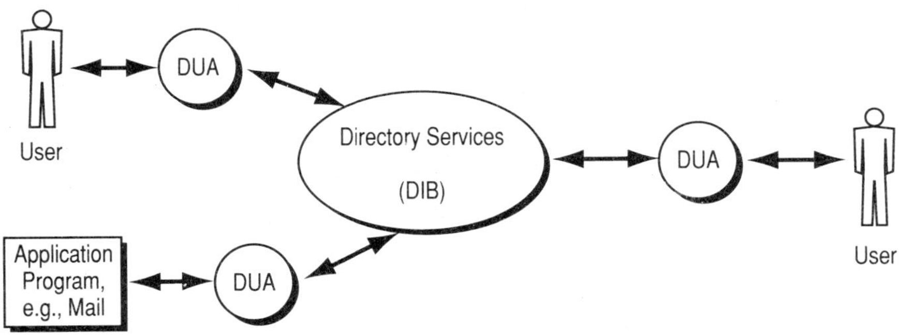

Figure 7.8 X.500 Directory functional components.

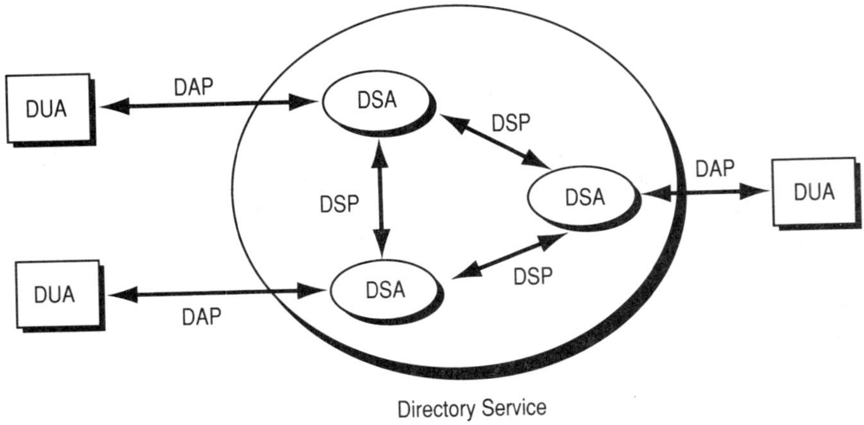

Figure 7.9 Distributed Directory environment.

are special naming attributes in that they make up the RDN of the entry. Naming attributes may be multivalued, but only a single value is used as the "distinguished value" to uniquely name the entry. Figure 7.10 depicts the structure of a typical X.500 DIB entry.

Logically the DIB is structured as a hierarchical information tree called the Directory Information Tree (DIT). Each entry of the DIB corresponds to a vertex of the DIT. The DIB refers to the physical realization of the Directory, while the DIT refers to the logical representation of the name space.

Each Directory entry is named by an ordered sequence of attributes called Relative Distinguished Names (RDNs). The sequence of RDNs that lead from the root of the DIT to the object being named constitutes what is called the object's Distinguished Name. Distinguished

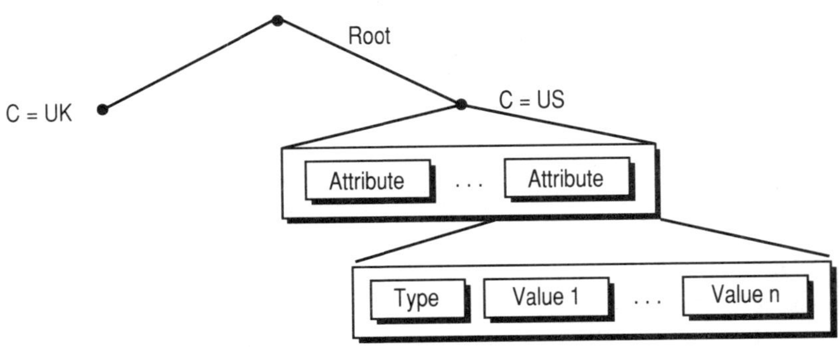

Figure 7.10 X.500 entry structure.

Names are unambiguous within the Directory and the entire OSI network environment.

Figure 7.11 shows a sample DIT made up of entries for three countries: UK, US, and Japan. The UK name space is further subdivided into an organizational level name space for a company called Widget, Ltd. Widget consists of two organizational units representing the sales department and the research and development (R&D) department, respectively. Individual persons as well as department resources are listed under each organizational unit name. Thus J. P. Smith is an individual within the Sales department, and A. Jones is an individual in the R&D department. In addition, the R&D department owns a printer called LaserPrinter.

The full Distinguished Name for each of the leaf nodes under Widget, Ltd., is obtained as follows:

1. The Distinguished Name for J. P. Smith is made up of the following naming attributes, each of which represents a Relative Distinguished Name:

CountryName	= UK
Organization	= Widget Ltd.
OrganizationalUnit	= Sales
CommonName	= J.P. Smith

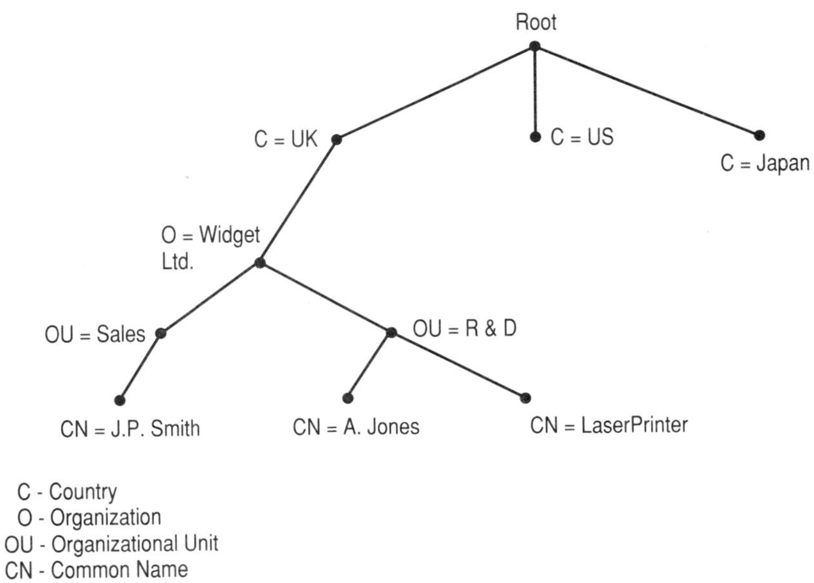

Figure 7.11 Sample DIT.

Although X.500 does not specify a particular syntax notation for expressing distinguished names, the following notational approach is commonly used:

```
{C=UK, O=Widget Ltd., OU=Sales, CN=J.P.Smith}
```

2. The Distinguished Name for A. Jones is given by

```
{C=UK, O=Widget Ltd., OU=R&D, CN=A. Jones}
```

3. The Distinguished Name for the printer LaserPrinter is given by

```
{C=UK, O=Widget Ltd., OU=R&D, CN=LaserPrinter}
```

Currently, distinguished names are always expressed in terms of an attribute type and a value. This is a fairly cumbersome approach, particularly as names get longer, and conflicts with X.500's stated goal of user-friendly naming. It is expected that in the future the standards bodies will explore the potential for a more compact notation for Directory names.

Directory names may also have alternative names, or *aliases*. Aliases provide a shorthand way of referring to an entry's name. Figure 7.12 gives an example of the use of aliasing. An entry E in the directory database may be accessed either through what is called its full distinguished name, in this case "B, C, E"; or through its alias name "A." Using the alias provides a shorthand way of addressing the entry but forces more processing on the Directory, which now has to resolve the alias pointer to the correct entry.

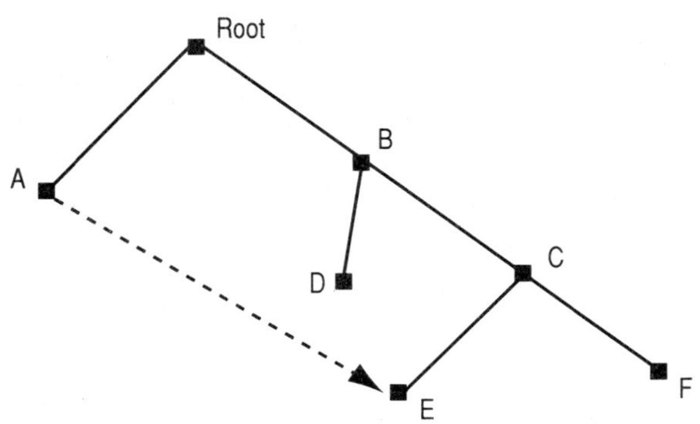

Figure 7.12 Alias example.

7.4.1.3 The global name space. Internationally, the Directory name space is managed by various Naming and Registration Authorities. Each naming authority has the responsibility for one or more branches of the DIT. These authorities may, in turn, delegate authority for subbranches of the name space to private organizations. Both ISO and CCITT share the vision of a single, unified, worldwide name space that encompasses all OSI entities, and supports worldwide message handling services. The presence of a unified, common name space is an important prerequisite to the development of integrated electronic messaging services, since it allows all MHS users and resources to be addressed in the same manner.

Figure 7.13 depicts the notion of the global name space where a global naming authority, most likely ISO and CCITT, agrees upon the naming conventions for each country's ADMD services. National standards organizations in each country, in turn, hand out subsets of the name space to private organizations for use within private networks. This simple process ensures that all OSI services share a common name space whether they are interconnected or not. Additionally, bilateral agreements may exist between countries at an international level to ensure that naming conventions and message routing are handled smoothly across different national boundaries.

The use of a common naming scheme and name space for all OSI resources makes it possible for MHS entities to address each other on a worldwide basis. The ability for worldwide addressing is independent of whether the various services are physically interconnected

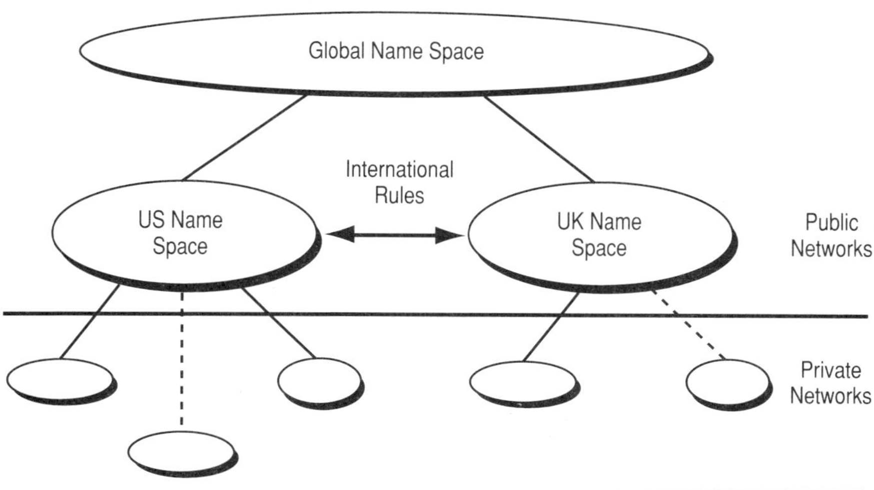

Figure 7.13 Global name space.

with each other or not. It ensures, however, that if a physical path is established between two networks that were previously unconnected, the names and addresses used in the two networks will be able to co-exist and will not need to change.

7.4.5 Attributes and object classes

Directory entries are made up of attributes that provide specific information about some particular characteristic of a network entity. An attribute is defined by specifying its type and assigning a syntax to it. The Attribute Macro is defined in X.500 to allow new attributes for MHS as well as other OSI applications to be defined. Attribute types may be internationally standardized (such as those defined in X.520), assigned locally by national or private organizations, or specific to a particular implementation.

Attributes may also be defined as belonging to a particular object class. An entry's object class restricts the types of attributes that may be present in the entry. Every Directory object (or entry) is considered to belong to at least one class, although an object class may be a subclass of another. Defining a new object class is also provided for in X.500 through the use of the OBJECT CLASS MACRO. Defining a new object class involves assigning a unique object identifier for the class, indicating if it is a subclass of another class, and listing any mandatory or optional attribute types for the class. X.500 defines a special object class, called Top, as the superclass for all Directory object classes.

The following macros can be used by MHS or other OSI applications to define new object classes or attribute types:

```
OBJECT-CLASS MACRO ::=
{ SUBCLASS OF some class,
  MUST CONTAIN some attribute,
  MAY CONTAIN some attribute }
::= { objectClass some integer }

ATTRIBUTE MACRO ::=
WITH ATTRIBUTE-SYNTAX some syntax,
SINGLE VALUE optional,
::= { attributeType some integer }
```

The OBJECT CLASS macro specifies that a new object class is defined by stating what other object class it is a subclass of (the default being the superclass Top), what mandatory attributes it "must" contain, and what optional attributes it "may" contain. The new object class is identified by assigning it a unique object identifier. Specifying dependency rules between object classes (i.e., by specifying what class they are a subclass of) has the effect of defining the relationship between DIT entries and therefore the structure of the DIT itself.

The ATTRIBUTE macro specifies that a new attribute type can be created by defining its intended syntax and specifying whether it will be a single-valued attribute or whether multiple values may be present. As was the case for new object classes, new attribute types are also identified through the assignment of a unique object identifier.

Below are two examples of MHS attribute types and object classes defined using the OBJECT-CLASS and ATTRIBUTE macros:

```
mhs-user OBJECT-CLASS
       SUBCLASS OF Top
       MUST CONTAIN {mhs-or-addresses}
              MAY CONTAIN {
              mhs-deliverable-content-length,
              mhs-deliverable-content-types,
              mhs-deliverable-eits,
              mhs-message-store,
              mhs-preferred-delivery-methods }
       ::= id-oc-mhs-user

mhs-or-addresses ATTRIBUTE
       WITH ATTRIBUTE-SYNTAX mhs-or-address-syntax
       MULTI-VALUE
       ::= id-at-mhs-or-addresses
```

The object class mhs-user is defined to be a subclass of Top and must contain as mandatory attribute the user's MHS O/R address (mhs-or-address). In addition, an object of type mhs-user may also contain attributes specifying the maximum content length of messages that the user is willing to accept (mhs-deliverable-content-length), the preferred content types the user is willing to receive (mhs-deliverable-content-types), etc.

The mhs-or-addresses attribute is defined to be of attribute syntax mhs-or-address-syntax and to be a multivalued attribute (e.g., multiple values may be present for the attribute type). Finally, the mhs-or-address attribute type is uniquely identified by assigning to it an integer object identifier called "id-at-mhs-or-addresses."

A number of object classes have been defined within the X.500 documents for use by all OSI applications. Figure 7.14 lists the set of Directory object classes and their relative dependencies as defined in X.521. Note that this is only a suggested set of object class dependencies and that particular implementations or user profiles may choose to adopt their own structure. For example, the North American Directory Forum (NADF) has suggested a DIT structure specific to the needs of North American service providers.

Most OSI applications will also define a set of object classes specific to their own needs in addition to those made available by the Directory DIT structure. The 1988 MHS defines for instance, a set of object classes specific to its own naming and addressing needs, as listed in Fig. 7.15 below.

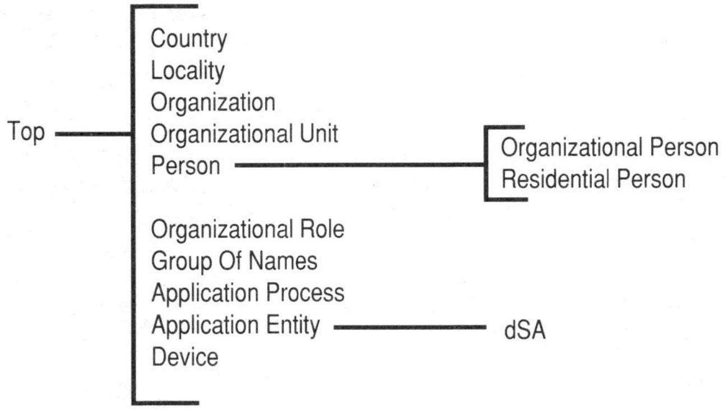

Figure 7.14 Dependency of Directory object classes.

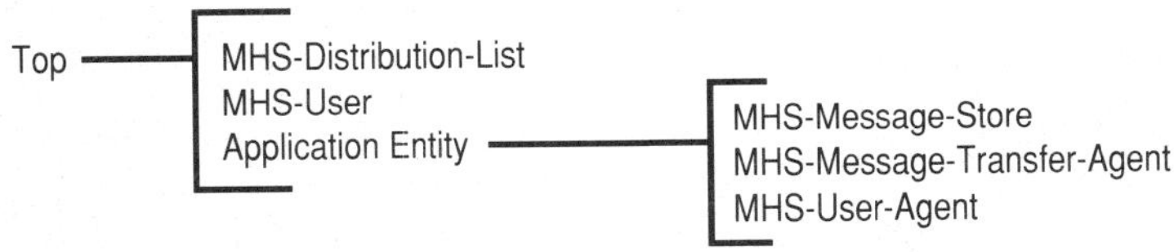

Figure 7.15 Dependency of MHS object classes.

7.5 MHS Use of Directory

The 1988 MHS relies on X.500 Directory services to provide the following services:

1. Naming and addressing
2. DL expansion
3. Authentication and security services
4. Capability assessment

Since the use of X.500 Directory services is optional in 1988 MHS, alternatives have been defined in the standard in order to handle most important functions even without an X.500 service on the network. This is true, for example, of DLs that may operate both in conjunction with, and in the absence of, X.500 Directory services. In general, however, when X.500 Directory services are present, the particular function is handled more elegantly and transparently from the point of view of the user. Again using DLs as the example, their expansion becomes much more effective in the presence of a distributed and replicated Directory service that allows the DL membership information to be available consistently from all parts of the network (assuming of course that a Directory entry exists for all members of the DL).

Figure 7.16 illustrates how a UA and DUA capability may be colocated to best serve the needs of an MHS user. The UA can rely on the colocated DUA capability to query the Directory and find the O/R address information and any relevant capability information associated with a given Directory name. The UA may also query the Directory, again through the local DUA component to browse through the Directory information base. Finally, the UA may rely on the DUA to access the Directory to perform authentication and validate an intended recipient's credentials.

Figure 7.17 shows how the DUA functionality can be colocated with an MTA on the same mail server. The MTA will use the DUA capability to query the Directory in order to determine the capabilities of the recipient UA before attempting message delivery to it, to look up its presentation address and perform password verification, as well as to expand any DL information that may be present in the list of intended recipients of the message. Where DLs are nested, it is possible that several MTAs will progressively need to query the Directory to expand the nested DL information in the course of transferring the message. In most network environments, DUAs will be colocated with both UAs and MTAs so that both kinds of entities may avail themselves of Directory services.

7.5.1 Naming and addressing

In 1988 MHS, O/R names can consist of a Directory name, an O/R address, or both. Users of Directory services may be UAs, MTAs, as well as MHS users themselves. A Directory name is merely one possible component of an O/R name. While 1984 MHS defined O/R names for

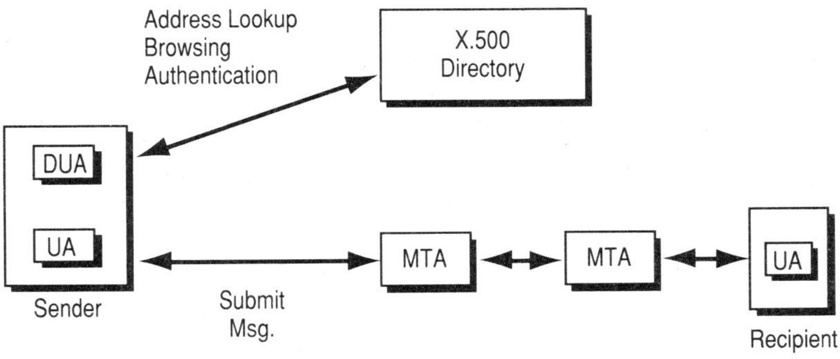

Figure 7.16 UA use of X.500.

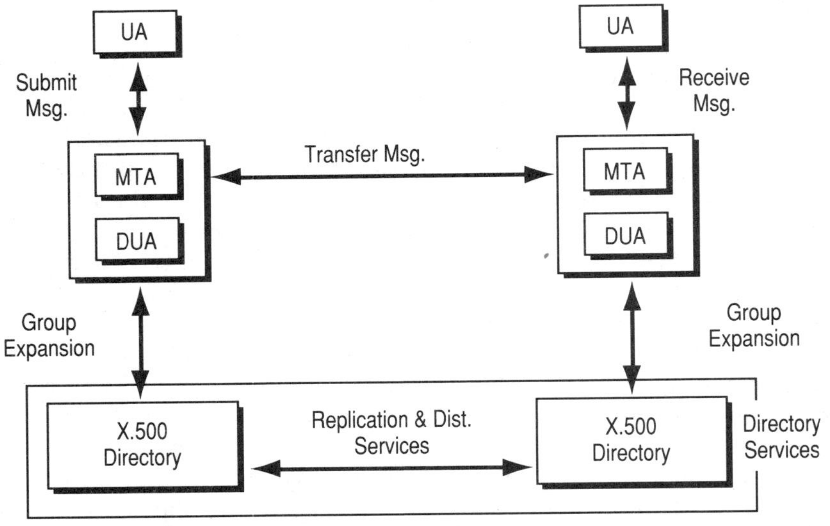

Figure 7.17 MTA use of X.500.

simplicity to be equivalent to O/R addresses, the 1988 MHS seeks to make use of Directory services to provide O/R names that are distinct from addresses. X.500 names are composed of an ordered sequence of attributes that largely reflect the actual name of the MHS user or application as well as giving some notion of its place in an organization or geographical location.

In order to obtain an O/R address, the Directory service user queries the X.500 database by providing a name (either an alias or the distinguished name) and requests the corresponding network address. If only the Directory name is present when submitting a message for delivery, the MHS accesses the Directory to obtain the correct O/R address, which it then uses to route and deliver the message. If the Directory name is absent, the MHS relies on the O/R address as given. When both the Directory name and the O/R address are present, the MHS uses the O/R address directly (without further Directory lookups). However, the Directory name is carried with the message and presented to the recipient along with the O/R address. If the O/R address proves invalid at any stage in the message transfer and delivery cycle, the MHS can rely on the Directory name to resolve it to an appropriate, valid O/R address.

Where an X.500 Directory is present on a network, MHS will use it to resolve X.500 names and return the corresponding O/R address. If an X.500 service is not available, MHS will use the O/R address as specified in the original recipient's name. For an interim period, while X.500 services are still not widely available, it is likely that some users and DLs will continue to rely on 1984 style O/R names based on O/R addresses. Recommendation X.402 provides a set of standard attribute types and syntaxes from which valid O/R addresses may be constructed.

7.5.2 Capability assessment

Beyond simply resolving Directory names to O/R addresses, the Directory also serves as an invaluable repository of information about MHS users and resources. As such it is used in MHS to discover the capabilities of an intended recipient which may affect successful message delivery. Any user, UA, or MTA can directly obtain information about the capabilities of an intended recipient by querying the Directory. The Directory stores all capability information relevant to message delivery in the form of attributes. The following Directory attributes are defined for use in representing particular capabilities of MHS users:

1. MHS deliverable content length
2. MHS deliverable content types
3. MHS deliverable EncodedInformationTypes (EITs)
4. MHS preferred delivery methods

The following Directory attributes are defined to represent Message Store capabilities:

1. MHS supported automatic actions
2. MHS supported content types
3. MHS supported optional attributes

7.5.3 Distribution lists

Distribution lists (DLs) provide the ability to address a message to a group of users by specifying a single name. The use of DLs is optional in MHS and is a service that is provided by the underlying message transfer system. DLs are a great convenience to MHS users because they allow users to address a message to a potentially very large group of users without having to list each recipient individually. In many instances, a user will not even need to know all the names of the users within a particular DL. DLs may be nested, such that a DL may itself be a member of a larger DL.

Distribution lists are realized in the Directory as entries whose content attributes hold the names of the members of the DL. The name of the entry corresponds to the name of the DL. DLs are identified by means of X.500 Distinguished Names. DLs may be nested indefinitely through a recursive use of attribute definitions. When an MHS user, UA, or MTA attempt to address and route a message to a DL, the MTS queries the Directory to obtain the list of attributes contained within the DL's entry. Generally, in a well-designed, replicated and distributed MHS environment, this kind of name resolution is handled by the MTA transparently to the UA or MHS user. Depending on the size and complexity of the DL, the first MTA involved in a message transfer may be able to completely resolve all the members of the DL. Whereas when a DL contains multiple nested DLs, several MTAs may need to progressively query the Directory to obtain the full set of DL members.

Replication and distribution of Directory information makes it possible for DL information to be accessed from anywhere within the network. This makes it possible for MHS users to move about the network and still continue to utilize the MHS facilities from different locations with the same ease of use and transparency.

DLs are characterized by the following properties:

1. *A set of members,* which consist of users or names of other DLs which are members of the DL.
2. *A DL submit permission,* which may be a list of users or other DLs that are allowed to send messages to this DL.
3. *A DL expansion point,* which is the O/R address of the MTA (or domain) where the DL can be expanded, which is where the full list of DL members is contained. If a distributed Directory is used on the network, this information is no longer necessary.
4. *A DL owner,* which is the name of the user or set of users who manage the DL. Owners are typically responsible for adding and removing users to and from DLs, as well as modifying submit permissions.

DL names are indistinguishable from other O/R names. They may consist of a Directory name, an O/R address, or both. A user need not be aware that an O/R name refers to a DL, nor does it need to know whether more DLs are nested within a DL name that it is using. A message originator, however, may set an indication upon message submission requesting that any DLs contained in the recipient name not be expanded. This may be done to avoid unnecessary processing when the originator knows that a number of nested DLs are present but is interested only in the top-level DL members.

A DL's properties may be stored and managed through the use of the Directory service. This is in fact the preferred way to support the implementation of DLs, since the Directory's replication capabilities make it possible for DLs to be more easily expandable from any point of origin in the MHS system. The DL's name corresponds to the object name, and a set of attributes is used to represent each of the DL properties listed above.

7.5.3.1 DL expansion. In order to expand a DL, an MTA will perform the following functions at the expansion point:

1. Look up the DL membership information and other relevant properties, such as the submit permissions. It may do so by querying the Directory or by using locally stored DL information if a Directory is not available on the network.
2. Verify the sender's right to send to the specified DL.
3. If expansion is allowed, it will add the names of all the DL members to the recipient list of the message.

Where DLs are nested, several expansion points may be involved in completing delivery of the message. A message will be forwarded for further expansion, from the expansion point of the parent to that of any member DLs. Throughout the expansion process, the identity of the parent DL is verified against the submit permissions of the member DLs to ensure that messages can be sent to the nested DLs.

7.5.3.2 Recursion control. It is possible that a DL may be structured to contain the same member DL at various levels in the nesting. This may result in the receipt by the user of multiple copies of the same message. The same phenomenon can also occur if a user's name is contained in multiple nested DLs. Duplicate messages can be suppressed by performing some additional processing at either the recipient UA or the recipient MTA. A DL expansion point, either the UA or the MTA, will typically add a DL expansion history similar to a trace information field to the message. This allows MTAs to recognize whether they have expanded a message before. An MTA must also remember which messages it has already received (and delivered to the user) so as to recognize and suppress duplicate messages. The message id and possibly some timestamp indication can be used to detect duplicate messages.

It is also possible for a message to originate in one domain and legitimately come back to it after the addressing information is successfully expanded in another domain. This occurrence is not treated as a routing loop, but rather it is accepted as valid behavior.

7.5.3.3 Notifications. Delivery and nondelivery notifications can be generated at both the DL expansion point (if, for example, submit permission is denied) or at the delivery point of the ultimate recipient. A message coming from a DL may generate a notification that is sent to the DL from which it came. The DL will then, depending on the policy of the list, forward the notification to either the owner of the list or the originator of the message, or both.

Notifications sent back to the originator, after DL expansion, may cause the originator to receive many delivery/nondelivery notifications per single recipient (the DL itself). The originator may even receive many notifications from an ultimate recipient, if the recipient received the message more than once through different lists.

7.5.3.4 DL handling policy. An MTA may or may not provide different policies for handling DLs. Such policies will control whether notifications should be propagated back through the previous DL, or to the originator if no previous DL is available, as well as to this list's owner. If the policy is such that notifications are sent only to the list owner, then the originator will receive requested notifications only during expansion of that DL.

7.6 The 1988 MHS Protocols

The 1988 MHS adopts a completely object-oriented view of the MHS environment. It depicts all the major functional components of the MHS model as objects that interact with each other via a set of service ports. Each port supports a different set of protocol operations that implement the services provided by that port. Figure 7.18 provides an object-oriented view of UAs, the Message Store, and the MTS.

The behavior of each MHS object shown in Fig. 7.18 is modeled as a set of ROS-based consumer-supplier actions. Each object supports one or more service ports which define the protocol operations that a consumer object can invoke on that supplier object.

1988 introduces some major stylistic differences in the way MHS protocols are described and how they relate to the underlying support-

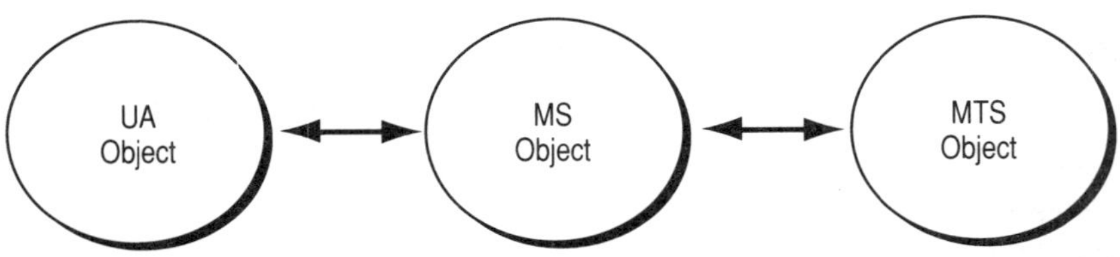

Figure 7.18 Object-oriented view of MHS.

ing protocols. These differences are not defined merely for cosmetic reasons, but rather because they accomplish two very important goals: they provide backward compatibility to the 1984 version of the protocols, and they allow alignment to the full 1988 OSI stack architecture.

The architectural mechanism that allows the 1988 protocols to cater to these two complex and seemingly conflicting requirements is the 1988 upper layer concept of Application Service Elements (ASEs). ASEs allow the services provided by various ports to be combined in a number of different ways to produce different Application Contexts (ACs).

Application Contexts comprise not only the MHS-level application service elements but also supporting upper-layer service elements such as ROSE, RTSE, etc. ACs therefore provide a method for "bundling" different service functions with different protocol layering requirements. This ability to mix and match protocol components in different ways allows the MHS protocols to achieve both backward compatibility with 1984 MHS, as well as alignment with the 1988 OSI architecture.

7.6.1 Application service elements

The 1988 MHS defines five service ports, or ASEs, that may be supported by the MHS objects:

1. The Submission Service Port
2. The Administration Service Port
3. The Retrieval Service Port
4. The Delivery Service Port
5. The Transfer Service Port

An additional ASE called the Indirect Submission Service Port is defined entirely in terms of the Submission Service Port but is used only in conjunction with the Message Store protocol to resubmit to the MTS messages already held in the Message Store. Figure 7.19 gives a detailed view of some MHS objects and shows what service ports are supported by each kind of MHS object.

Access to the MTS is supported through three service ports: the Message Delivery Port, the Message Submission port, and the Administration port. The MTS is a supplier of Submission and Administration services, whereas it is a consumer of Delivery services. This means that it is able to initiate delivery actions on the MTS user, but it can only accept submission and administration actions from the MTS user.

Access to the Message Store is supported through the Message Re-

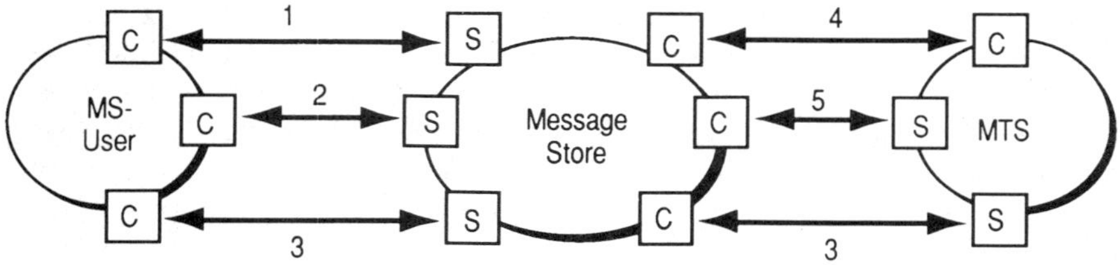

1 – Retrieval Port
2 – Indirect Submission Port
3 – Administration Port
4 – Delivery Port
5 – Submission Port

Figure 7.19 Refined Message Store object model showing the Message Store consumer-supplier relationships.

trieval port, the Administration port, and the Indirect Message Submission port. Indirect submission refers to the fact that the UA submits messages first to the Message Store for submission to the MTS. The operations defined by the indirect submission port service are identical to those defined for the submission port service.

At the MTA level (not shown in Fig. 7.19), the Transfer Service Port is used to transfer messages between MTAs.

7.6.1.1 Submission Port Services. The Message Submission Service Element (MSSE) supports operations for submitting messages, probes, or reports to the MTS for transfer within the MHS environment. It comprises the following protocol operations:

1. *Message-submission,* which allows an MTS user to submit a message to the MTS for transfer to one or more intended recipients.
2. *Probe-submission,* which allows the MTS user to submit a probe message in order to determine the viability of the MTS.
3. *Cancel-deferred-delivery,* which enables the MTS user to request the cancellation of a previously submitted message intended for deferred delivery.
4. *Submission-control,* which allows the MTS to control the use of the submission operations by the MTS user.

The Message Store (P7) indirect submission port is exactly analogous to the MTS (i.e., P3) submission port, but its semantics are extended to allow a UA to refer to messages already in the Message Store and forward them rather than resubmit all over again. It is defined in ASN.1 simply as

```
indirectSubmissionPORT ::= submission
```

The indirect submission port allows UAs to submit messages to the Message Store, which immediately submits them to the MTS for transfer within the MHS environment. A submission is not complete until the message has been submitted to the MTS.

7.6.1.2 Administration Port Services. The Message Administration Service Element (MASE) is supported by MTA objects, as well as MS objects. It consists of the following operations:

1. *Register,* which enables an MTS user to set or change any long term service parameters that the MTS may have defined for it,
2. *Change-credentials,* which enable either the MTS user to change its credentials with the MTS, or the MTS to change its credentials with the MTS user.

7.6.1.3 Retrieval Port Services. The Message Retrieval Service Element (MRSE) consists of operations designed to summarize, list, fetch, and delete messages held in the Message Store. In addition, it also comprises an operation (register-MS) that allows users to register various kinds of information with the Message Store relating to its operation. The services of the Retrieval port are defined in more detail in Chap. 8 (the Message Store Protocol, P7).

7.6.1.4 Delivery Port Services. The Message Delivery Service Element (MDSE) is used to transfer messages at the MTA level. It supports the following operations:

1. *Message-delivery:* This operation is used by the MTS to deliver a message to the MTS-user. The MTS-user in this case may be either a Message Store or a UA. The MTS-user may not refuse delivery of a message unless it violates some previously established control restrictions.

2. *Report-delivery:* This operation allows the MTS to inform the MTS-user of the outcome of a previous message or probe submission operation. In the case of a previously submitted message, the report-delivery operation indicates the successful or unsuccessful delivery of the message to the intended recipients. In the case of a probe, the report-delivery indicates simply whether a message could be successfully delivered and whether the distribution lists to which it is addressed, can be successfully expanded. A single message or probe submission can result in several instances of the report-delivery operation for each of the intended recipients. Also, a message or probe

submission by an MTS-user can cause the occurrence of a report-delivery operation at another recipient, in the case where a report delivered to the owner of a distribution list rather than the originator of the message.

3. *Delivery-control:* This operation can be used by the MTS-user to limit temporarily the operations that the MTS can invoke on the delivery port. It can also limit the messages that the MTS can deliver via the message-delivery operation. The MTS will hold delivery operations that cannot be performed until the specific time at which they are allowed. It will not discard any information it is about to deliver. The controls set up by the delivery-control operation are in force for the duration of the association during which they were set up.

7.6.2 Protocols

The Application Service Elements described so far are combined with Upper-Layer ASEs (e.g., ACSE, ROS, etc.) to produce the 1988 MHS protocols. Four protocols are defined:

1. A revised P1 protocol which incorporates 1988 security features, plus some new service elements which support the new 1988 MHS functionality, such as distribution lists.
2. A slightly revised P2 protocol which is now called P22.
3. A completely revised P3 protocol which supersedes the 1984 P3. Remember that 1984 P3 was never really implemented.
4. A completely new protocol, called P7, which supports the interactions between the Message Store and the Message Store user.

7.6.2.1 The MTS Access Protocol: P3. Access to the MTS is defined by three Application Service Elements which correspond to different service ports:

1. The Message Submission Service Element (MSSE)
2. The Message Delivery Service Element (MDSE)
3. The Message Administration Service Element (MASE)

The MTS-User and the MTS object can both act as either the supplier or consumer of these service elements. The above Application Service Elements are combined with the underlying application layerASEs (e.g., ROSE, ACSE, etc.) to produce four Application Contexts which together implement the P3 protocol. These are

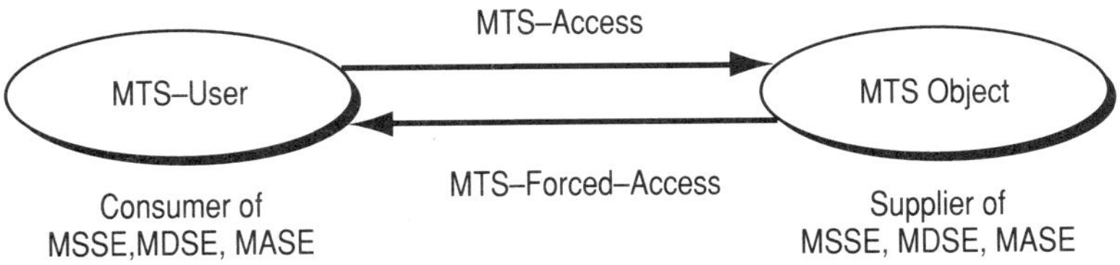

Figure 7.20 Object-oriented view of the P3 protocol.

1. An mts-access AC
2. An mts-forced-access AC
3. An mts-reliable-access AC
4. An mts-reliable-forced-access AC

Figure 7.20 gives an object-oriented view of the ACs and ASEs that make up the P3 protocol. The following table summarizes which Application Service Elements are combined to produce each P3 Application Context:

Application context	Constituent Application Service Elements
mts-access:	MSSE(c), MDSE(c), MASE(c), ROSE, ACSE
mts-forced-access:	MSSE(s), MDSE(s), MASE(s), ROSE, ACSE
mts-reliable-access:	MSSE(c), MDSE(c), MASE(c), ROSE, RTSE, ACSE
mts-reliable-forced-access:	MSSE(s), MDSE(s), MASE(s), ROSE, RTSE, ACSE

MTAs must support both the mts-access AC and the mts-forced-access AC. The remaining two ACs are optional. However, if the MTA supports one of them, then the other must be supported as well. On the MTS-user side, all four ACs are optional.

In summary, the P3 protocol supports the following set of operations:

MTS Bind and Unbind

MTS-bind
MTS-unbind

Message Submission Service Element (MSSE)

message-submission
probe-submission

cancel-deferred-delivery
submission-control

Message Delivery Service Element (MDSE)

message-delivery
report-delivery
delivery-control

Message Administration Service Element (MASE)

register
change-credentials

Conformance to the P3 protocol is given by the following table:

AC	MTA	MTS-User
mts-access	Mandatory	Optional
mts-forced-access	Mandatory	Optional
mts-reliable-access	Optional*	Optional
mts-forced-reliable-access	Optional*	Optional

*If mts-reliable-access is used by the MTA, then mts-forced-reliable-access must also be used, and vice versa.

The 1988 P3 differs from the 1984 version in a number of ways. For instance, 1988 places constraints on all types of definitions. This includes size constraints on the length of strings, number of items that can be contained within sets and sequences, and permissible value ranges for integer definitions. The assignment of these boundaries was based on similar size constraints established within the P1 and P2 protocols. The content field of messages is the only exception and has been left of undefined size.

A number of type changes are also significant in 1988 P3. The most important one is the fact that OR names can now include X.500 Directory names as well as what are called *extension-attributes*. The extension attributes allow the inclusion in the name of the teletex character set, postal addresses for physical delivery, and terminal addresses.

The content type has also changed to accommodate the inclusion of externally defined body parts. These are body parts whose content type is defined by an ASN.1 definition that specifies the syntax of the information. The ASN.1 definition is external to the MHS standards and may therefore be proprietary in nature as well as simply bilaterally agreed upon between two distinct management domains. The content type is identified by an object identifier that allows implementations to recognize which external ASN.1 definition is to be applied to the contents of the message.

The operations of 1988 P3 change largely to accommodate the new security features defined in MHS as well as the greater flexibility in content type definitions. The Bind operation takes an additional optional parameter that allows security contexts to be specified. Security contexts, as we will see in Chap. 9, allow two parties to agree on a common security level to be used in the course of their interaction. The Bind operation also restricts credentials of type ANY to be either simple-credentials or strong-credentials. The definition of simple and strong credentials is consistent with the specification of simple and strong authentication provided by the X.500 standards (i.e., X.509—the Authentication Framework). These are explained further in Chap. 9 on MHS security.

The message-delivery operation has been made into a confirmed operation that now contains a RESULTS clause. The operation also takes an optional content-identifier. The report-delivery operation has also been made a confirmed operation. It has also added new values for the type-of-MTS-user to reflect possible new kinds of users such as the Message Store, distribution lists, Physical Delivery Access Units, and physical recipients (i.e., for postal delivery). The delivery-control operation has new parameters to define the permissible content types that may be delivered and the security context. The message-submission, register, probe-submission, submission-control, and change-credentials operations also undergo parameter changes to accommodate security and content type information. Figure 7.21 summarizes the protocol mapping options defined for the 1988 P3.

7.6.2.2 The MS access protocol: P7. The functionality of the Message Store access protocol, P7, is given by three Application Service Elements:

1. The Message Submission Service Element (MSSE)
2. The Message Retrieval Service Element (MRSE)
3. The Message Administration Service Element (MASE)

The Message Store is always the supplier of the above services, while the Message Store user is always the consumer. The above Application Service Elements are combined to produce two Application Contexts that implement the functionality of the P7 protocol:

1. An ms-access AC
2. An ms-reliable-access AC

Figure 7.22 provides an object-oriented view of ASEs and ACs that make up the P7 protocol. The following table summarizes the application service elements that are combined to produce each P7 application context:

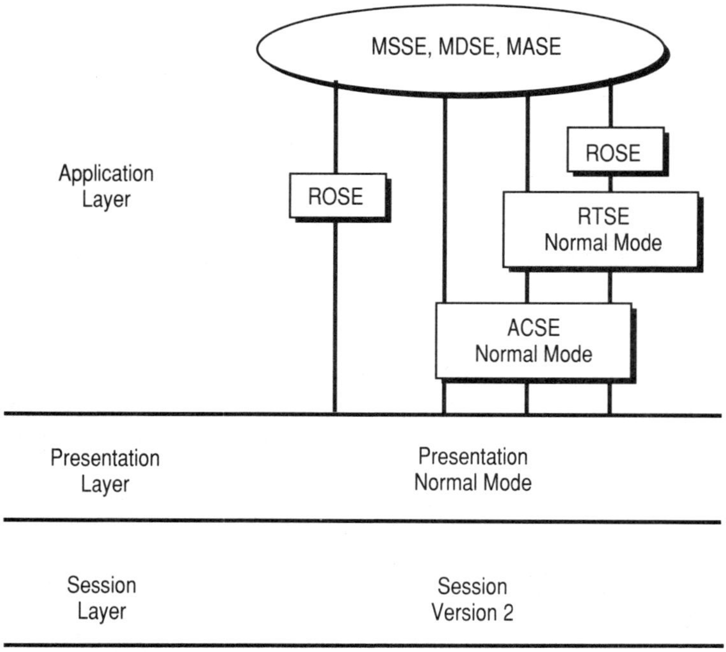

Figure 7.21 P3 protocol mappings.

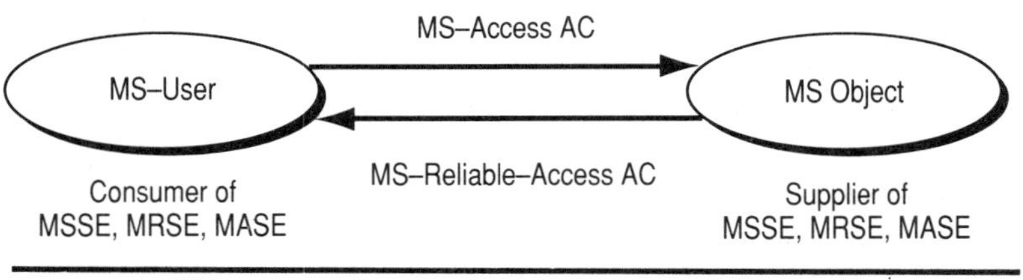

Figure 7.22 Object-oriented view of the P7 protocol.

Application Context	Constituent Application Service Elements
mts-access:	MSSE(c), MRSE(c), MASE(c), ROSE, ACSE
mts-reliable-access:	MSSE(c), MRSE(c), MASE(c), ROSE, RTSE, ACSE

Message Stores must support the ms-access AC, while the ms-reliable-access AC is optional. Both ACs are optional for the Message Store user.

In summary, the P7 protocol supports the following set of operations:

MTS Bind and Unbind

MS-bind
MS-unbind

Message Submission Service Element (MSSE)—same as in P3

message-submission
probe-submission
cancel-deferred-delivery
submission-control

Message Retrieval Service Element (MRSE)

summarize
list
fetch
delete
register-MS
alert

Message Administration Service Element (MASE)—same as P3

register
change-credentials

Conformance to the P7 protocol is given by the following table:

AC	MS	MS-User
ms-access	Mandatory	Optional
ms-reliable-access	Optional	Optional

Figure 7.23 shows the possible protocol mappings defined for P7.

7.6.2.3 The MTS transfer protocol: P1. The message transfer protocol, P1, which operates between MTAs is defined in terms of a single Application Service Element: the Message Transfer Service Element (MTSE). As you may recall from Chap. 6, the P1 protocol is the only one in the 1984 version of the standard that uses RTS. In 1988 MHS, RTS evolves to become RTSE, and a new set of upper-layer OSI standards are defined including Presentation and ACSE. The 1988 version

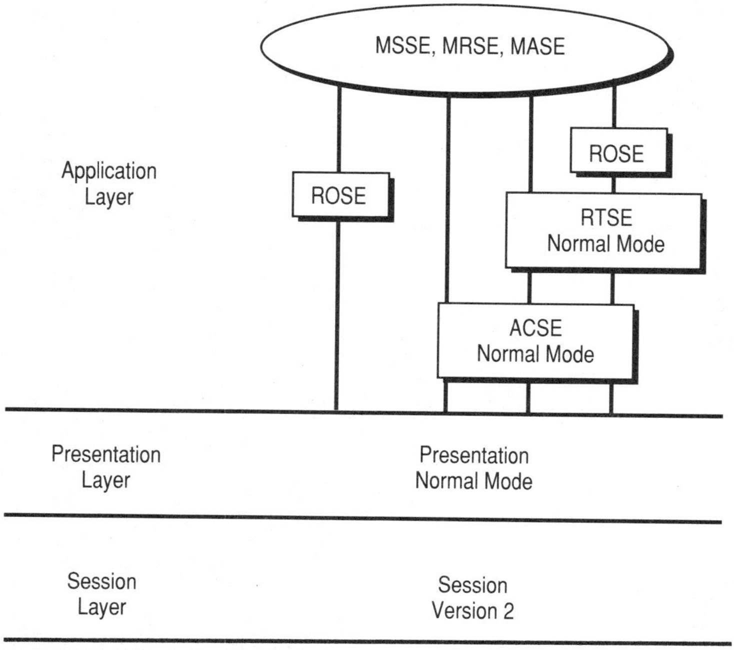

Figure 7.23 P7 protocol mappings.

of P1 must therefore not only accommodate the new upper-layer architecture, but must do so in a manner that is backward-compatible with the 1984 standards. This led the designers of 1988 P1 to define three different Application Contexts:

1. The mts-transfer-protocol-1984 AC, which is exactly compatible with 1984 P1. It defines 1984 P1 operating over the 1984-style stack.
2. The mts-transfer-protocol AC, which allows the new 1988 version of P1 to operate over the old 1984-style stack.
3. The mts-transfer AC, which allows the new 1988 version of P1 to operate over the new 1988-style stack. This version of the stack is also called *normal mode.*

Use of the X.410-1984 RTSE implies the lack of ACSE and presentation as defined by the 1984 version of the standards. Use of the 1988 RTSE implies use of the 1988 ACSE and presentation.

The following table summarizes the three Application Contexts that make up the 1988 P1:

Application Context	P1	RTSE-mode
mts-transfer-protocol-1984:	1984 P1	X.410-1984
mts-transfer-protocol:	1988 P1	X.410-1984
mts-transfer	1988 P1	RTSE normal mode (i.e., 1988 stack)

The mts-transfer-protocol-1984 and mts-transfer-protocol ACs are both mandatory in 1988 MHS. The mts-transfer AC is defined as mandatory in the ISO standards, while it is optional in the CCITT recommendations. We will discuss in greater detail what impact this has on interoperabilty in Chapter 10 (Advanced Topics).

The 1988 P1 protocol supports the following operations:

MTA Bind and Unbind

MTA-bind
MTA-unbind

Message Transfer Service Element (MTSE)

message-transfer
probe-transfer
report-transfer

The 1988 P1 protocol incorporates changes similar to the P3 protocol in terms of establishing size constraints on most fields, defining the fundamental types supported and the addition of security parameters particularly on the bind operation. New operation parameters to support the enhanced 1988 functionality have been added as "EXTENSIONS" to the 1984 version of the P1 operations. EXTENSION parameters have been added to:

1. The Message-transfer-envelope
2. The Probe-transfer-envelope
3. The Report-transfer-envelope
4. The Report-transfer-content

Two optional parameters have been added to the per-report transfer fields of the Report-Transfer-Envelope. These are original-encoded-information-types and the content-type. An optional private-domain-identifier has been added to the per-domain-bilateral-information parameter of message and probe envelopes. This allows bilateral information to be sent between PRMDs as well as ADMDs. Additional parameters have also been added to the trace-information field to indicate whether a message has been redirected or expanded by a particular management domain. Chapter 10 discusses how the differences between the ISO and CCITT specification of P1 affect interoperability at the MTA level.

Figure 7.24 summarizes the possible protocol mappings defined for the 1988 P1. Figure 7.25 summarizes the 1984 and 1988 MHS protocol stack combinations defined by the 1988 MHS recommendations for the P1, P2, and P3 protocols. Note that while ACSE is shown in the figure as positioned below RTSE and ROSE, it is in fact accessed directly by the MSSE, MDSE, MRSE, and MASE application service elements in establishing and terminating associations.

7.6.2.4 The interpersonal messaging protocol: P22. The editorial format of the interpersonal messaging protocol P2 is changed considerably in the 1988 version of the standard but incorporates relatively few technical changes. The content type assigned to P2 changes to P22, where P22 denotes the 1984 P2 protocol plus 1988 extensions to the header information. The use of P2 as defined in the 1984 MHS is still valid in 1988. Therefore, both P2 and P22 content types are valid in 1988 MHS.

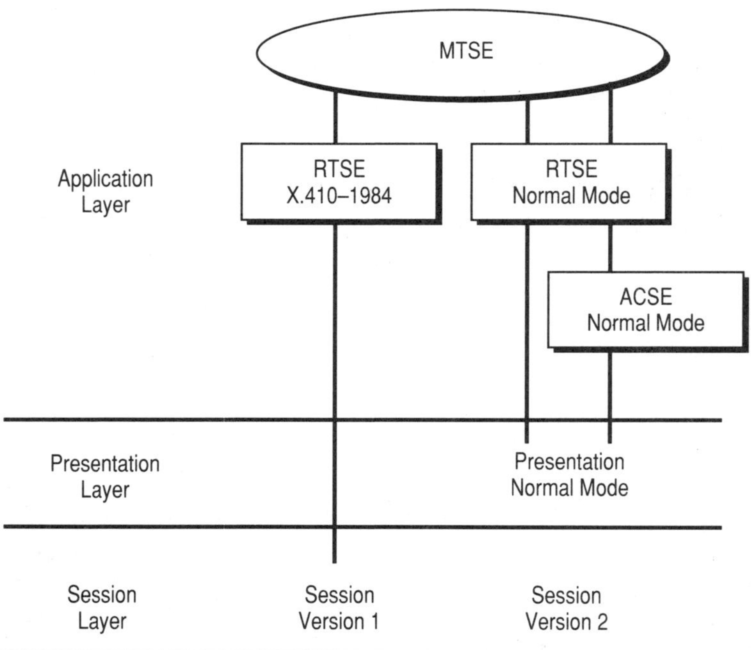

Figure 7.24 P1 protocol mappings.

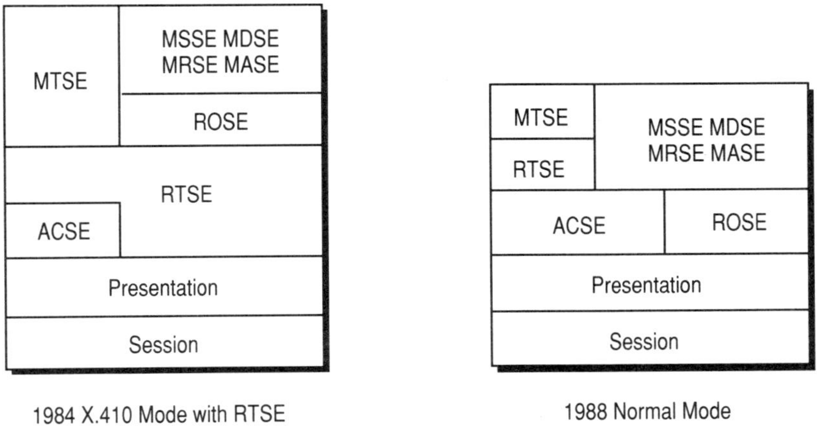

Figure 7.25 1984 vs. 1988 MHS stacks.

The header information in P22 contains extensions to accommodate new definitions for ORName and ORAddress to accommodate the new name forms adopted in the 1988 MHS. Extension parameters are present on the message delivery envelope, the Encoded Information Types field, and the Supplementary Information field. Also, heading extensions have been defined to support

1. Incomplete copy, which indicates that one or more body parts or heading fields are absent from the IPM.
2. Language indication, which identifies the languages used in the IPM's subject heading field and body. Each language is identified by a two-character language code as defined in ISO 639.2.

The Telex and Simple Formattable Document body parts have been abandoned in 1988, and it is now possible for message body parts to be bilaterally or externally defined. Similarly to the other 1988 protocols, upper bounds have been placed on variable-length protocol elements. Most of the upper bounds derive from the 1984 X.400 Implementor's Guide, which was developed after the adoption of the 1984 protocols to enhance interoperability between implementations from different vendors. The upper bounds constraints are mandatory in the CCITT version of the standard, while they are only optional in the ISO version. Another difference between the ISO and CCITT texts is that ISO defines a general text body part, while CCITT does not.

References and for Further Study

The 1988 X.400 MHS architecture and protocols are defined in the Blue Book (CCITT X.400, 1988). The Directory service and its related protocols and object definitions are defined in the X.500 standards (CCITT X.500, 1988). Radicati (1989) provides an in-depth overview of the distributed operations aspect of X.500. Schicker (1988) gives a good overview of some of the major differences between 1984 and 1988 X.400, particularly in the protocol layering approach. Manros (1988) provides a very detailed description of the 1988 protocols and architecture.

Chapter

8

The Message Store Protocol, P7

The Message Store functionality makes it possible for UAs of different levels of sophistication to reliably access and benefit from the MHS services. In particular, it allows smaller systems, such as personal computers, to attach more easily to MHS services by allowing them to rely on the Message Store as the intermediary system for message retrieval and submission. This chapter looks in detail at the services that the Message Store provides to its users, as well as the protocol operations that can be carried out on messages held by the Message Store.

The Message Store provides the following set of services to user agents:

1. A secure, reliable, and continuously available stable storage message repository.
2. A continuously available mechanism for accepting message delivery. Without a Message Store, UAs have little control over message receipt and have to be constantly available to receive mail. This is of course usually impractical in most small systems.
3. A set of sophisticated mechanisms to selectively view, forward, retrieve, and delete delivered messages or parts thereof.
4. In addition, the Message Store is able to send alerts back to the UA upon receipt of particular messages.

From a logical standpoint, a Message Store acts on behalf of a single user and possesses a single O/R address; it does not provide a shared capability to multiple users. From an implementation standpoint, however, multiple users can access the MS services provided by a single physical system, although each user will have the impression of dealing with a dedicated Message Store repository.

The P7 Message Store protocol acts between the UA and the Message Store. It allows UAs to obtain information about and manipulate stored messages in a number of different ways. Users may, for example, get counts on the number of messages held in the Message Store, list messages according to a particular set of criteria, or selectively fetch and delete messages.

From the MTS perspective, messages are considered to have been successfully delivered when they are accepted by the Message Store. A UA attached to a Message Store does not receive messages directly but can be alerted automatically by the Message Store of the arrival of messages that match certain preestablished criteria. These criteria are set up by the UA through operations defined in the P7 Message Store protocol.

Message submission is generally transparent to the Message Store. The exception is when the UA requests that a previously received message be forwarded or replied to by the Message Store. In these cases, the Message Store can automatically expand the message to include the appropriate recipient header information. Users can also request that messages received from the MTS be forwarded automatically upon receipt by the Message Store.

8.1 Organizational Considerations

From an organizational point of view, Message Stores may be owned by either ADMDs or PRMDs. Where they are operated by a PRMD, they need not be colocated with a PRMD-provided MTA; that is, the PRMD need not also own an MTA. A privately owned Message Store could be a stand-alone entity, which attaches directly to an ADMD MTA. Figure 8.1 shows a private PRMD-based UA and Message Store that attach directly to a publicly provided ADMD MTA. Figure 8.2

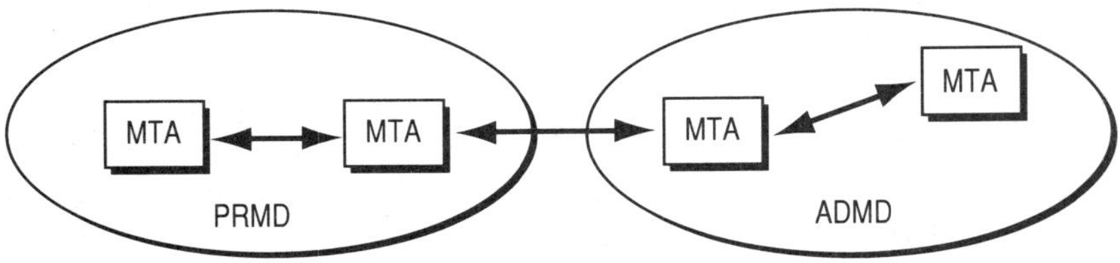

Figure 8.1 Private MS attaching to an ADMD MTA.

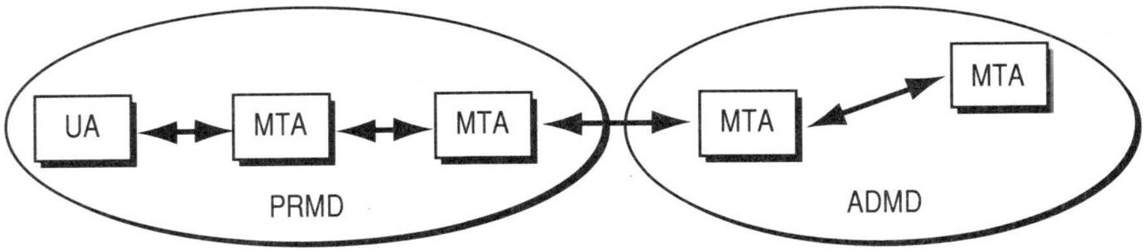

Figure 8.2 Private UA, MS, and MTA attaching to public ADMD.

shows a private PRMD that includes UA(s), a Message Store, and an MTA that attaches to an ADMD at the MTA level.

8.2 The Message Store Model

The MHS conceptual model defines the Message Store as an object that acts as an intermediary between a UA and the MTS. The Message Store accepts delivery of messages from the MTS on behalf of the UA and provides a pass-through service to the UA for the submission of messages. In particular, the Message Store allows the UA to handle "indirect" submission of messages, that is, forwarding messages which reside within the Message Store. The Message Store acts only on behalf of a single user and does not provide services to support the sharing of Message Store information among multiple users. From the point of view of authentication and security, the Message Store constitutes a separate identity with its own security key, or keys.

As with the other 1988 MHS protocols, the behavior of the Message Store is modeled as a set of consumer-supplier actions. The Message Store is a consumer of the MTS services in that it relies on the MTS for message submission and delivery. The UA object communicates with the MS object via the P7 protocol, while the Message Store object communicates with the MTS environment via the P3 protocol.

The Message Store supplies the following services to the UA:

1. Retrieval
2. Indirect-submission
3. Administration

It is a consumer of the following MTS services:

1. Delivery
2. Submission
3. Administration

The behavior of the Message Store object can be formalized by the following ASN.1:

```
mS OBJECT
    PORTS {     retrieval [S],
                indirectSubmission [S],
                administration [S],
                delivery [C],
                submission [C],
                administration [C] }
    ::= id-ot-ms
```

8.3 The Information Model

The information held by the Message Store is modeled as a collection of information bases, each of which consists of a collection of entries and attributes. The CCITT Blue Book describes a single information base called the stored-messages-information-base. This information base consists of information derived from message deliveries and report deliveries to the Message Store across the MTS delivery port. The definition of the Message Store information model closely resembles the description of the X.500 DIB.

A future addendum to the ISO version of the standard will define additional information-bases specialized for logging, called the *inlog* and the *outlog*. These information bases are defined only in the context of the ISO version of the standard and are not specified in the CCITT version of the standard. A major reason for diverging in this area lies in a different perception between ISO and CCITT of what the Message Store is about. CCITT designers believe that the Message Store should define only a basic stable storage facility, whereas ISO designers believe it should define a set of database-like facilities for handling the information it maintains. This difference of opinion has led to an on-going debate between ISO and CCITT over just what is the right level of complexity that should be specified for the Message Store.

The Message Store information base definition can be summarized in ASN.1 as follows:

```
informationBase ::=  INTEGER {
      stored-messages     (0),
      inlog               (1),
      outlog              (2) (0 . . ub-information-bases) }
```

Each information base is organized as a sequence of entries, where each entry corresponds to a single object (e.g., a delivered message). Each entry in the information base is identified by a sequence number that is unique to that information base. Sequence numbers are generated sequentially, in ascending order, and are never reused. They are, therefore, unique to that information base for all time and provide a foolproof way of distinguishing one message from another.

An entry consists of a set of attributes, as shown in Fig. 8.3. Each attribute provides a piece of information about or derived from the data to which the entry corresponds. Examples of such information are the sequence number of the entry itself and the creation time of the entry in the MS. Attributes consist of a type and one or more values. Attributes may be internationally standardized or may be defined locally by national or private authorities. New attribute types may be defined using the Attribute MACRO defined in the X.500 standards (see Chap. 7).

Entries in the Message Store are generally independent of each other. However, the Message Store information model defines the existence of child entries and parent entries. A child entry is created when a message arrives with a body part of type message. An entry that is not a child entry is called a main entry. By default, Message Store operations act only on main entries. Two attributes are defined to express relationships between entries:

1. The parent-sequence-number attribute is a single-valued attribute that holds the sequence number of the parent of a child entry (i.e., the sequence number identifying the parent entry). It is absent from a main entry.
2. The child-sequence-number attribute is a multivalued attribute that holds the sequence numbers of all child entries of a parent entry. It is absent from nonparent entries.

One of the most important properties of messages stored in the Message Store information base is its entry status. This attribute is cre-

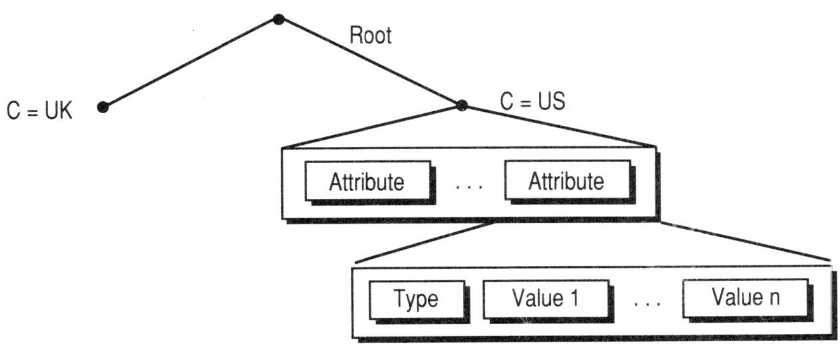

Figure 8.3 Message Store entry model.

ated and maintained by the Message Store, and serves to record whether a particular message has been accessed by the UA or not. The entry-status attribute may take on any of the following values:

1. *New,* indicating that the message has neither been listed by a UA nor has yet been automatically processed by the Message Store.
2. *Listed,* which indicates that information about the message has been returned to the UA in response to a list or a fetch operation; however, the message has not been completely processed yet.
3. *Processed,* which indicates that the UA has completely fetched the message, or the Message Store has performed some autoaction on it. The entry-status attribute of a (non)delivery notification takes on the value processed, when the delivered-report-envelope is retrieved.

8.4 Auto-Actions

The Message Store supports the concept of auto-actions, which are activities that will be carried out automatically whenever some predefined criterion has been met. The result of an auto-action is typically visible externally from the Message Store in that it results in the sending of a message or alert. Auto-actions are registered by UAs with the Message Store, using the Register-MS operation.

Each class of auto-action is identified by an auto-action-type. Associated with an auto-action registration there is a corresponding auto-action-registration-parameter. These parameters are needed by the Message Store to perform the registered action automatically. Registration of an auto-action requires the use of an auto-action-registration-identifier which serves to identify the particular registration. The following ASN.1 summarizes the above relationships:

```
AutoActionRegistration :: SEQUENCE {
      type                       AutoActionType,
      registration-identifier     [0] INTEGER (1..ub-per-auto-
      action)
                                      DEFAULT1,
      registration-parameter      [1] ANY DEFINED BY type}

AutoActionType ::= OBJECT IDENTIFIER
```

Auto-action types may be internationally standardized, as well as defined by national or private administrative authorities. Each auto-action type is uniquely designated by an object identifier when it is first defined.

Defining a new auto-action type requires specifying an ASN.1 datatype to which the auto-action-registration parameter must conform.

The data type is defined using an object identifier which denotes the auto-action-type.

The auto-action-type is defined by

1. Assigning an object-identifier to the auto-action-type
2. Indicating the ASN.1 data type of the auto-action-registration-parameter.

The following macro can be used to define a new auto-action-type:

```
AUTO-ACTION MACRO  ::=
BEGIN
      TYPE NOTATION  ::=  Registration
      VALUE NOTATION ::=  value (VALUE OBJECT IDENTIFIER)
      Registration   ::=  ''REGISTRATION PARAMETER IS''
                          type
END
```

where

1. Registration gives the data type of the registration parameters associated with the auto-action.
2. Value represents an object identifier which is used to identify the auto action.

The macro currently provides no support for defining relationships or possible interactions between different registrations of the same (or different) auto-actions.

A number of general-purpose auto-actions are defined in recommendation X.413; these are known as general-auto-action-types. They include the Auto-forward, and Auto-alert auto-action-types.

8.4.1 Auto-forward

The Auto-forward auto-action type enables the Message Store to forward automatically a message that has been delivered to the Message Store which meets certain predefined criteria. A number of Auto-forward parameters may be registered for this purpose with the Message Store by the UA. Each parameter is uniquely identified by its Auto-forward-registration-identifier. The same delivered message may be auto-forwarded many times depending on whether it matches multiple sets of forwarding criteria.

8.4.2 Auto-alert

The Auto-alert auto-action type allows the Message Store service to automatically alert the Message Store user of the acceptance on the part of the Message Store of a particular message delivered to it. A set of Auto-alert parameters may be registered by the Message Store user with the Message Store for this purpose. The Message Store will attempt to match each message it receives with the predefined Auto-alert parameters and will generate alerts to the Message Store user accordingly. Alerts are only sent to the user after the user has successfully bound to the Message Store.

8.5 P7 Protocol Operations

As described earlier in Chap. 7, the P7 Message Store protocol consists of three service ports:

1. A retrieval port
2. An indirect submission port
3. An administration port

The indirect submission and administration ports of P7 are common to the equivalent MTS-level ports defined in recommendation X.411. The ISO version of the standard defines additional Message Store management services for logging incoming and outgoing messages, called the inlog and outlog information-bases. It also provides services for automatically correlating incoming notifications with logged information about outgoing messages. As mentioned earlier, however, CCITT has chosen not to adopt the inlog and outlog information-bases.

Generally, services provided by the Message Store are invoked by the Message Store user and performed by the Message Store. The exceptions to this rule are the alert functions provided by the retrieval port and the submission-control function provided by the indirect submission port.

8.5.1 The MS-bind

The MS-bind operation serves to bind the indirect-submission, retrieval, and administration ports of the Message Store user to the Message Store supplier. Only one association may exist at any one time between the Message Store and the Message Store user. The Message Store authenticates the Message Store user before allowing it to make use of any of the retrieval capabilities. Similarly, the MTS authenticates the MTS user before extending its services to it.

The Bind operation also carries a number of security parameters that include a field called the security-context. The security-context comprises one or more security labels that define the sensitivity of the interactions between the Message Store user and the Message Store service for the duration of the association, these must be in line with the security policy in force. The security-context must match one that has been registered by the Message Store user with the Message Store through the registration of the appropriate security labels.

The arguments of the MS-bind operation serve to identify a Message Store user to the Message Store. They also serve to authenticate the Message Store user and set the security-context for the association. The bind arguments may also contain a set of restrictions for entries that can be returned as a result of fetch operations, and a request to be informed of the auto-action types, attribute types, and content types which are supported by the Message Store.

Fetch restrictions represent a set of possible restrictions on the contents that will be returned by the Fetch operation. They include

1. Allowed-content types, which identify the content types that the MS user is prepared to accept.
2. Allowed-EITs, which denote the set of encoded information types the MS user is prepared to accept as a result of a Fetch operation. If a message contains EITs other than those specified, a filtering will take place so that the disallowed EIT parts are not returned with the message text.
3. Maximum-content-length, which represents the maximum content length that the MS user is prepared to accept as a result of the Fetch operation. Any message with a content length greater than that specified by this parameter will not be returned.

The MS-configuration-request parameter is used to get information on which auto-actions and optional attributes are supported by the Message Store.

8.5.2 Submission Port Services

The Message Store (P7) indirect submission port makes use of the services defined in the MTS (i.e., P3) submission port; however, its semantics are extended to allow a UA to forward messages already in the Message Store rather than resubmit them all over again. It is defined using the ASN.1 formal notation as

```
indirectSubmissionPORT ::=  submission
```

The operations supported by the submission port are described in Chap. 7.

8.5.3 Administration Port Services

The administration port is also common to P1 MTS-level administration port. The operations of the administration port are described in Chap. 7.

8.5.4 Retrieval Port Services

The Retrieval port is the only service port whose functions are proper to the Message Store. It provides both operations to gain information about and to manipulate stored messages. The ASN.1 definition of the Retrieval port is as follows:

```
retrievalPORT
        CONSUMER INVOKES {
             Summarize,
             List,
             Fetch,
             Delete,
             Register-MS}
        SUPPLIER INVOKES {
             Alert }
        ::= id-pt-retrieval
```

The operations that are made available by the Message Store through the retrieval port are Summarize, List, Fetch, Delete, Register-MS, and alert.

8.5.4.1 The summarize operation. The summarize operation is used to obtain a count of the number of entries held in the information-base that match certain specified filter criteria. It may also be used to obtain the lowest and highest sequence numbers of the entries selected. Several distinct counts may be requested covering different ranges of entries in the information base.

The arguments of the summarize operation permit the Message Store user to specify on which information base to execute the operation. The default information-base is the stored-messages information base; however, this allows the ISO version to specify use of the inlog or outlog information bases. The set of entries to be summarized is selected on the basis of a set of filtering criteria that allow the MS user to specify whether both main entries and child entries or only child entries are to be summarized. The operation allows the specification of a range of contiguous entries within either a specified sequence number range or a specified creation time range.

The summarize operation will only succeed if the information-base allows the MS user to access it according to the security context and the enforced security policy.

8.5.4.2 The List operation. The list operation is used to search the information base for entries that match a particular set of criteria and to return a set of selected information regarding those entries.

Like the summarize operation, the list may act on any specified information-base. By default, it will operate on the stored messages information-base. If the operation succeeds, it will return the set of requested information types and attributes from each entry that matched the filter criteria, in ascending order of sequence numbers. If no entries matched the specified filter, the operation will return an empty set.

The list operation will succeed only when the information-base permits access according to the security-context and the enforced security policy.

8.5.4.3 The Fetch operation. The fetch operation is used to return selected attributes from a specific entry in the information-base. It may also be used to return selected information from the first entry among several that match the specified filter criteria. In the latter case, it also returns the sequence-numbers of the other entries that also matched the filtering criteria.

The fetch operation will only succeed on information-bases permitted by the security-context and the security policy in force.

Like the preceding operations, if a particular information base is not specified, the fetch operation will operate on the stored-messages information base. It is possible in the fetch operation to request that it execute only on a specified entry, or a set of entries. In the latter case, the entry with the lowest sequence number will be fetched.

A parameter called *requested-attributes* indicates what information from the selected entry will be returned with the result. If the parameter is absent, the operation will return whatever set of attributes were predefined by means of the register-MS operation (see Sec. 8.6.4.5).

8.5.4.4 The Delete operation. The delete operation is used to delete selected entries from an information-base. A parent-entry and its child entries may only be deleted together. This is accomplished by specifying only the main-entry as the argument of the operation.

The delete will succeed only when it operates on the information-bases permitted by the security-context and the security-policy in force.

Like the other Message Store operations, the delete allows a particular information-base to be specified, the default being stored-messages. Depending on the information-base specified in the operation, different restrictions may apply on which entries can be deleted. In the stored-messages information-base, for example, no entry may be deleted if its status is set to "new."

Entries can be deleted by specifying either a set of filter criteria or an unordered list of sequence-numbers. When the delete succeeds, it returns a null set of parameters.

8.5.4.5 The Register-MS operation. The register operation is used to register or unregister various kinds of information with the Message Store. These may include

1. Auto-actions.
2. A default list of attribute types.
3. New credentials.
4. A new set of user-security labels.

The registration of auto-actions includes the specification of an auto-action type. If an auto-action type is not included in the register-MS operation, then no new auto-actions are being registered. Auto-actions may be de-registered by specifying their auto-action type.

The register-MS operation allows a Message Store user to

1. Register a set of attributes to be returned as defaults on any list or alert operation where the entry-information-selection argument is absent.
2. Specify a set of default attributes for the fetch operation to be used in the event that the entry-information-selection argument is absent.
3. Register a new set of authentication credentials.
4. Change the set of security-labels that apply to that particular user.

8.5.4.6 The Alert operation. The Alert operation is used by the Message Store to inform the MS-user (i.e., the UA) that a new entry has entered the MS and that the attributes of the new entry match the selection criteria preestablished by one of the auto-alert registrations preformed earlier via the Register-MS operation.

The alert operation may be invoked only over an existing association, and then only as a result of new entries created after the establishment of the association.

Entries matching a set of preestablished selection criteria that are created between associations will be indicated to the MS-user as a result of the next bind operation which establishes a new association. No alert operation will be invoked for these entries, prior to the MS-user initiating a new bind operation.

The alert operation will succeed only if the information-base allows access according to the security-context and the enforced security policy.

The alert takes as arguments an alert-registration-identifier that indicates which of the auto-alert-registrations resulted in the invocation of the alert operation. It also takes a new entry argument, which conveys the information from the new entry which was requested in the auto-alert-registration parameter. It is absent when the Message Store user did not specify an auto-alert-registration-parameter. If the alert operation succeeds, it returns a null result.

References and for Further Study

The Message Store protocol and information base architecture are defined in the Blue Book (CCITT X.400, 1988). An excellent and very detailed explanation of the Message Store is available in the *Blue Book Companion* by Carl-Uno Manros (1989).

Chapter

9

Security in 1988 MHS

The 1988 MHS provides two different kinds of security services: Secure Access Management and Administration services, as well as Secure Messaging.

1. *Secure Access Management and Administration:* This refers to a set of services which ensure that associations are established only among two authenticated parties. It also defines services that are used to set up the security parameters necessary to guarantee the secure use of an association. These security services apply between any MHS components in a pairwise manner, and include associations between UAs and MTAs, MTAs and MTAs, Message Stores and MTAs, as well as UAs and Message Stores.
2. *Secure Messaging:* This refers to a set of mechanisms used to verify the origin and content integrity of electronic mail messages. These security services also include mechanisms to prevent the disclosure of message contents to unauthorized parties.

For the most part, security services in the 1988 MHS are designed to function primarily between adjoining system entities. That is, they operate on a peer-to-peer basis between two MHS components rather than on an end-to-end basis between message handling users. While some end-to-end mechanisms have been defined, such as digital signatures, more research is required before comprehensive end-to-end security schemes can be specified for use in large distributed messaging systems, such as X.400.

This chapter provides an overview of 1988 MHS security services and describes in detail the X.509 authentication framework on which they are based. Additional work on security is currently underway as part of the 1992 study period.

9.1 The X.509 Authentication Framework

X.400 security is based extensively on the authentication framework defined in recommendation X.509 of the Directory standards. X.509 defines an asymmetric encryption mechanism that can be used for peer-to-peer authentication, as well as to support digital signatures. Asymmetric encryption schemes rely on a pair of keys, one secret and one public, to encrypt and decrypt information. Symmetric encryption schemes, on the other hand, use a single secret key to perform both encryption and decryption. The 1988 standards left the possible future use of symmetric encryption schemes within MHS for further study.

The standards also allow implementations to dynamically register different encryption algorithms through the inclusion of external ASN.1 definitions. This allows the "grandfathering" of preexisting security schemes, as well as allowing for the graceful addition of new enhanced security schemes in the future.

The Directory is used to store what are called "certified" public keys of MHS users. These keys, which are held in the form of encrypted certificates, can be read from the directory using the Directory Access Protocol (DAP).

The X.509 authentication framework specifies three basic security services that can be used by all application-layer OSI services: simple authentication, strong authentication, and digital signatures. Simple and strong authentication allow two communication parties to reliably verify each other's identity. Digital signatures, on the other hand, provide end-to-end data integrity by making it possible for a message recipient to reliably verify that the message contents have not been altered or otherwise tampered with during transfer.

9.1.1 Simple authentication

Simple authentication is the least secure form of authentication defined by the current standards. However, it is often sufficient in environments where security is not a major concern. X.509 defines three options to support simple authentication:

1. *Option 1* involves transferring the user's name (i.e., typically the X.500 Distinguished Name) and a password in the clear. This is a very weak form of security, but nonetheless it provides a bare-minimum level of security for very low-risk environments.

2. *Option 2* involves transferring what is called a secure token, consisting of the user's name, a password, a random number, and a

timestamp. The token is protected by a one-way hash function, as follows:

```
f1 (Name, Password, r, t)
```

In the function above, r and t are, respectively, a random number and a timestamp indicating when the token was generated. In order for two entities to authenticate each other in this manner, they must share the same hash function (Appendix D of the X.509 standard provides a sample hash function for use in simple authentication).

3. *Option 3* is similar to option 2 above; however, the security token is further protected by a second hash function (denoted as f2). Option 3 is expressed by the function

```
f2 [ f1 (Name, Password, r, t) ]
```

The use of the second hash function may seem somewhat redundant; however, it adds some increased protection because two entities need to share two similar hash functions, rather than just one, in order to communicate.

Option 1 works by having a user (user A) send its name and password in the clear to another user (user B). User B queries the Directory to check that the password it received from A matches the one held in A's Directory entry. The UserPassword attribute type is defined to store user password information within directory entries. If the comparison succeeds, the Directory confirms the validity of A's credentials to B. B, in turn, conveys the success of the operation to user A. If the comparison fails, B conveys a failure indication to user A. Figure 9.1 summarizes this sequence of operations.

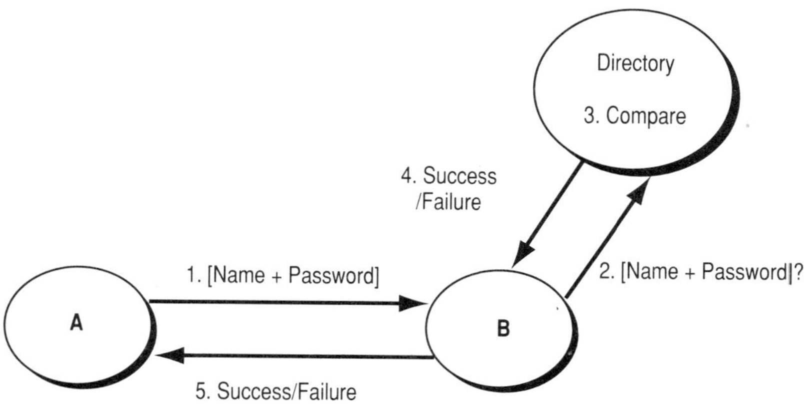

Figure 9.1 Authentication interactions.

In option 2, the set of exchanges between users A and B and the Directory are very similar to those in option 1. However, the information exchanged is better protected through the use of a one-way hash function. In this case, user A generates a token called Protected 1, which is derived from applying the one-way hash function to the following information: A's name, A's password, a random number, and a timestamp. Protected 1 is defined by:

```
Protected1 = f1 [ t1, r1, Name, Password ]
```

Protected 1 can then be used to create an authentication token, called Authenticator1, which is defined as:

```
Authenticator1 = [ Protected1, Name, t1, r1]
```

User A sends Authenticator1 to B, which uses the information contained in it to reconstruct Protected1. User B queries the directory to obtain user A's password and hashes the password with the values for user name, r1 and t1, which it received from user A. If the result matches Protected1, then the authentication has completed successfully and user B notifies user A of that; otherwise authentication has failed.

In option 3, the sequence of events is largely the same as in option 2, with the addition that Protected1 is hashed further with a second hash function called f2, in order to yield Protected2. Protected2 is defined by the following function:

```
Protected2 = f2 [t2, r2, Protected1]
```

Authenticator2 is defined as:

```
Authenticator2 = [t1, t2, r1, r2, Protected2]
```

Again in this scenario, user A sends Authenticator2 to user B, which reconstructs its value locally with information it reads from the directory and information it receives in the token.

9.1.2 Strong Authentication

The X.509 strong authentication scheme is based on what are called asymmetric public key encryption techniques. The standard does not mandate a particular encryption algorithm; however, the RSA (Rivest, Shamir, and Adleman) algorithm is heavily implied. RSA is an example of what are called *public key* (or asymmetric) cryptosystems. These types of encryption mechanisms mandate that each entity possesses two keys: a public key and a secret key. RSA has the additional property that both keys can be used for encipherment. If the secret key was used to encrypt the information, the public key can be used to decrypt it; and vice versa, if the public key was used to encrypt, the secret key can be used to decrypt.

Public keys are typically stored in a central repository accessible to multiple entities in the network. The Directory therefore represents an ideal such repository. There is no particular need to protect public keys. A sender who wishes to send information to a recipient in a secure manner obtains the recipient's public key from the Directory and uses it to encrypt the information. The encrypted information is then sent to the intended recipient who proceeds to decrypt it using the secret key.

The above mechanism is strictly a point-to-point scheme and relies on the concept of an "unbroken chain of trust." This means that if system A trusts system B and system B trusts system C, then system A trusts system C. In this manner, an entity may base its trust of a remote entity on the mutual trust of any number of intermediate entities.

9.1.2.1 Certificates. Public keys are generally stored in the directory in the form of a package of information, called a *certificate.* Certificates are constructed by "signing" a set of information that includes the user's name and its public key. Certificates are also used to convey a copy of the asymmetric public key of the user to which the certificate pertains. A certificate will typically include the following information:

1. *Signature-Algorithm-Id:* An object identifier which denotes the algorithm that was used to sign the certificate.

2. *Issuer:* The Directory name (i.e., the distinguished name) of the Certification Authority which issued the certificate. In most cases, where the Certification Authority is implemented through the use of a Directory service, the name of the Certification Authority corresponds to the distinguished name of the DSA which signed the certificate.

3. *Validity:* A predefined period of time during which the certificate is considered to be valid.

4. *Subject:* The Directory name of the subject of the certificate (i.e., the User to whom the certificate pertains).

5. *Subject-Public-Keys:* One or more asymmetric public keys of the subject of the certificate.

6. *Algorithms:* One or more algorithm identifiers associated with the public key of the subject of the certificate.

7. *Signature:* An asymmetrically encrypted, hashed version of all the above parameters computed by the Certification Authority that issued the certificate. It is computed by applying the algorithm used to sign the certificate plus the Certification Authority's secret key.

Certificate information may be expressed using the following notation:

```
CA < A >  = CA {SN, SI, CA, Ta, A, Ap, Al, S}
```

Where SN is the serial number of the certificate, SI is the signature algorithm identifier, CA denotes the Certification Authority for user A, Ta is a preestablished period of validity of the certificate, A is the user's Distinguished Name, Ap is the public key for user A, Al identifies the algorithm used to produce the signature, and S represents the signed data.

Certificates have the following properties:

1. Any user who has the public key of the Certification Authority, can recover the public key of users served by that Certification Authority. This is because the public key of the Certification Authority is necessary to access the information held in the user's certificate.
2. No party other than the Certification Authority can modify a user's certificate without it being detected.

Certificates for each user can be held in the Directory as attributes contained within that user's Directory entry. X.500 defines the following attributes for this purpose:

1. UserCertificate, which serves to store each user's public key.
2. CACertificate, which serves to store the public key of the user's certification authority.
3. CrossCertificatePair, which serves to store the public keys of other certification authorities which may be involved in an authentication exchange between two parties.

The public key of a user A can be found by any user who knows the public key of the Certification Authority for user A. A certification path is a list of certificates that allows a user to get the public key of another user. Each item in the list of certificates is a certificate for the Certification Authority of the next item in the list. In this way, a certification path constitutes an unbroken chain of trust.

In the most general case, in order to reciprocally authenticate each other, users must obtain from the Directory the complete forward and return certification paths. That is, they must possess all the public keys of the Certification Authorities in each other's domains in order to be able to access the public key information signed by those Certification Authorities. A number of useful optimizations, however, are defined to this general scheme. In particular, it can be expected that in most cases two entities wishing to authenticate each other will share the same Certification Authority and therefore will not need to rely on certification paths as both have the public key for the same Certification Authority.

Where two entities do not share the same Certification Authority, it is usually simpler for them to exchange each other's Certification Authority public key through some off-line mechanism, as well as the public key of any intermediary Certification Authorities that may be in the communication path between the two entities. Alternatively, certification paths may be stored in the Directory, and the two entities may rely on a series of Directory queries to obtain the full certification path. When this method is selected, implementations are usually designed to cache the results of Directory lookups for later reuse.

9.1.2.2 Digital signatures. Digital signatures provide the basic mechanism for ensuring data integrity. Information is signed by appending to it an enciphered summary of itself. The summary can be produced by means of a one-way hash function which guarantees that false information cannot be substituted. Appendix D of the X.509 recommendation provides a sample hash function that may be used for this purpose.

The encipherment of information is carried out by using the secret key of the signer. This guarantees that digital signatures cannot be forged. The digital signature function is summarized as follows:

```
X { Info } = Info, Xs [ h(info) ]
```

where h represents the hash function, Info is the information to be signed, and Xs is the secret key of the signer.

The recipient of signed data can perform the following steps to verify the validity of the signature:

1. Apply the one-way hash function to the information.
2. Compare the results obtained, with the results obtained by deciphering the signature using the public key of the signer.

This works because in order for the results of step 1 to match those of step 2, the information could only have been signed with the user's correct secret key.

9.1.3.2 Tokens. A token is a package of security-related information that is exchanged between two or more parties during authentication. Typically tokens are exchanged as parameters of the bind operation between two parties. Only asymmetric tokens are defined in the 1988 version of MHS; however, future versions of the standard will also attempt to define tokens suited for symmetric authentication exchanges. A 1988 MHS token contains the following kinds of information:

1. *Signature-Algorithm-Id:* The algorithm used by the originator of the token to compute the signature.
2. *Recipient-Name:* The O/R address or Directory name of the intended recipient of the token.
3. *Time:* The time at which the token was generated.
4. *Signed-Data:* The information that is being signed.
5. *Encryption-Algorithm-Id:* An identifier for the algorithm used by the originator of the token to compute the encrypted data.
6. *Encrypted-Data:* The information encrypted by the originator of the token using the algorithm specified by the Encryption-Algorithm-Id and the public key of the intended recipient of the token.
7. *Signature:* An asymmetrically encrypted, hashed version of the above parameters computed by the originator of the token using the algorithm specified by the Signature-Algorithm-Id and the secret key of the originator.

9.1.2.4 Authentication procedures. Authentication information is exchanged between two parties when an association is established. It is provided within the bind parameters and is mapped onto the mechanisms provided by ACSE for the secure transfer of authentication information. X.509 defines three possible procedures for strong authentication:

1. A one-way exchange
2. A two-way exchange
3. A three-way exchange

In the one-way authentication exchange, a single transfer from entity A to entity B establishes the identity of A and that the authentication token originated at A. By implication it also establishes the identity of B and the integrity (and nonreplay) of the authentication token that was sent from A to B. Two-way authentication is similar to one-way, except that entity B sends a reply token back to entity A. The reply token establishes in a more reliable manner the identity of B. The three-way authentication is similar to the two-way authentication, but relies on a third exchange between A and B to supplant the need for timestamping the tokens. The three-way authentication is therefore less dependent on mutually synchronized time clocks. This is important because OSI lacks a synchronized time protocol. However, the three-way exchange cannot really be used with ROS-based protocols since it does not fit well with ROS's two-way request-reply style of exchange. The three-way authentication exchange is defined in the standard more for the sake of full generality rather than with the expectation that it will really be adopted in ROS-based systems such as X.500 and X.400.

9.1.2.5 Generation and management of key pairs. The administrative process required to generate and distribute key pairs is, of course, outside the scope of the international standard. However, the standard does establish some general guidelines for the secure management and generation of key pairs. In particular, it states that key pairs may be produced by any of the following means:

1. A user may generate his or her own key pair, so the secret key is never released to foreign entities.
2. The keys are generated by a secure third party, in which case they must then be transferred to the user in a secure manner.
3. The keys are generated by the Certification Authority (in most cases this is synonymous to the Directory). In this case a secure data transfer to the Certification Authority is not necessary but it is needed to transfer the secret key to the user.

Since a certificate associates a user's name with a public key, the Certification Authority must be reliably sure of a user's identity before generating a certificate for it. The Certification Authority must also take care not to issue certificates for two users with the same name. Since the certificate stored in the Directory is public, no security is necessary to transport it to the Directory.

Certificates are valid only for a predefined time period, after which they expire and must be removed from use. The Certification Authority is responsible for the timely replacement of certificates that have expired, as well as issuing certificates in a way such that they do not all expire at the same time. Since timestamps are based on coordinated universal time, some clock synchronization is required. Certification Authorities must also be able to revocate certificates prior to their expiration date in the event that a certificate is found to have been corrupted.

9.2 MHS Security Threats

The 1988 X.400 identifies a number of potential security threats that can arise in an MHS environment. These are categorized as follows:

1. *Access Threats:* These are threats which involve the invalid access to the MHS environment by unauthorized users. Mechanisms are provided to detect and prevent such unauthorized access.

2. *Intermessage Threats:* These are threats that can arise when unauthorized agents external to the communication exchange maliciously interfere with the exchange. They can manifest themselves in a variety of ways, including

a. Masquerading: A user or entity in the MHS pretends to be a different entity so as to maliciously gain information or solicit behavior from another entity in the MHS. It may include impersonation of the MTS, falsely acknowledging a message receipt, falsely claiming to originate a message, impersonation of an MTA to an MTS user, or impersonation of an MTA to another MTA.

b. Message modification: A genuine message may be maliciously modified by an unauthorized agent during its transfer through the MHS system. This may involve modification of the contents of the message, as well as its destruction.

c. Replay: A message whose originators and contents are genuine may have been recorded and may be played back to the intended recipient at a later date to confuse or trick the recipient into revealing information. This kind of threat may involve both replaying and reordering of messages.

d. Traffic analysis: Analysis of message traffic by an eavesdropper can yield valuable information regarding the nature of an exchange between MHS users, even if the actual contents of the exchange are not revealed.

3. *Intramessage Threats:* These threats may be performed by one or more of the actual participants in the message communication. They involve

a. Denial of Service: This occurs when an entity fails to perform its functions or prevents other entities from performing theirs. An MTS-user may provoke this by flooding the MHS system with more messages than the system can handle. This threat can manifest itself through denial of communications by MTAs and other components, MTA failures, or flooding of the MTS by too many messages.

b. Repudiation of messages: One of the communication participants can deny involvement in the communication. This has particularly serious implications if the exchange relates to financial transactions. Repudiation occurs if either the MTS-user or the MTS itself deny submitting or receiving a particular message (or set of messages). It can include denial of origin of the message, denial of submission of the message, as well as denial of delivery of the message.

c. Security level violation: If a management domain within the

MHS has different security clearance levels (e.g., public, private, personal, company confidential), users must be prevented from sending or receiving messages at a level for which they are not authorized. This may involve an originator not using the valid message label, an MTA or MTS-user not using the appropriate security context (see Sec. 9.3.3), as well as different security labeling policies in use between the MTS and the MTS-User.

4. *Data Store Threats:* The MHS holds a number of data stores that must be protected from corruption. Protection is required against the following kinds of threats:

a. *Modification of routing information:* Unauthorized modification of the Directory's contents may lead to messages being misrouted or lost. Modification of the deferred delivery data store or the hold for delivery data store can be used to mislead or confuse an intended recipient. This can involve corruption of routing information, as well as misrouting of information.

b. *Preplay:* An unauthorized agent can make a copy of a deferred delivery message and send it to the intended recipient while the original is still being held for delivery in the MTA. This can lead the message recipient to reply to the message, prior to the originator's expected reply, or simply confuse the intended message recipient. This threat may involve the preplay of messages or delays in message delivery.

9.3 Implementation of the Security Services

Authentication between parties in MHS is carried out by exchanging some form of secret data, such as passwords or encrypted tokens. The initiator and responder credentials parameters and results in the MTS-Bind, MS-Bind and MTA-Bind operations are used to transfer these passwords and tokens. As a result of this exchange, the two parties are sure of each other's identity. The two parties may also implicitly agree to transfer some confidential data element for the duration of the association as an ongoing verification of identity with each request-response exchange. A secure communication path is typically accomplished through the use of the lower layer services provided by ACSE.

9.3.1 Security labels

Security labels are a series of security classifications that help establish a hierarchy of security levels. They may be associated with any

MHS entity including messages, probes, reports, MTAs, management domains, and MTS-Users. They may also be used to characterize an association between an MTS-User and a management domain (or MTA), as well as associations between management domains and MTAs.

Security-labels comprise a set of security attributes that are used to define the various security levels. The following attributes have been specified to allow MHS users to define an open-ended set of security labels that can meet the real-life security needs of organizations:

1. *Security-Policy-Identifier:* An identifier of the security policy to which the label applies.
2. *Security-Classification:* This serves to specify a particular security classification from a hierarchy that consists of the following possible classifications: unmarked, unclassified, restricted, confidential, secret, top-secret.
3. *Privacy-Mark:* A printable string, which may be used to provide security designations such as "in confidence," "in strictest confidence," etc.
4. *Security-Categories:* When present, security categories provide further restrictions within a particular security classification, such as "personal," "staff," "commercial," etc.

Basically, security labels provide a way of establishing a common security level between two parties before an information exchange occurs between them. The security level description must then be carried along to designate each piece of information exchanged between the two parties.

9.3.2 The Message Origin Authentication Service

The Message Origin Authentication Service enables the recipient, or an MTA through which the message passes, to verify the identity of the originator of the message. It is used to verify that the originator is indeed who it says it is on the message envelope information. Similarly, a Report Origin Authentication Service and a Probe Origin Authentication Service are also provided. In addition, a Non-Repudiation of Origin Service is provided to protect against attempts by the originator to falsely deny sending a message.

Message origin authentication for messages, reports, or probes is provided through the computation of what is called a *Message Origin Authentication Check*. The Message Origin Authentication Check is a function of the message contents, the content identifier, and the message security label. In order to additionally obtain content confidentiality, the Message Origin Authentication Check can be computed as a function of the enciphered message content. This allows MHS entities (i.e., MTAs or MSs) to verify the overall integrity of the message without having to examine the plain-text message content. Where content confidentiality is being used, however, the Message Origin Authentication Check cannot be used to provide the non-repudiation of origin service, because it verifies origin but cannot assume that the message is not being replayed.

9.3.3 The Proof of Submission Service

The Proof of Submission Service enables the originator of a message to verify that the message was submitted to the MTS for delivery to the specified recipients.

Proof of Submission is implemented via a request for proof of submission argument which is sent with the message at submit time, and the actual proof of submission result which is returned by the MTS once it has successfully accepted the message. The proof of submission is computed as a function of all the arguments of the message, including the Message Submission Identifier and the time at which the message was submitted.

9.3.4 The Proof of Delivery Service

The Proof of Delivery Service enables the originator of a message to request authentication of the delivered message, its contents, and the identity of the recipients. It is used primarily to verify that a message was successfully delivered to its intended recipients.

This service is provided by having the originator of the message include a proof of delivery request with the submitted message. The request is delivered to each recipient with the message. A recipient who receives such a request should compute the proof of delivery as a function of the arguments associated with the message. The proof of delivery is returned by the MTS to the message originator as part of a report on the results of the original message submission.

9.3.5 The Secure Access Management Service

The Secure Access Management Service provides authentication between peer entities (i.e., adjacent communicating components). It allows two communicating entities to set up a number of parameters that define a common security context, or security level, that will be used throughout the rest of the exchange.

At the time when an MTS-user binds to an MTA, or an MTA binds to another MTA, the Bind operation allows the specification of a security context that serves to limit the passage of messages on the association to only those containing the specific security labels agreed upon for that association. The security context itself consists of one or more security labels which define the level of sensitivity of the interactions that may occur over the particular association. By setting up a security context, two entities agree that only messages of a particular security level will be allowed over the association. This fits well with the military model of selectively restricting access to information on the basis of privilege levels.

The Register service allows an MTS-user to preestablish set permissible security labels with the MTA. An MTS-user may also use the Register operation to change the arguments held by the MTS that define what level of messages it can deliver to the MTS-user. The MS-Register service also allows the establishment of permissible security labels between the Message Store and its users.

9.3.6 Content Integrity Service

The Content Integrity Service enables a recipient to verify that the original content of a message has not been tampered with. This service is provided through the use of one or more cryptographic algorithms. The specification of the algorithm, keys, and other necessary initializing data are conveyed in the message using the Message Argument Confidentiality and the Message Argument Integrity fields. Once the algorithm and keys are applied to the message, a Content Integrity Check is generated, which is then sent in the message envelope. Depending upon the local security policy, if the Content Integrity Check is protected using the Message Argument Integrity security element, it may also be used to help provide the Non-Repudiation of Origin service.

9.3.7 The Content Confidentiality Service

The Content Confidentiality Service prevents the unauthorized disclosure of the contents of a message to anyone other than the intended recipients. This security service relies on the use of an encipherment algorithm to ensure that only the recipient and the sender of the message know the plaintext contents of the message. The encipherment algorithm and the key(s) used plus any other necessary initializing data are conveyed to the recipient by means of the Message Argument Confidentiality and the Message Argument Integrity security elements. Possession by either party of the algorithm and key allow the message contents to be enciphered or deciphered as needed.

9.3.8 The Message Sequence Integrity Service

The Message Sequence Integrity Service allows the originator to provide the recipient with proof that the correct sequencing of a set of related messages has been preserved. In addition, the Message Flow Confidentiality Service allows the originator of a message to conceal the flow of the message through the MHS.

This service is provided by associating a message sequence number with each individual message, which identifies the relative position of the message in a sequence of messages. Each originator-recipient pair involved in this type of exchange has to maintain a consistent set of sequence numbers. No mechanisms are defined to support the initialization or synchronization of the message sequence numbers.

9.3.9 Non-Repudiation Services

Non-Repudiation Services include the following services:

1. *Non-Repudiation of Origin Service:* Provides the recipient of a message with proof of the origin of the message and its content. It is designed to protect against attempts by the originator to falsely deny sending the message.

2. *Non-Repudiation of Delivery Service:* Provides the originator of a message with proof of delivery of the message. It protects against attempts by the recipient to falsely deny delivery of the message or its contents.

3. *Non-Repudiation of Submission Service:* Provides the originator of a message with proof of submission of the message. It protects against attempts by the MTS to falsely deny that the message was submitted for delivery to the originally specified recipients.

No specific services are defined to support the non-repudiation of origin of either messages, probes, or reports. These services are provided in conjunction with a set of local security policies and in combination with the message arguments specified by the security context.

9.3.10 Message Security Labelling Service

The Message Security Labelling Service provides a capability to categorize messages by indicating their sensitivity. This allows a message to be handled in accordance with the security policy in force, as specified by the agreed upon security context.

Messages may be labeled with data specified by the prevailing security policy. The Message Security Label is also made available to intermediate MTAs, so as to ensure that messages with a particular label will only pass through MTAs that service information conforming to that security level.

A message security label may be sent as argument in a message, or it may be protected by the Message Argument Integrity or Message Origin Authentication security element (same as other message arguments). If both confidentiality and integrity are used, the Message Security Label can be protected by using the Message Argument Confidentiality security element. In this case, the label is an argument that is exchanged between the originator and the recipient and may differ from the Message Security Label in the message envelope.

9.3.11 Double enveloping

Double enveloping allows one message to be completely embedded in the body of another message. This allows greater confidentiality in transferring the original message through the MTS. This is a common electronic mail technique that was discussed earlier in Chap. 2. It allows messages to travel through messaging domains that rely on very different security policies.

9.4 The NIST Security Agreements

The ISO/CCITT base standard defines only an asymmetric encryption technique. However, the ISO/CCITT implementor's guide permits the use of both symmetric and asymmetric techniques for signed data and encrypted data. The NIST implementor's agreements are designed to permit the implementation of all mandatory security facilities in terms of either symmetric or asymmetric encryption techniques. The actual technique employed is dependent on the algorithm chosen, which is registered with the MHS domain by a security authority.

If asymmetric techniques are used for content integrity, they can also be used for UA-to-UA Non-Repudiation of Origin. If symmetric techniques are used, content integrity can provide this via a trusted (i.e., secure) third party "notary" function. A notary function relies on a third-party system to maintain records of any encrypted information which was issued by the sending party so as to be able to corroborate that event at a later time.

Peer entity authentication is provided using strong authentication on the Bind operation, via either symmetric or asymmetric encryption techniques. The actual key management policy, however, is outside the scope of the standard. End-to-end (i.e., UA-to-UA) message origin authentication is provided through content integrity. Some of the NIST security classes make this more stringent by requiring support of message origin authentication by the MTAs which handle the message as it passes through the MTS.

9.5 1984 to 1988 Security Interworking

The most expedient way to achieve interoperability between 1988 secure MHS environments and 1984 nonsecure environments is through the use of the double-enveloping technique. Double enveloping in this case means enclosing a secure (i.e., signed or encrypted) message into the body of a nonsecure message of 1984 vintage. This allows 1988 messages to be transported transparently within 1984 MTS environments.

In summary, a message (MSG1) can be encrypted via any technique available in 1988 MHS. Its contents and envelope will then make up the content portion of a new message, called MSG2, which has as its envelope a message envelope that conforms to the 1984 encoding rules. If the 1984 MHS system to be traversed supports a predefined security scheme specific to that environment, the envelope of MSG2 will reflect whatever appropriate security parameters are required to support that security scheme.

Double enveloping represents a very powerful technique that makes it possible for messages to traverse a number of diverse and possibly hostile domains without needing to have their contents altered or mapped into complex other encodings. Implementation of a double-enveloping function is usually considerably simpler and more secure than attempting to match potentially very different security parameters encoding schemes.

References and for Further Study

The X.509 authentication framework is part of the X.500 Directory standards (CCITT X.500, 1988). The RSA public key encryption scheme on which X.509 is based is described by Rivest, Shamir, and Adleman (1978). The specification of the security services proper to MHS and how the X.509 services relate to message handling services can be found in the X.400 MHS recommendations (CCITT X.400, 1988). The NIST implementor's agreements on the use of security in the context of X.400 message handling systems are found in the NIST Stable implementor's agreements (1988).

Chapter 10

Advanced Topics

Chapters 6, 7, and 8 focused primarily on describing the X.400 MHS standards as defined by the 1984 and 1988 MHS recommendations. This chapter looks at the complex issue of backward compatibility between 1988 and 1984 implementations. Since 1984 is still the predominant commercial implementation of X.400 in use today, the designers of the 1988 MHS were under a great deal of pressure to produce a set of recommendations which would be fully backward compatible with 1984 implementations. It describes the provisions made available by the designers of 1988 MHS to allow it to interwork gracefully with 1984 MHS implementations.

This chapter also looks at some of the pragmatic issues that affect the way in which electronic mail systems are evolving today, such as the development of gatewaying techniques between X.400 and RFC-822 systems; support for Electronic Data Interchange (EDI); and the development of industry-standard application programming interfaces (APIs) for X.400-based systems. Finally, it provides a brief overview of the work items currently under study as part of the CCITT 1992 study period on X.400 MHS.

10.1 1988 to 1984 Interoperability

The 1988 MHS standards deal extensively with the issue of interoperability between 1988 systems and 1984 systems. Since 1984-based systems were already being deployed commercially at the time 1988 was under development, a great deal of effort was made in the specification of 1988 to ensure that it would be fully backward compatible with the 1984 standards. The 1988 MHS achieves backward compatibility with 1984 MHS through two principal mechanisms:

1. The inclusion in the 1988 protocol definitions of Application Contexts based on the 1984 version of the stack (i.e., the use of X.410-1984 mode). Chapter 7 dealt extensively with the different protocol application contexts that have been defined to satisfy both the 1984 and 1988 protocol stack requirements.

2. The use of an EXTENSION qualifier to denote 1988 fields as "deltas" to the 1984 fields. Tagging new fields as "extensions" allows systems to deal with them more easily when converting back to 1984-compliant protocol data units. Extensions that are marked "critical" indicate that they are essential to the informational value of the protocol data unit and cannot be removed or converted to the 1984 equivalent.

When dealing with interoperability between MHS systems of different vintage, the concern is not merely whether a 1984 can talk to a 1988 system, but more importantly whether a message can successfully traverse a mixed environment comprised of both 1984 and 1988 MTAs. The interoperability features specified in 1988 MHS, therefore, focus primarily on the interoperability requirements at the MTA level. The process of converting 1988 MTA operations and APDUs down to the 1984 version of the standards is called *downgrading*. The following issues must be addressed when downgrading from 1988 to 1984 operation:

1. 1988 security fields
2. 1988 extension fields
3. Conversion of 1988 ORNames to 1984 ORNames
4. Conversion of 1988 basic-encoded-information-types to 1984 Encoded Information Types
5. Handling redirection and DL information
6. Dealing with the APDU size constraints imposed by 1988 MHS

10.1.1 Association establishment

When an association is established between a 1988 and a 1984 MTA, the 1988 system must rely on the use of the mts-transfer-protocol 1984 application context. This ensures that the protocol encoding generated by the 1988 system conforms to that expected by 1984 systems. Section 10.1.8 describes the conformance requirements specified by both ISO and CCITT for the support of X.410-1984 mode application contexts.

10.1.2 Security

Since security was not specified in the 1984 MHS, a 1988 MTA must refrain from generating security context information as part of the bind operation parameters. Only simple authentication is supported when binding to 1984-based systems.

10.1.3 Extension fields

When a 1988 MTA transfers a message to a 1984 MTA, it must first downgrade the 1988 application protocol data units to the equivalent 1984 APDUs. Downgrading requires that all 1988 extension fields be removed. If the downgrading process fails, it is equivalent to the whole transfer failing. Critical extension fields cannot be removed and therefore will cause the downgrading process to fail.

10.1.4 ORName conversion

1988 ORNames are downgraded by deleting the Directory name and downgrading the ORAddress to contain only the components mandated by the 1984 version of the standard. Teletex strings are deleted if they are present as both teletex strings and printable strings. If, on the other hand, the ORAddress contains teletex strings but the corresponding printable strings are absent, the ORAddress cannot be downgraded. Also, when the ORAddress is a numeric-OR-address, or a terminal-OR-address containing a private-domain-name, the ORAddress cannot be downgraded to 1984.

10.1.5 Encoded Information Types conversion

The international standard defines a set of rules for mapping 1984 Encoded-Information-Types to 1988 basic-encoded-information-types. If the content-type is an object-identifier (as defined by 1988 MHS), it must be mapped into an integer compatible with the 1984 MHS before the ADPU is transferred. The mapping may cause 1984 systems to receive values for integer protocol elements that are unknown to them, since not every 1988 object identifier will map to a known 1984 integer.

10.1.6 Redirection and distribution lists

The use of redirection and distribution lists in 1988 MHS may cause problems when traversing 1984 domains, including:

1. Recipients may not be able to know whether they received a message because of redirection or expansion, since much of the forwarding information is lost.
2. The message expansion and redirection history is lost.
3. 1984 MTAs will return notifications back to the message originator directly, rather than back through the distribution list's expansion path.

10.1.7 APDU size constraints

Another potential concern is that APDUs generated by 1984 systems may override the size constraints placed on 1988 APDU fields. This is unlikely, however, since 1988 size constraints were adopted largely as a way to legitimize the size restrictions recommended by the 1984 MHS Implementor's Guide. It is unlikely that 1984 implementations will generate ADPUs which exceed the size constraints imposed on 1988 APDUs.

10.1.8 ISO and CCITT conformance

Interoperability between 1988 and 1984 MHS is further complicated by the fact that ISO and CCITT specify different conformance requirements for backward compatibility to 1984 systems. CCITT makes it mandatory for 1988 implementations to interwork with 1984 implementations. ISO, on the other hand, leaves backward compatibility with 1984 as optional. In CCITT, support for X.410-1984 mode is mandatory and support for RTSE normal mode (i.e., RTSE over 1988 ACSE and presentation) is optional. ISO mandates the reverse: RTSE normal mode is mandatory, and X.410-1984 mode is optional. Finally, to complicate matters even further, CCITT specifies in detail how MHS services map onto lower-layer protocols and of course mandates the use of transport class 0 at the lower layers. ISO, on the other hand, leaves it open to individual implementations or functional standards groups such as NIST to adopt whatever protocol layering approach suits them best.

The following table summarizes the contrasts between ISO's and CCITT's conformance requirements:

	ISO	CCITT
X.410-1984 mode	Optional	Mandatory
1988 normal mode	Mandatory	Optional
1988 to 1984 interworking	Optional	Mandatory
Use of lower layers	Undefined	Defined

CCITT's choices were motivated by the fact that most service providers were just putting in place 1984-based MHS services at the time 1988 MHS was being specified. Service providers were therefore hesitant to invest immediately in upgrading to the 1988 version of the standards. ISO, on the other hand, was aggressively promoting the 1988-based upper-layer architecture and wanted to accelerate the convergence of all OSI application layer standards to a common architectural model.

These discrepancies between ISO and CCITT depict what may seem like a horrible situation from the point of view of interoperability, and justifiably makes one wonder how vendors and service providers will ever succeed in interoperating. In reality, however, most vendors will implement all the options listed above as though they were mandatory. This approach will ensure interoperability with both service providers as well as other vendors. While vendors do not like to have to support these many options in their products, it is in their best interest in this case to do so.

10.2 Gatewaying between X.400 and SMTP

Since the community of mail users using RFC-822 is very large and growing, it is highly desirable to identify ways in which these networks can interwork effectively with X.400 networks. A considerable amount of work has been done in the Internet and the UK academic community to develop techniques for gatewaying between X.400 systems and RFC-822-based systems. As you will recall from Chap. 3, RFC 822 defines the messaging standard that is largely in use within the Internet today. Its function is roughly comparable to the P2 or P22 protocols in X.400. A number of RFCs have been published by researchers that define a preferred gatewaying approach between RFC 822 and X.400 MHS environments. These include:

1. RFC 987 (and its addendum RFC 1026), which defines the mapping between 1984 X.400 and RFC 822
2. RFC 1148, which defines the mapping between 1988 X.400 and RFC 822

It is very important to note that RFC 1148 does not attempt to obsolete RFC 987. Rather, it is envisioned that just as 1984 and 1988 X.400 MHS systems will coexist side by side, so will the need to gateway to both of them independently. This chapter describes primarily the requirements for gatewaying between 1988 X.400 and RFC 822 (as defined in RFC 1148). The gatewaying between 1984 MHS and RFC 822 (RFC 987) is very similar in nature, but constitutes a simpler subset of the issues encountered when interworking with 1988 systems.

While gateways have always been designed and implemented in an ad hoc manner, it was recognized early on that the need to interwork between X.400 and RFC 822 systems would become so prevalent as to warrant the specification of a common gatewaying approach. This was particularly important in order to provide a consistent level of service to users on both sides of the gateway, as well as to minimize data loss where multiple gateway traversals are involved. It is a particular property of electronic mail that a message may actually travel through numerous different domains in its transfer from a sender to an intended recipient. The challenge presented to designers of messaging systems is to be able to support the necessary transformations required to allow a message to pass through a system without sacrificing too much of its intended information content.

The RFC 822 gateway model is very simple and attempts as much as possible to map RFC 822 header information into X.400 P2 (or P22) protocol elements. It also maps the RFC 822 mail transport (also called RFC 822 P1) into 1988 X.400 P1. The architecture of the two messaging systems, however, is sufficiently different that protocol elements do not map quite as cleanly at the P2 and mail transport levels. The gateway must therefore place more effort in collecting information from various levels in order to do the mapping. It is generally easier to map from RFC 822 to X.400 because the RFC 822 functionality is simpler and can be more conveniently embedded into equivalent fields on the X.400 side. The following top-level mapping rules generally apply:

1. When going from RFC 822 to X.400, the RFC 822 message and the RFC 822 P1 information are always mapped onto an X.400 interpersonal message.
2. When going from X.400 to RFC 822, the RFC 822 message and RFC 822 P1 information may be obtained from either X.400 MTS level reports, interpersonal notifications at the MTS or IPMS level, or interpersonal messages.

X.400 probes are not mapped by the gateway because the equivalent concept does not exist in RFC 822 messaging environments. The new features of 1988 X.400 provide generally a cleaner mapping to RFC 822 than is possible with 1984 MHS.

When mapping from X.400 to RFC 822, there are some X.400 services that do not have an equivalent in RFC 822. In these cases a new RFC 822 header is defined using the "X-" extension notation (see Chap. 3). These fields are transported along with the message but are transparent to the RFC 822 environment. X-fields are registered so as to be known to cooperating RFC 822 gateway systems. This mechanism allows some X.400 information to travel unused through the RFC 822 environment, and later be reconstructed by the gateway when it crosses again into an X.400 environment. This makes it particularly important that the receiving gateway also be designed according to RFC 1148.

1988 security services are not mapped onto RFC 822. If any security elements in an X.400 message are marked critical, the gateway returns a nondelivery notification and the message is not delivered. If the security elements are not critical, they are simply ignored and the message is transferred regardless of the specified security services.

Not all X.400 body types are supported across the gateway. However, IA5 generally is and provides a good common ground for conversion of all message content fields. The gateway interprets all IA5 as ASCII and vice versa.

10.2.1 Address mapping

Perhaps one of the more complex aspects of conversion between X.400 and RFC 822 formats is that of naming and addressing. A great deal of emphasis is placed in RFC 1148 on how to map X.400 addresses to RFC 822 and vice versa. In doing so, RFC 1148 specifies a textual representation for X.400 addresses which can then be dealt with more easily by the RFC 822 environment. The reader who needs to understand address mapping in detail is encouraged to read RFC 1148, we will relate here a couple examples to give an intuitive feeling for how address mapping works.

When mapping X.400 addresses to RFC 822, the general approach is that the X.400 country attribute maps to the top-level domain in RFC 822. The remaining ADMD, PRMD, ORG, and other X.400 attributes map to the following RFC-822 subdomains. The X.400 personal name is mapped to the "local part" of the RFC 822 address. The following example shows a conversion between an X.400 address and an RFC 822 address.

The RFC 822 string:

```
smith@marketing.widget.com
```

must be encoded into an X.400 MHS ORAddress which consists of the following attributes:

```
CountryName                = UK
AdministrationDomainName   = BT
OrganizationName           = Widget
OrganizationalUnitName     = Marketing
Surname                    = Smith
```

Widget.COM maps to UK and BT because the gateway knows that Widget.COM is a commercial network in the UK. This knowledge must be set up and managed by the gateway administrators. Within the RFC 822 environment, a message is routed to the intended recipient in the standard manner using the domain mechanisms to select the appropriate gateway for the corresponding ORAddress space. When mapping from RFC 822 to X.400, care must be applied to ensure that top-level domains like uucp, earn, or bitnet are not mapped to "Country." This case is handled by maintaining correspondence tables in the gateways which provide the appropriate conversions for the top-level domains. The higher levels of the name space are internationally registered across implementations and managed by a central Internet distribution facility. The gateways perform most of the mapping at the lower levels of the name space.

In going from X.400 to RFC 822, the reverse mapping applies. The X.400 address:

```
CountryName                = XY
AdministrationDomainName   = PTT
OrganizationName           = Widget Corporation
Surname                    = Soap
Given Name                 = Joe
```

maps to the following RFC 822 string:

```
jsoap@widget.ptt.com
```

10.3 X.400 Application Programming Interfaces

Application programming interfaces, called APIs for short, refer to the "internal" interfaces defined between software modules operating within the same machine. By standardizing these interfaces, vendors provide an open software environment where software modules can be developed independently of each other, usually by different vendors, and yet can be linked together into a unified system because each module adheres to a commonly agreed interface. A great deal of emphasis is being placed today in the computer industry on developing APIs for all the major aspects of software functionality which run on typical host systems. These APIs represent de facto standards, in that they are usually developed by a single vendor or a small group of vendors and become standards by virtue of being published and made publicly available to everyone in the industry.

The popularity of X.400 as an electronic mail interchange standard has led over the past couple years to the development of standard application programming interfaces (APIs) for X.400 products. In 1988 a group of North American vendors and service suppliers formed an organization called the X.400 API Association. The association's goal was to develop and publish a set of "standard" interfaces for X.400 software products. The goal of developing these standard APIs was to enable vendors and service suppliers to incorporate X.400 modules developed by other suppliers within their own products. By adhering to a common interface, it is possible for vendors to develop X.400 modules independently of any other software components that may interface to it. This allows, for example, a vendor to develop an MTA while another vendor develops a gateway that interfaces a preexisting proprietary mail service to it.

As the prevalent choice in the industry to date has been to develop gateways between proprietary electronic mail systems and X.400, the API Association decided to focus its initial efforts on the development of a Gateway API. This API allows certain vendors to develop the X.400 MTA capability independently, while other vendors merely interface their proprietary electronic mail systems to it via the common programming interface. Figure 10.1 illustrates the basic idea behind the gateway API. It shows how a proprietary electronic mail system can interface to an X.400 MTA "engine" developed independently by another vendor. The API breaks the gateway server into two portions: a standard X.400 module which implements the MTA capability, and a module which implements the proprietary electronic mail capabilities and appears as a native mail server to the proprietary messaging environment. The two modules work with each other through the common interface provided by the standard API. This capability is likely to have a great deal of impact on the industry since it makes it easier for vendors or systems designers to build gateways from proprietary electronic mail systems to X.400 without having to develop any extensive X.400 expertise in-house.

The initial gateway API developed by the X.400 API Association

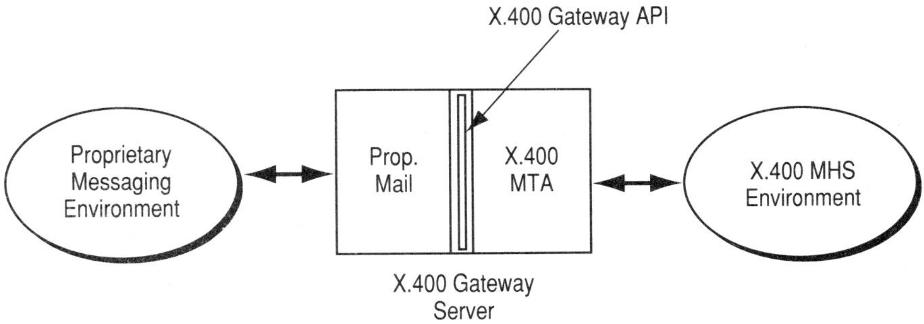

Figure 10.1 MHS gateway API.

turned out to be actually two distinct APIs: a Gateway API for moving messages, probes, and reports across the the gateway interface, and an Object Management API. The Object Management API was designed to be a generic module for dealing with data structures. The Object Management API is intended to be common to other APIs beyond the initial X.400 gateway API. Figure 10.2 gives an internal view of the software architecture of an X.400 gateway server that uses standard APIs. The gateway makes available two interfaces: an object management API and a Message Transfer API. A full X.400 MTA is implemented underneath these two interfaces.

Figure 10.3 illustrates another way in which the Gateway API can be used. It shows how the X.400 MTA can be on a separate machine from the proprietary electronic mail server. The mail server can communicate with the MTA server via local API calls. This arrangement actually allows several different proprietary electronic mail systems to use the same X.400 MTA service as long as each implements the standard API calls.

In 1989, the X.400 API Association began working on its phase two set of APIs. This time it was joined in its efforts by a group called X/Open. X/Open is an international consortium of vendors, including many U.S. vendors, which have long been developing standards to cover major aspects of applications portability in UNIX-based computing environments. X/Open was interested in developing X.400 APIs and in addition, was also beginning work on an X.500 API. The cooperation between the X.400 API Association and X/Open was a natural one since many of the larger vendors were already members of both

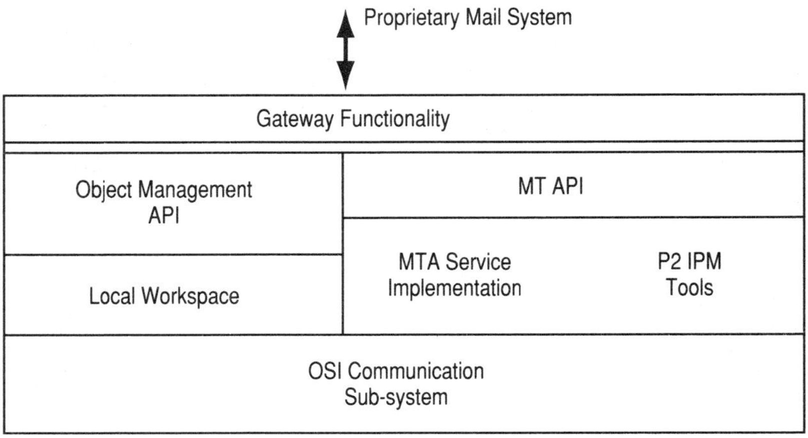

Figure 10.2 Internal view of the APIs within an X.400 MTA.

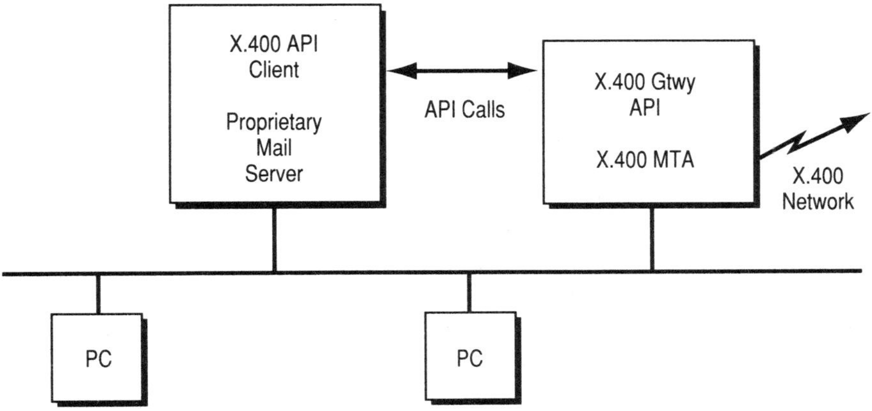

Figure 10.3 Uses of the MHS gateway API.

groups. Jointly, the two groups embarked on the development of an X.400 Application API, an X.500 API, and a revised Object Management API common to the entire set of APIs. Figure 10.4 summarizes the goals of the Application API. It serves to standardize the internal interface through which an X.400 UA interfaces to an MTA.

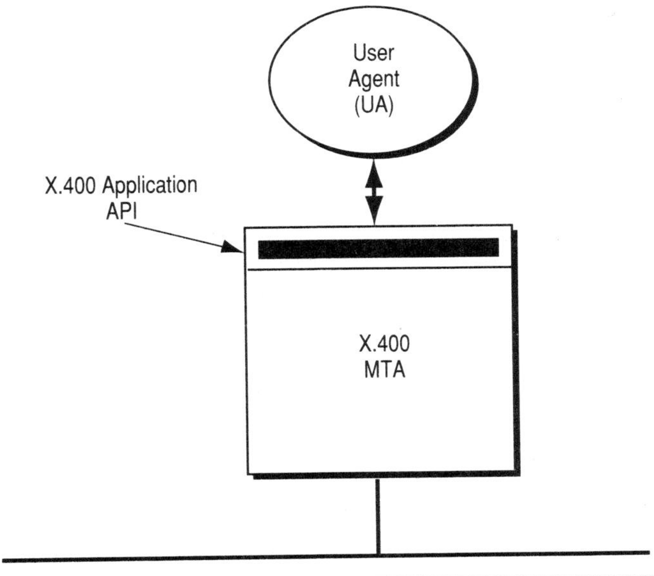

Figure 10.4 Application API.

Work is currently under way on additional APIs specific to the Message Store and EDI. The X.400 API movement has been so powerful in the industry that even the international standards bodies are beginning to show a strong interest in publishing the API standards. ISO and IEEE are both initiating work items on X.400 and X.500 APIs. Their stated intent is to adopt much of the API work that has already been done by the X.400 API Association and X/Open with very little change. The adoption of these APIs by the international standards bodies is significant since it allows these technologies to be officially referenced by government procurement guidelines, such as GOSIP.

10.4 Electronic Data Interchange

Electronic Data Interchange (EDI) represents an automated way for businesses to exchange highly structured business data such as invoices, purchase orders, and other financial documents. EDI messaging users are primarily computer processes, although some human intervention may also be allowed. Where organizations rely on computer-based systems to produce business documents that must then be forwarded to an external company for processing, it has become increasingly desirable to provide mechanisms which allow these documents to be transferred directly in electronic form from the originator's computer to the recipient's computer. EDI has grown tremendously in popularity over recent years both in the United States and in Europe, mainly out of a growing desire on the part of many businesses and corporations to streamline their business processes and take better advantage of computer automation. Clearly for this kind of financial exchange between two companies to be meaningful, both companies must be able to rely on a similar document format. The EDI standardization work has addressed precisely this need. The EDI work thus far has focused primarily on the information formatting aspects of the business exchange, rather than worrying about the underlying communication requirements. Communication of EDI transactions, as they are called, has thus far taken place through ordinary data transfer mechanisms, ranging from mailing computer tapes to the use of private leased lines between host computers.

Standards for EDI have emerged in recent years both in the United States and in Europe which define both the syntax and the semantics of EDI information. In the United States, the EDI format that is usually employed is that defined by ANSI X12. In Europe the EDI standard that has prevailed is based on the ISO standard 9735, "Electronic Data Interchange for Administration, Commerce, and Transport," and is called EDIFACT. The United Nations has also defined an EDI standard called United Nations Data Trade Interchange (UNTDI). All the above standards deal exclusively with the way in which business information is structured and make no assumptions regarding how it's transferred between computers.

Because the exchange of EDI information is an asynchronous form of communication, many people have come to view X.400 as a natural transport mechanism for use with EDI. The fact that X.400 is an international standard with a stated intent to provide widespread interworking between open computer systems makes it a natural candidate for use as the underlying transport mechanism for EDI transactions. From the X.400 perspective, EDI represents the most interesting and commercially viable application of electronic messaging. While EDI and X.400 have so far developed independently of each other, the convergence between the two technologies represents the best opportunity for success for both.

In recognition of this, work has been completed as part of an accelerated study to define explicitly how EDI interactions will be supported by MHS systems. In addition, although 1984 and 1988 MHS were developed without specific thought to support for EDI, special provisions have been established by NIST and other functional standards groups for the interim use of the existing X.400 protocols to support the transfer of EDI messages.

10.4.1 EDI with 1984 and 1988 MHS

While the design of the 1984 and 1988 MHS standards did not take EDI use into any account, as X.400 gains popularity, it became increasingly desirable to use it as a medium for exchanging EDI information. The NIST agreements have attempted to foster this application by defining ways in which EDI documents can be transported with the existing X.400 messaging protocols. NIST's analysis of the problem was of course initially geared to meet primarily the needs of the North American market and has therefore adopted the ANSI X12 version of EDI. The NIST standardizers felt that the P2 IPMS protocol was not well suited for EDI because it was designed to handle mostly small messages, exchanged between human users who did not require extensive confidentiality. As it is being used in North America, EDI requires the exchange of large documents between companies or central EDI communication agencies and a high degree of confidentiality. NIST, therefore, felt that the appropriate place to handle EDI transactions in the X.400 architecture was at the MTS level. The NIST approach is very simple and essentially supports the embedding of EDI messages within P1-level messages. It used the undefined content type called P0 which allows EDI messages to be directly embedded within P1 envelopes. They are then transferred transparently by the

MTS, as is the case for all P2 messages, and reconstructed at the receiving end only if users comprehend messages of content type 0. Otherwise, they are not delivered.

European users approached the problem differently, largely because EDI is used differently in Europe than in the United States. EDI usage in Europe makes less use of large single transfer agents but relies more on smaller direct EDI exchanges between computers. European designers, therefore, decided to embed EDI messages within P2 IPMS messages and make use of some P2 fields to carry EDI header information. The P2 approach has the advantage that EDI interchanges can be annotated by text, graphics, and other valid P2 body types.

In order to harmonize these differences and better promote the use of EDI, in 1988 the CEC (European Community) under the TEDIS (Trade Electronic Data Interchange Systems) program established a number of guidelines for the use of EDI in conjunction with X.400. These are known as the TEDIS guidelines and were defined in cooperation between European and North American users and experts. The TEDIS guidelines confirmed that the use of P2 IPMS was recommended in Europe. However, they strongly discouraged the use of P2 protocol service elements implementing the P2 approach. This makes it easier for EDI communications between Europe and the United States to occur through the use of simple gateways. Figure 10.5 below

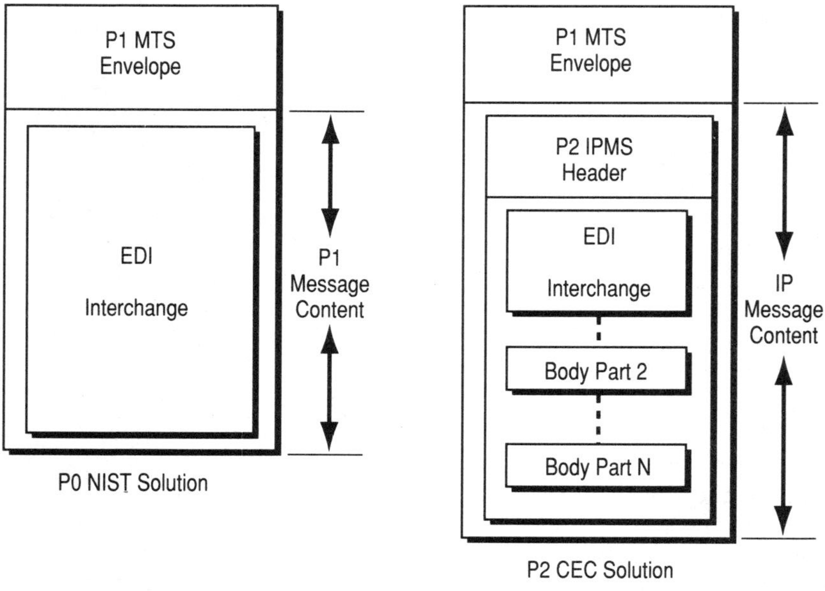

Figure 10.5 NIST P0 vs. the European P2 approach.

illustrates the differences between the NIST P0 approach and the European P2-based approach.

Both the NIST and the CEC approach will soon be replaced with an international agreement that defines a completely new content type designed specifically to support EDI transactions.

10.4.2 EDI in 1990 MHS

EDI is one of the major new work items under development during an accelerated study period. 1990 MHS has chosen to develop a new protocol called Pedi to specifically support EDI data interchanges. Pedi represents essentially a new message content type which has been optimized to meet the needs of EDI transactions. 1990 MHS is also defining an architectural model which embeds EDI applications within the MHS environment. The CCITT work on Pedi is currently available for approval as recommendation X.435 "MHS: EDI Messaging Systems." An F-series document has also been published by CCITT, called F.435, "MHS: EDI Messaging Service."

10.4.2.1 EDI model. The 1990 MHS defines the concept of EDI-UAs which are analogous to the IPM-UAs defined by 1984 and 1988 MHS. EDI-UAs create messages (EDIMs) with a content type specific to EDI. The heading of an EDIM contains information fields that are present in the EDIFACT interchange header segments (or corresponding ISA or STX segments for ANSI X12 and UNTDI EDI exchanges). It also carries additional service requests which may have been set by the message originator. Figure 10.6 illustrates how the Pedi protocol fits into the architecture relative to the other MHS protocols. Figure 10.7 illustrates the architecture of an MHS environment encompassing EDI services.

The 1990 MHS also defines Message Store facilities specifically tailored to the needs of the EDI-UA users. A number of EDI-specific Message Store attributes and auto-actions are defined in X.435. The

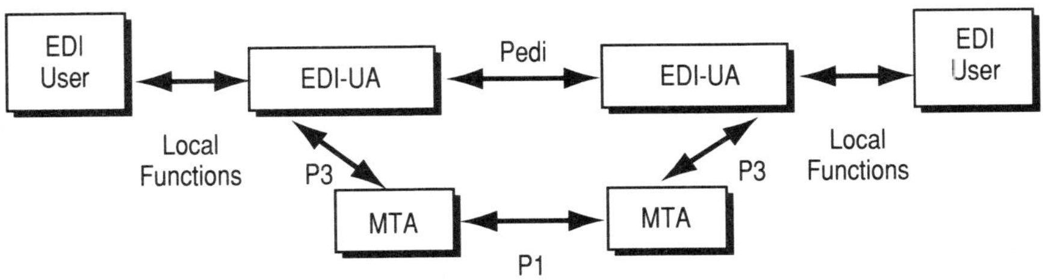

Figure 10.6 The Pedi protocol in MHS.

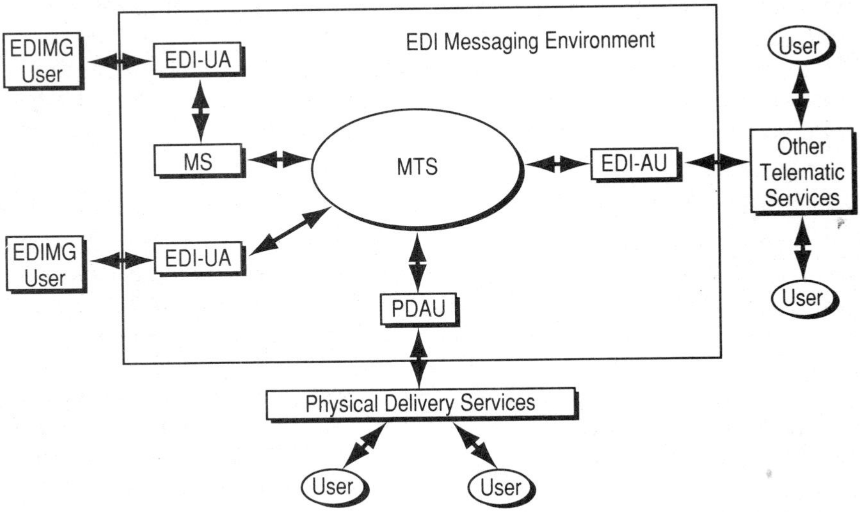

Figure 10.7 The EDI messaging environment.

EDI-MS service element "stored EDI message auto-forward" provides Message Store auto-forwarding for EDI messages.

10.4.2.2 EDI names. EDI messages are routed within the MTS on the basis of the O/R Address in the same way as any other MHS message. In addition, however, EDI messages also carry naming information that is specific to the EDI environment. EDI users, or trading partners as they are called, identify each other by a name which is an arbitrary alphanumeric string. EDI names are usually unique within a particular EDI user community but are not necessarily globally unique. EDI communities may be organized by

1. Industry group
2. Private trading groups of a large corporation
3. Third-party EDI service providers

The EDI names used by any of these communities may be either names issued by an international naming authority, names issued by a multinational company, or free-form names assigned by the trading partners themselves. EDI names usually contain no geographic element. However, the EDI standards allow the use of a qualifier along with the EDI name in order to identify the naming authority which assigned the alphanumeric string that makes up the name. The use of the qualifier in conjunction with the EDI name makes it possible to achieve globally unique EDI naming.

Information about EDI users will typically be stored in the Directory along with other useful information about network users (e.g., MHS users) and resources. A new object class called EDI-user is defined to contain attributes for the name of the EDI user and the capabilities that pertain to a particular user. Entries that belong to the object class EDI-user are represented in the directory DIT structure underneath entries for either organization or organizational unit. This is the same level as entries that belong to the object class organizational person. The capabilities that may be associated with an EDI-user entry include information about what EDI standard is supported, by what user, what EDI character set is supported, and any specific versions or releases of EDI documents that are supported.

10.4.2.3 EDI Messages. EDI messaging (EDIMG) consists of the exchange of two kinds of messages:

1. EDIMs, EDI messages containing business transactions
2. EDINs, EDI notifications containing information pertaining to the successful or unsuccessful delivery of an EDI interchange. These are analogous to receipt notifications in P2.

EDI messages are members of a special class of information objects conveyed between users of EDI messaging: they are defined in ASN.1 as

```
EDIM :: SEQUENCE OF {
          heading        Heading,
          body           Body }
```

The heading component corresponds to a sequence of information fields which characterize the EDI message, whereas the body component is a sequence of one or more body parts. The body of an EDIM is defined to consist of one "Primary Body Part" which contains the EDI information object. The primary body part may be either an EDI interchange or a forwarded EDIM. EDI interchanges may contain EDI information objects defined by either EDIFACT, the United Nations Data Trade Interchange (UNTDI), or ANSI X12.

Additional body parts may be present beyond the primary body part, but these can contain only different (non-EDI) body types that can be associated with the EDI interchange. This information may include textual information, voice annotations, graphics, etc. The body of an EDIM is defined as:

```
Body :: SEQUENCE {
      primary-body-part          PrimaryBodyPart,
      additional-body-parts      OtherBodyParts OPTIONAL }

PrimaryBodyPart :: = CHOICE {
      edi-body-part              [0]  EDIBodyPart,
      forwarded-EDIM             [1]  EDIMBodyPart }

OtherBodyParts :: = SEQUENCE OF EDIM-ExternallyDefinedBodyPart

EDIM-ExternallyDefinedBodyPart :: = SEQUENCE {
      body-part-reference        [0]  BodyPartReference OPTIONAL,
      external-body-part         [1]  ExternallyDefinedBodyPart
                                               — from IPMS —}

BodyPartReference :: = INTEGER    – shall be unique within an EDIM —
```

Externally defined body parts carry information objects whose semantics and abstract syntax (i.e., their ASN.1 definition) are identified by an object ID which is carried with the body part. The standard explicitly states that externally defined body parts may not include other EDI interchanges, since only one EDI interchange is permitted per message. Figure 10.8 depicts the structure of an EDI message. EDI can also be used to send information to physical delivery units for postal delivery, as well as the facsimile machines.

10.4.2.4 EDI notifications. The equivalent of P2's notion of receipt notifications was considerably modified in EDI to better suit the needs of EDI users. Since EDI deals with financial transactions, it was particularly important that notifications operate on an end-to-end basis. While this is also true of IPM exchanges, the receipt (i.e., responsibility acceptance) of messages is more succinctly defined in X.435 to in-

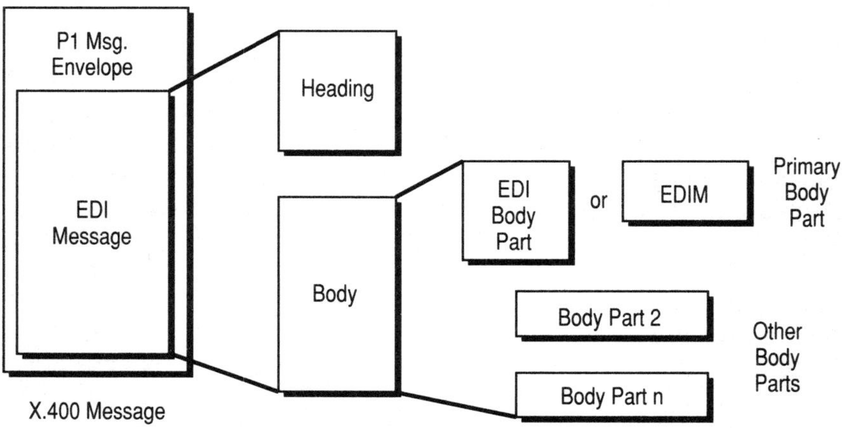

Figure 10.8 EDI message structure.

dicate when the end recipient has truly taken possession of the message.

EDI messaging users can request the return of notifications regarding the disposition of the message received. These notifications may be generated by a recipient EDI-UA, EDI-MS, or AU. EDI notifications cannot be forwarded, and of course notifications cannot be obtained for preceding notifications.

The 1990 MHS concept of "EDIM responsibility" provides a method for tracing the "acceptance" of EDIMs as they leave the MHS environment. Responsibility for EDIMs may be either accepted, refused, or forwarded. The element of service "EDI Notification Request" allows an originator to request notification from each recipient EDI-UA indicating whether the EDIM was accepted, refused, or forwarded. Notifications can be requested independently, or on a per recipient basis, or the request can be omitted altogether.

It is often desirable for organizations to receive all EDI messages at a central location, or EDI user agent, which will then forward them to the final destination EDI-UAs. This is particularly useful in large organizations where it enables them to perform functions such as logging and auditing of all EDI message traffic at a central location. An EDIM may therefore be accepted by an intermediate EDI-UA before being forwarded on to the final intended recipient EDI-UA.

If the notification returned is a negative notification (NN), the message will not be processed by the EDI message user. If the notification is positive (PN), the EDI message is made available to the EDI message user. If the notification indicates that the message has been forwarded (FN), it indicates that the EDI message along with EDIM responsibility have been forwarded to one or more EDI-UAs.

If an intermediate EDI-UA accepting responsibility for an EDIM changes the content of the message by adding or removing body parts from it, these are replaced with place holders that serve to indicate the type of body part that was removed.

10.4.2.5 EDI security. Additional security elements have been defined in 1992 MHS to specifically support the security requirements of EDI messaging. These include the following security elements:

1. *Proof of EDI notification:* This security element allows the recipient of an EDIM to create a notification that serves to authenticate the recipient.

2. *Non-repudiation of the EDI notification:* This security element provides the recipient of an EDI notification proof of origin of the no-

tification. It serves to protect against attempts by the originator of the notification to falsely deny having sent it.

3. *Proof of content received:* This security service element enables the originator of an EDI message to authenticate that the content of the message received is the same as that which was originally sent by the originator.

4. *Non-repudiation of content originated:* This security service protects the recipient from attempts by the originator to deny having originated the message contents.

5. *Non-repudiation of content received:* This service protects against the recipient falsely denying receipt of the message contents.

10.5 1992 MHS Work Items

ISO and CCITT are currently continuing work on the X.400 standards as part of the 1992 study period. The outcome of this new round of standardization, however, is not expected to be as major as the architectural and protocol changes that were made between the 1984 and the 1988 version of the standard. The major new addition to 1988 MHS is represented by the definition of services to support EDI as defined in CCITT recommendation X.435.

1992 MHS work items generally deal with minor enhancements to the 1988 standards. Some of the work items currently under consideration are:

1. The development of conformance tests for 1988 MHS implementations.

2. Restructuring the standards documents themselves to more clearly separate the content-type-independent MTS services from content-specific services such as IPM and EDI.

3. Deciding on what additional character sets should be supported in MHS.

4. Defining additional Message Store extensions to enable the Message Store to provide long-term storage facilities.

5. Developing secure messaging extensions to allow symmetric (i.e., single private key) encryption techniques to be used in X.400 MHS, as an alternative to the asymmetric techniques currently defined in 1988 MHS.

6. Support for voice messaging. Most of the service providers are clearly very interested in merging electronic messaging services with voice messaging services.

7. The inclusion of Fax store and forward services within the MHS model.

8. Updating the 1988 version of the MHS Implementor's Guide.

9. Defining a standard representation for O/R addresses.

10. Developing techniques and protocols to support group-oriented messaging communications, such as bulletin boards and message-based computer conferencing. Bulletin boards provide a way for a user to post a message to a bulletin, much like a distribution list for later perusal by other users who may wish to search through the bulleting information. Computer conferencing, on the other hand, refers to the development of a set of facilities to support an organized exchange of messages between a group of users on a particular subject matter.

References and for Further Study

The rules for gatewaying between 1984 X.400 and RFC 822 are defined by Kille (RFC 987, and RFC 1027). The rules for gatewaying between 1988 X.400 and RFC 822 are also defined by Kille (RFC 1148). A good overview of the major issues encountered in designing gateways between X.400 and RFC 822 is given by Kille (1986). Shivji (1988) provides a good overview of the general issues involved in designing gateways between proprietary systems and X.400.

An overview of the development of EDI in the context of MHS and some of the technical as well as political issues which still remain is given by Genilloud (1990). The EDI standards for message handling systems are defined in draft international standard X.435 (CCITT X.435), and the corresponding service definition is given in draft recommendation F.435 (CCITT F.435).

Appendix

A

GLOSSARY

A-ASSOCIATE An operation defined by the Association Control Service Element (ACSE) protocol that serves to initiate an OSI communication connection between two application level entities.

AC (Application Context) A set of protocol operations used between two application layer entities to communicate and carry out some predefined set of functions.

Access Units (AU) Network interface units that allow access to the MHS environment to a generic set of entities which wishes to avail themselves of messaging services.

ACSE (Association Control Service Element) A standard developed by ISO/CCITT to enable the establishment-termination of OSI associations by application entities (ISO 8649 and CCITT X.217, X.227).

ADMD (Administration Management Domain) A collection of MHS entities managed by a common public administrative authority, or messaging service provider.

Administrative Authority An entity that has administrative control over the set of entries stored within a DSA, or a set of MHS entities.

Alias An alternative name for an object.

ANSI American National Standards Institute, the national organization responsible for the definition and adoption of standards for use within the United States.

APDU (Application Protocol Data Unit) Unit of information exchanged between application layer entities.

API (Application Programming Interface) Formalized and fully documented interface to a software module or set of modules. An API is usually published and promoted within the computer industry as a standard interface.

Application API Application level standard interface; allows client message handling software to be developed independently of the messaging protocols actually used to convey messaging information between a client and the message handling environment.

A-RELEASE An operation defined by ACSE to terminate an OSI communication connection between two application level entities.

ARPANET Computer communications research network sponsored by DARPA in the late 1960s.

ASE (Application Service Element) An application layer entity that provides a particular set of services.

ASN.1 (Abstract Syntax Notation One) A standard developed by ISO/CCITT to define the syntax of the information exchanged by application level entities (ISO 8824, 8825, and CCITT X.208, X.209).

Association Manager An entity within the message transfer agent (MTA) that is responsible for establishing and managing associations to other MTAs, as well as to user agents (UAs), or other clients of the MTA service.

Asymmetric Nonsymmetric exchange of information used in the context of security algorithms to denote the use of different keys to encrypt and decrypt information.

Attribute Information of a particular type concerning an object represented by a Directory entry.

Attribute Type That component of an attribute which indicates the class of information given by the attribute.

Attribute Value An instance of the class of information indicated by an attribute type.

Auto-Action An activity or set of activities that may be carried out automatically on behalf of a messaging user by the Message Store when a certain predefined set of criteria are met.

Bind Protocol operation used to set up an association between two application entities.

BITNET Research computer network established in the early 1980s in cooperation between Yale University and the City University of New York (CUNY).

Blue Book The 1988 version of recommendations approved by CCITT in its 1988 plenary session in Melbourne, Australia.

BNF (Backus Naur Form) Notation used to define the ASN.1 syntax.

Body The content portion of an electronic mail message.

Body Part One instance of possibly several pieces of information associated with a single electronic mail message.

Browsing A technique for looking up information in the Directory database.

Capabilities A generic term that refers to all the possible properties associated with a given MHS user or entity.

CCITT International Telephone and Telecommunications Organization responsible for developing and approving international standards for use by public service providers (i.e., PTTs).

Certificate The public key of a user together with some additional information, which is rendered unforgeable by encipherment with the secret key of the certification authority that issued it.

Certification Authority An authority trusted by one or more users to create and assign authentication certificates.

Certification Path An ordered sequence of certificates of objects in the DIT which together with the public key of the initial object in the path can be processed to obtain the public key of the final object in the path.

Client A computer process responsible for accessing a set of electronic services on behalf of a human user or another application process.

Content Type The type of contents conveyed in an electronic mail message.

Credentials Information used to establish the identity of a user or resource; typically it consists of a name and a public key.

CSNET Experimental computer network similar to the ARPANET established by the NSF (National Science Foundation).

DAP (Directory Access Protocol) The protocol used by a DUA to access the Directory Service.

Delivery Reports Status report messages that convey information regarding the successful or unsuccessful delivery of a message.

Delivery Report MPDUs The unit of information used to exchange delivery reports.

DIB (Directory Information Base) The collection of information held by the Directory.

Digital Signature A mechanism to ensure the integrity and authenticity of the originator of a piece of electronic information.

DIT (Directory Information Tree) The logical hierarchical structure of Directory information.

Directory Entry A part of the DIB that contains information about an object.

DIS (Draft International Standard) The draft version of an international standard under development by ISO.

Distinguished Name Directory term used to denote the sequence of RDNs leading from the root of the DIT to the Directory object of interest.

Distribution List (DL) Group of users or resources that may be addressed as a whole via a single electronic mail message.

Domain A portion of the message handling environment or the distributed directory service environment which is managed by a particular administrative authority.

Downgrading The process of converting 1988 protocol data units to 1984 protocol data units.

DP (Draft Proposal) A draft version proposal for a standard being developed by ISO.

DSA (Directory Service Agent) An OSI application process that provides the Directory functionality.

DSP (Directory System Protocol) The protocol used by a DSA to cooperate with other DSAs in carrying out the distributed Directory services.

DUA (Directory User Agent) An OSI application process that represents a user in accessing the Directory.

EDI (Electronic Data Interchange) Automated way to exchange structured business data such as invoices, purchase orders, etc.

EDIMS (EDI Messaging System) An X.400 MHS system that includes support for EDI transactions.

EDIN (EDI Notification) Notification message used to report the successful or unsuccessful delivery of an EDI transaction. Similar to the role provided by delivery reports in the P2 interpersonal messaging protocol.

EDI-UA (EDI User Agent) A user agent specifically designed to handle EDI information.

EITs (Encoded Information Types) MHS message contents identified by a particular type. Replaces the 1984 definition of content types.

Envelope A set of information that is prepended to a message in order to successfully route it within the message handling environment.

Extension Parameters New message fields that have been added to the MHS protocols to reflect the new features and services defined in 1988 MHS.

F Series A set of CCITT recommendations that parallels the CCITT Blue Book but provides more specific information regarding the actual deployment of the standards in actual system implementations.

FTP (File Transfer Protocol) An Internet protocol defined within the TCP/IP architecture to handle the transfer of files between different systems.

Gateway A network component that provides message translation services between two diverse electronic messaging environments.

Gateway API A standard interface to the software modules that provide the gateway service.

Global Domain Identifier A message identifier used to uniquely distinguish one message from another.

Header Addressing and other routing information carried along with a message.

IA5 (International Alphabet Number 5) A standard for representing textual and numeric information. Very similar to ASCII.

IM-UAPDUs (Interpersonal Messaging User Agent Protocol Data Units) The unit of information exchanged between user agents at the user level through either the P2 or the P22 protocols.

Interface Documented boundary between software modules residing within the same computer host or network node.

IP-Messages Interpersonal messages exchanged between individuals using the MHS system.

IPMS (Interpersonal Messaging Service) The portion of the MHS that is designed to support the exchange of user-level messages between individuals using the MHS system.

IPM-Status-Reports (Interpersonal Messaging Status Reports) Reports generated to provide the sender of an interpersonal message with information regarding the successful or unsuccessful delivery of the message.

IPM-UA (Interpersonal Messaging User Agent) A user agent specifically designed to handle the creation, display, and exchange of messages between human users of the MHS.

IPM-UAE (Interpersonal Messaging User Agent Entity) The element of the user agent responsible for implementing the actions of the IPM-UA.

IS (International Standard) An international standard developed by ISO.

ISO (International Standards Organization) An international standards organization responsible for developing and approving international standards.

LAN Local area network.

MACRO Mechanism for defining new, nonstandard object types.

Mail Server Network node or computer host responsible for receiving, relaying, and forwarding electronic mail messages.

MASE (Message Administration Service Element) Set of protocol operations used by the MTS-user to set or change MTS service parameters.

MDSE (Message Delivery Service Element) Set of protocol operations used between MTAs to deliver messages to the MTS-user.

Message Store (MS) Entity responsible for the receipt and storage of messages on a long-term basis on behalf of the end user.

Message Transfer Agent (MTA) An OSI application process, defined as part of X.400 MHS, which denotes an active component involved in the transfer of electronic mail messages.

Message Transfer System (MTS) The collection of MTAs and MTA-level protocols necessary to support the transfer of electronic mail between a sender and a set of recipients.

MHS (Message Handling System) A collection of protocols and network entities designed to support the exchange of electronic mail.

MHS Implementor's Guide An informal document published by the CCITT to aid implementor's in constructing MHS implementations. Documents errors found in the specification of the MHS protocols or services.

MOTIS (Message Oriented Text Interchange Service) ISO's version of the X.400 protocols.

MPDU Identifier Unique identifier used to recognize one Message Protocol Data Unit (MPDU) from another.

MRSE (Message Retrieval Service Element) A set of protocol operations used by a Message Store user to query the Message Store.

MSSE (Message Submission Service Element) A set of protocol operations used by the MTS user to submit messages for transfer by the MTS.

MTAE (Message Transfer Agent Entity) The entity within the MTA that actually implements the MTA functionality.

MTL (Message Transfer Layer) The layer responsible for transferring messages in the MHS.

MTSE (Message Transfer Service Element) A set of protocol operations used to transfer messages between MTAs.

Naming and Registration Authority An organization responsible for allocating OSI names and addresses. ISO and CCITT will share this role at the international level, while a number of local administration authorities will perform this function at a regional level.

Normal Mode The 1988 version of the MHS protocol stack.

Object Class An identified family of objects that share certain common characteristics.

Object Management API A standard interface to a set of software modules that are responsible for creating and managing MHS objects.

Octet OSI terminology used to denote a byte.

OPDUs (Operation Protocol Data Units) Units of information exchanged between application layer entities using ROS.

OR Address Address of the originator or recipient of an MHS message.

OR Name Name of the originator or recipient of an MHS message.

Originator The sender of an electronic mail message.

P1 Protocol used to relay electronic mail messages between MTAs.

P2 Protocol used to exchange interpersonal mail messages between human users of the MHS.

P3 Protocol used by user agents to submit messages to MTAs.

P7 Protocol used to submit and retrieve messages between user agents and the Message Store.

P22 1988 version of the protocol used to exchange interpersonal mail messages between human users of MHS.

PDAUs (Physical Delivery Access Units) Logical entities in 1988 MHS that allow postal delivery services to access the MHS.

Pedi Protocol under development as part of the 1992 MHS work to support the exchange of EDI transactions between EDI users of message handling services.

Ports Concept used to denote a set of operations used to access a particular MHS entity.

PRMD (Public Management Domain) A collection of MHS entities managed by a common private administrative authority.

Probe A message used to test the viability of the MTS.

Probe MPDUs Units of information used to carry probe messages.

Protocol A set of operations carried out between two remote network entities.

Protocol Elements A set of parameters carried as part of the message header or envelope information.

Public Key The publicly known security key of a user key pair.

Query A request for Directory information initiated by a DUA.

Recipient An intended recipient of electronic mail may be either a human user or an application process.

RDN (Relative Distinguished Name) Directory term used to refer to the name of a vertex of the DIT.

Red Book The 1984 set of CCITT recommendations.

Report MPDUs Units of information used to exchange reports.

RFC (Request for Comment) Internet technical specification for protocols used within the TCP/IP family of networking standards.

Root Directory term used to refer to the initial vertex of the DIT.

ROS (Remote Operations Service) A standard developed by ISO/CCITT to allow a request-response information exchange between application level entities, X.219/X.229.

ROSE (Remote Operation Service Element) The 1988 version of ROS.

RPC Remote procedure call.

RSA (Rivest, Shamir, Adleman Algorithm) A public key based encryption algorithm.

RTS (Reliable Transfer Protocol) 1984 MHS protocol defined to reliably transfer message handling data over the session layer.

RTSE (Reliable Transfer Service Element) The 1988 version of RTS.

SDE (Submission and Delivery Entity) Entity that resides within the user agent and relies on the P3 protocol to submit messages for transmission to the MTA.

Security Labels A set of classifications that serve to establish a hierarchy of security levels.

Secret Key The key of a user key pair known only to that user.

SEQUENCE An ASN.1 term used to denote an ordered collection of objects.

Service A computer process responsible for providing a set of services in a network environment.

Service Elements MHS features usually expressed as information in the MPDU header.

Service MPDU Unit of information used at the MTL layer to carry status information about the delivery of other messages.

SET An ASN.1 term used to denote an un-ordered collection of objects.

SMTP (Simple Mail Transport Protocol) Popular mail protocol used within the Internet and other TCP/IP-based network environments.

SR-UAPDUs Interpersonal messaging service (P2) level notifications regarding the successful or unsuccessful receipt of an interpersonal message.

Symmetric Security scheme where the same key is used both to encrypt and decrypt information.

TCP/IP Transmission Control Protocol over Internet Protocol in use within the Internet. It is roughly equivalent to transport class 4 in the OSI architecture.

Token A security object containing a set of security credentials. It is exchanged between two parties who are trying to establish a secure communication channel.

Top The special Directory object class of which every other class is a subclass.

Trace Information Historical information regarding the path which a message has taken within the MHS environment. It is used to detect potential routing loops or other inappropriate message routing situations.

UA (User Agent) An OSI application process, defined as part of X.400 MHS, which denotes a user accessing MHS services.

UAL (User Agent Layer) The set of protocols and functions that implement the user-level message exchange functionality.

UAPDUs (User Agent Protocol Data Units) The unit of information exchanged between user agents.

UDP User datagram protocol.

Unbind Protocol operation used to release an association between two application entities.

User MPDUs The unit of information at the P1 level that is used to transport the user-level information exchanged between messaging entities.

Uucp UNIX to UNIX copy program, informal computer network originated at Bell Laboratories and widely in use within universities and other academic or research institutions.

X.400 APIA An association made up of a group of vendors and service providers that have joined together to define standard APIs for X.400 and X.500 implementations.

X.410-1984 Mode The 1984 style of operations including the 1984 version of the MHS protocol stack.

X-Fields A set of extension fields available in the RFC-822 protocol to add user-definable parameters to be carried along with a mail message.

X/OPEN An association of vendors and service providers that have joined together to develop standards for UNIX-based computing environments, including X.400 and X.500 services.

BIBLIOGRAPHY

Bressler, R. D., and Thomas, R.: "Mail Retrieval via FTP," Cambridge, MA: Bolt Beranek and Newman, February 1973, RFC 458.

CCITT: "Data Communication Networks: Message Handling Systems," Recommendations X.400-X.430, CCITT Red Book, Vol. viii, Fasc. viii.7, Malaga-Torremolinos, 1984.

CCITT, ISO/IEC: "Data Communication Networks: Message Handling Systems," Recommendations X.400-X.420, CCITT Blue Book, Vol. viii, Fasc. viii.7, Melbourne, ISO/IEC 10021-1 to 10021-7, 1984.

CCITT: "Reference Model of Open Systems Interconnection for CCITT Applications," Recommendation X.200.

CCITT, ISO/IEC: "Specification of Abstract Syntax Notation One (ASN.1)," Recommendation X.208, ISO/IEC 8824, April 1988.

CCITT, ISO/IEC: "Specification of Basic Encoding Rules for Abstract Syntax Notation One (ASN.1)," Recommendation X.209, ISO/IEC 8825, April 1988.

CCITT, ISO/IEC: "Association Control: Service Definitions," Recommendation X.217, ISO/IEC 8649, April 1988.

CCITT, ISO/IEC: "Reliable Transfer Model: Service Definition," Recommendation X.218, ISO/IEC 9066-1, April 1988.

CCITT, ISO/IEC: "Reliable Operations Model: Notation and Service Definition," Recommendation X.219, ISO/IEC 9072-1, April 1988.

CCITT, ISO/IEC: "Directory—Overview," Recommendations X.500–X.521, 9594-1 to 9594-8, April 1988.

CCITT: "Message Handling: EDI Messaging Service," Draft recommendation F.435, version 5.0, June 1990.

CCITT: "Message Handling Systems: EDI Messaging System," Draft recommendation X.435, version 5.0, June 1990.

Comer, D. : "Internetworking with TCP/IP: Principles, Protocols, and Architecture," Englewood Cliffs, NJ: Prentice-Hall, 1988.

Crocker, D. H.: "Standard for the Format of ARPA Internet Text Messages," August 1982, RFC 822.

DARPA: "A History of the Arpanet: The First Decade," Bolt Beranek and Newman, Report no. 4799, April 1981.

Genilloud, G.: "X.400 MHS: First Steps Towards an EDI Communication Standard," Computer Communication Review, vol. 20, pp. 72–86, April 1990.

GOSIP: U.S. Government Open Systems Interconnection Profile (GOSIP) version 1.0, GOSIP Advanced Requirements Group, National Institute of Standards and Technology (NIST), April 1989.

ISO: International Standard 7498, Information Processing Systems, Open Systems Interconnection—Basic Reference Model, 1984.

Kille, S. E.: "Gatewaying between X.400 & Other Message Protocols," Pinner, UK: Online Publications, 1986, pp. 239–247.

Kille, S. E.: "Mapping between X.400 and RFC 822," RFC 987, 1986.

Kille, S. E.: "Addendum to RFC 987," University College London, September 1987, RFC 1026.

Kille, S. E.: "Mapping between X.400 (1988)/ISO 10021 and RFC 822," March 1990, RFC 1148.

Manros, C. U.: "The X.400 Blue Book Companion," Technology Appraisals, 1989.

NIST: "Stable Implementor's Agreements," National Institute for Standards and Technology, 1988.

Perry, D. G., Blumenthal, S. H., and Hinden, R. M.: "The ARPANET and the DARPA Internet," Library Hi Tech, Vol., No.2, April 1988.

Postel, J. B.: "Simple Mail Transfer Protocol," August 1982, RFC 821.

Radicati, S.: "Distributed Aspects of the X.500 Standards for Directory," Proceedings of the International Open Systems Conference, London: Online Publications, March 1989.

Rivest, R. L., Shamir, A., and Adleman, L.: "On a Method for Obtaining Digital Signatures and Public Key Cryptosystems," Commun. ACM, Vol. 21, pp. 120–126, February 1978.

Schicker, P.: "Message Handling Systems, X.400 (An Overview)," IFIP WG 6.5 International Working Conference Message Handling Systems and Distributed Applications, Costa Mesa, CA, 1988.

Shivji, A., and Koorland, N. K.: "Implementing X.400 Gateways—Identifying the Issues," IFIP WG 6.5 International Working Conference Message Handling Systems and Distributed Applications, Costa Mesa, CA, 1988.

Tanenbaum, A. S.: "Computer Networks," Englewood Cliffs, NJ: Prentice-Hall, 1988.

Watson, R. W.: "Mail Box Protocol," Menlo Park, CA: Stanford Research Institute, Augmentation Research Center, July 1971, RFC 196.

Index

To stay current with the latest developments in the messaging industry, you may wish to subscribe to:

The Messaging Technology Report

The Messaging Technology Report is a monthly report authored by Dr. Sara Radicati, a prominent spokesperson in the messaging industry, in cooperation with other leading industry experts. It provides in-depth analysis of the latest trends in the design and use of message handling systems, including: directory services, EDI, authentication and security, workflow automation, and related messaging applications.

The Messaging Technology Report provides up-to-date information on the development of international and industry standards, as well as a detailed explanation of the technologies and their implications on the messaging industry from both a vendor and a customer perspective. Reports include information on: the Lotus Open Messaging Interface (OMI), the 1992 X.400 Message Handling standards, X.500 products and services, the 1992 extensions to the X.500 Directory standards, government procurement requirements (GOSIP) for messaging and directories, LAN-based messaging systems and applications, and more.

For subscription information, please write or call:

ABOUT THE AUTHOR

Dr. Sara Radicati is a leading expert in the fields of Message Handling Systems and Directory Services. She has been actively involved with the development of electronic mail technologies and standards for the past ten years, and has been an active contributor to numerous OSI standards organizations such as ISO, CCITT, ANSI and NIST. Dr. Radicati was one of the principal designers of the X.500 standards for Directory Services.

Dr. Radicati is currently responsible for messaging product strategies at Novell, Inc. Prior to joining Novell, Dr. Radicati held senior level architecture and product planning positions at 3Com and Xerox Corporation, where she was responsible for the development of the XNS applications architecture, communication protocol design and distributed systems architectures. Dr. Radicati has published numerous articles and has lectured widely in topics relating to her field of expertise both in the U.S. and abroad.